CW00924738

SHAW AND HIS
CONTEMPORARIES

SHAW AND HIS CONTEMPORARIES

THEATRE ESSAYS

by
RONALD BRYDEN

edited by
DENIS JOHNSTON

mosaic press

The Academy of the Shaw Festival
Niagara-on-the-Lake, Ontario

National Library of Canada Cataloguing in Publication Data

Bryden, Ronald-
    Shaw and his contemporaries: theatre essays / Ronald Bryden
edited by Denis Johnston

Co-published by Mosaic Press.
ISBN 0-9699478-4-4 (Academy of Shaw Festival). --
ISBN 0-88962-791-6 (Mosaic Press)

    1. Shaw, Bernard, 1856-1950--Criticism and interpretation. 2. English drama--20th cen-
tury--History and criticism. 3. American drama--20th century--History and criticism. 4. Theatre--
Reviews. I. Johnston, Denis, 1950- II. Academy of the Shaw Festival III. Title.

PR732.B79 2002   822'.91209   C 2002-902161-8

No part of this book may be reproduced or transmitted in any form, by any means, electronic
or mechanical, including photocopying and recording, information storage and retrieval sys-
tems, without permission in writing from the publisher, except by a reviewer who may quote
brief passages in a review.

Published by Mosaic Press, offices and warehouse at 1252 Speers Road, Units 1 and 2, Oakville,
Ontario, L6L 5N9, Canada and Mosaic Press, PMB 145, 4500 Witmer Industrial Estates, Niagara
Falls, NY, 14305-1386, U.S.A.

Mosaic Press acknowledges the assistance of the Canada Council and the Department of Canadian Heritage, Government of Canada for their support of our publishing programme.

Cover design and photo layout by Scott McKowen
Photos by David Cooper
Text design and layout by Natasha Hunt
Associate Editor: Jean German
Copyright © Ronald Bryden, 2002

Printed and Bound in Canada.
ISBN 0-9699478-4-4
ISBN 0-88962-791-6

Le Conseil des Arts   The Canada Council
du Canada   for the Arts

Co-Published by Mosaic Press and the
Academy of the Shaw Festival
Box 774, Niagara-on-the-Lake,
Ontario, L0S 1J0, Tel. 1-800-657-1106
Fax: 905-468-5438

Mosaic Press in Canada:
1252 Speers Road, Units 1 & 2,
Oakville, Ontario
L6L 5N9
Phone/Fax: 905-825-2130
mosaicpress@on.aibn.com

Mosaic Press in U.S.A.:
4500 Witmer Industrial Estates
PMB 145, Niagara Falls, NY
14305-1386
Phone/Fax: 1-800-387-8992
mosaicpress@on.aibn.com

CONTENTS

EDITOR'S NOTES
by Denis Johnston

As Publications Editor for the Shaw Festival, one of my pleasant responsibilities each autumn is to commission programme notes for the next year's plays. In a decade of this, I've commissioned about a hundred such essays from a wide range of writers, including some of the foremost theatre scholars in the world. A pattern has emerged: first I offer Ronald Bryden, The Shaw's Literary Adviser since 1992, his choice of plays on which to write, then Ron and I collaborate in constructing a wish-list of essayists for all the other plays. I reason that he gets few enough perks as Literary Adviser, so this is one I can cheerfully throw his way.

A Ronald Bryden essay is the gold standard of programme notes. Only occasionally have I lavished my highest compliment on other writers – "it reads like a Ron Bryden piece"– and only then on people who will understand what I mean. Ron's essays are always erudite, wide-ranging, jargon-free, accessible without being simplistic, and enriched by a lifetime of seeing, pondering and writing about the theatre. Sometimes at the end he seems to pull a rabbit out of his hat, leaving me shaking my head and muttering something like, "gosh I wish I could write like that." His essay on *The Apple Cart* provides one such example, but there are several others in this collection.

Though the forty essays in this book span forty years, they focus mainly on Ronald Bryden's writings of the past two decades. Half of essays first appeared in Shaw Festival house programmes between 1992 and 2002, and there are also programme notes from the Royal National Theatre, the Stratford Festival, and other theatre companies in Toronto and San Francisco. The collection includes eight book reviews on theatrical topics, including three originally published in the *London Review of Books* and reprinted by permission. Finally, the six essays here that date from the 1960s (including the only theatre review, a hymn of praise to Laurence Olivier's landmark *Othello* at the National Theatre) all appeared in an earlier collection of Bryden essays, *The Unfinished Hero* (1969). As these pieces are long out of print, it seemed appropriate to include some of them in this new collection, as they represent a time when Ronald Bryden was one of the leading theatre critics in the English language. Most of these are in the final section, which I rather desperately entitled "Critic at Large," partly to acknowledge its departure from the Shaw Festival's mandate and from my own chosen theme of Shaw and his contemporaries. Once the essays for this section were in place, however, I found it intriguing to note how the protean figure of Olivier ran through them like a golden thread.

Finally, because Ronald Bryden always writes about his topic and not about himself, a biographical sketch is in order. He was born in Trinidad in 1927, a fourth-generation colonial of British stock – indeed, this heritage contributes some insights to his essays on *Point Valaine* and *The Cherry Orchard*. He was sent to boarding school in St Catharines, Ontario – the nearest city to the yet-unborn Shaw Festival! – then took a degree in English literature at the University of Toronto. While he had seen some good amateur theatre in Trinidad, it was in Toronto that he saw his first professional theatre, mostly touring shows at that city's venerable Edwardian playhouse, the Royal Alexandra Theatre. In 1951 he went to England and took an MA at Cambridge University, after which a series of jobs in journalism led to his making his reputation as literary editor for the *Spectator*, drama critic for the *New Statesman* and then the *Observer*, and dramaturg for the Royal Shakespeare Company. He returned to Canada in 1976 as a Visiting Professor at the University of Toronto's Graduate Centre for Study of Drama, and decided to remain in Toronto, where he still resides. He served on the boards of several theatre companies in the 1970s and '80s, including the

Stratford Festival; and when he retired from the university in 1992, the Shaw Festival's artistic director, Christopher Newton, eagerly invited him to join the company as Literary Adviser.

Ronald Bryden is retiring from The Shaw this year, and so far I have been unable to talk him out of it. It has been an enormous pleasure to work with him over the past ten years, and to edit this collection as well. I can't help but think the experience has made me a better writer, and I know it has made me both a humbler and a prouder one at the same time. If you can find a copy of *The Unfinished Hero*, Ron's Foreword will give you some idea of the forces that, at mid-century, brought a colonial lad to the centre of the old Empire, where he became one of the major interpreters of its culture. And why the theatre? He writes: "Perhaps it's because the stage is almost the last really public art, the one which depends not on a private, solitary response but a shared one, common to neighbours not of one's choosing. In this, it is still, as someone said, like the world."

FOREWORD
by Ronald Bryden

Caveat emptor: buyer beware! Welcome, come on inside, but I think I should warn you that most of the pieces in this collection started life as programme notes written for various theatres, the majority for the Shaw Festival at Niagara-on-the-Lake, Ontario. I'm not saying that lessens their value or importance – I wrote them – but a programme note by its nature is a form with limits. It can't be theatrical criticism. It can't tell a director how to stage a play or actors how to play it – it's often written before the play is cast. It shouldn't even try to tell what kind of experience the play in performance will give an audience. If it turns out to be wrong, everyone feels cross and foolish, especially its writer.

What a programme note perhaps can tell you is why a playwright threw a stone of that particular shape into that particular historical pond, and what ripples it caused in the world where he or she wrote it. I like that kind of information because it's what we used to call "hard news" when I was a journalist, and specific in its detail. Plays are highly individual transactions between playwrights and their times, whose meaning is created jointly by the text, the text's theatrical interpreters, and the minds of the audiences who come to see it. Generalizations about them, attempts to consider them in groups, seem to me largely a waste of time. If you believe that the highest purpose of theatrical scholarship is to arrive at grand theoretic formulae which enable you to label works post-modern, post-colonial, neo-feminist or even palaeo-patriarchal, you will find little here to interest you.

It's been a happy privilege, having the chance to study and think about these plays individually, and then to see how they worked on audiences in performance. Many of them I've been able to see in productions by a director whose care for the play's individuality, for the past it grew out of and for the detail which is its life, makes him in my view one of the finest I've encountered anywhere – Christopher Newton. Most of them I have seen performed by the company which is his most extraordinary achievement: the best in Canada, perhaps in North America. They are living proof of the value of the classics. By performing the great plays of one of the three great centuries of Western drama – the century of Ibsen, Shaw and Chekhov (the others are the Athenian fifth century BC and the century of Shakespeare, Lope and Molière) – they've found a discipline that teaches the skills needed to play them. Its actors are the only ones I've found in North America who seem to have learned how to point a line, a craft no longer taught in most acting schools. They're also the only company I've met anywhere who, when a show is unfinished or unsatisfactory on opening night, go on working together unasked, in their own time, until it has reached a quality they think worthy of them and their artistic director. To borrow an adjective from one of Shaw's heroines, I think they're bloody marvellous. This collection, carefully chosen and scrupulously edited by their head of publications, Denis Johnston, is dedicated to Christopher and to them.

BERNARD SHAW

MRS WARREN'S HOME ADDRESS

Programme note for the Shaw Festival's 1997
production of *Mrs Warren's Profession*

According to his first biographer, Bernard Shaw originally intended to call his third play *Mrs Jarman's Profession*. Shaw later denied the story, but may simply have wished to deny that he was ever so young, envious and piratical. For the point of that title would have been to put a shot across the bow of Arthur Wing Pinero, the most popular and admired playwright in London since the huge success in May 1893 of *The Second Mrs Tanqueray*. Pinero's play was the story of a Woman with a Past – specifically, a past of being supported by wealthy men in return for sexual services. When she marries Aubrey Tanqueray and tries to lead a new life, society will not let her. Too many people remember her queening it on a loose-living aristocrat's yacht in the Mediterranean, going under the name of Mrs Jarman.

Whatever its title, Shaw certainly intended his play to show up Pinero's as pious flapdoodle; to "offer a counter-portrait to the general image of the romantic, sentimentally attractive courtesan of the stage." His objection to *Mrs Tanqueray* was that people took it seriously as a discussion of sexual morality. In his view, it left wholly untouched the real problem of the world's "fallen women"– lack of money. He wanted to write a play about the reality of prostitution and prostitutes, most of whose lives bore little resemblance to the genteel boredom of Paula Tanqueray, driven to despair by the empty round of arranging flowers, playing the piano and changing expensive frocks to receive visitors who never called. By surrendering to the beauty and sadness of Mrs Patrick Campbell's performance as Paula, Shaw considered, the British public continued to ignore and so, in effect, to connive at the real squalor and exploitation of the trade of prostitution.

Shaw did not frequent prostitutes – he remained a virgin, as he declared, until his twenty-ninth birthday and continued for the next thirteen years to live under his mother's roof. But he knew what he was talking about. In his first job, collecting slum rents for a Dublin land agent, he had to descend on prostitutes so early in the day that their overnight clients, usually soldiers, were still struggling into their breeches and boots. As a penniless scribbler in London, he walked everywhere – to the British Museum Library, to newspaper offices, concerts, free lectures and the handful of Soho restaurants where he could get a vegetarian meal for less than a shilling. No one who used the streets of London as a pedestrian, by day or after dark, could fail to recognize the enormous extent of prostitution in the city.

Nobody born after 1918, said the Austrian writer Stefan Zweig in his autobiography *The World of Yesterday*, could imagine the armies of women who walked the streets of Europe's great cities before the First World War.

> Then the sidewalks were so sprinkled with women for sale that it was more difficult to avoid than to find them. To this was added the countless number of "closed houses," the night clubs, the cabarets, the dance parlours with their dancers and singers, and the bars with their "come-on" girls. At that time female wares were offered for sale at every hour and at every price, and it cost a man as little time and trouble to purchase a woman for a quarter of an hour, an hour or a night, as it did to buy a package of cigarettes or a newspaper.

In a real sense, Zweig concluded, prostitution was the dark underground vault over which the gorgeous edifice of bourgeois society, with its twin cults of female purity and unswerving monogamy, reared itself. Middle-class European civilization could deny the erotic so long as eroticism seethed and bubbled elsewhere, unavowed and readily available, in the mean streets.

Where did Shaw get the name, in the end, of his play's central character, Mrs Warren? One possibility is that he found it across from his mother's apartment on Fitzroy Square, whose north side is closed by Warren Street. The corner of London where the Shaws lived has a raffish history and stood on the borderline between respectability and bohemianism. Lady Castlemaine, Charles II's most demanding mistress, secured the future of her second royal bastard Henry Fitzroy by gaining for him the hand of the heiress to Tottenham Court manor, and to go with it the titles of Earl of Euston and Duke of Grafton. When builders in the late eighteenth century developed the Tottenham Court lands for housing, the obvious names for the new district's streets were those of its semi-royal squire and his mother, who died the Duchess of Cleveland. The main thoroughfares surrounding Fitzroy Square were Fitzroy Street, Grafton Way and Cleveland Street, backing the square on the west side.

In the later nineteenth century the neighbourhood became a kind of northern annex to Soho, London's Latin Quarter, full of cheap foreign restaurants and artists' studios. Among the painters who worked in what later became known as Fitzrovia were Constable, Bonington, Maclise, Landseer, Rossetti, Holman Hunt, Whistler and Sickert. One of the attractions of the area to them may have been the ready availability of models. At least, that was what the Earl of Euston, Henry Fitzroy's successor, said he expected to find when he knocked one evening in 1886 on the door of 19 Cleveland Street, a block or two southwest of the Shaws' home. He said he had been handed a card by a man in Piccadilly advertising *poses plastiques* at that address. What he found instead was a male brothel offering the services of post-office messenger boys, among others, at ten shillings a time.

The earl found himself testifying to all this in a witness box two years later. In that time, the Cleveland Street affair had become a national scandal, shedding a searching light on the whole neighbourhood. Among the clients named by the boys who tipped off the police was Lord Arthur Somerset, son of the Duke of Beaufort and master of horse to the Prince of Wales, the future Edward VII. Lord Arthur fled to France on learning that a warrant was out for his arrest, hinting to friends that he did so not to protect himself but someone much nearer the throne. He could not have faced under oath, he implied, any questions about visits to the house in Cleveland Street by the Prince of Wales' eldest son Albert Edward, third in line of succession to Queen Victoria.

Albert Edward's death from pneumonia a few years later kept him from the throne, the succession passing to his blameless brother George V, and Lord Arthur's sacrifice of his reputation kept the prince's name out of the newspapers. But the rumours which flew around the case were sufficient to make it London's biggest scandal for some years. If you left out Jack the Ripper's murders of prostitutes in 1887 (no culprit was ever charged), there had been nothing to compare to it since the Crawford divorce case in 1885 had ruined the career of the statesman Sir Charles Dilke. On that occasion, Mrs Crawford testified that Sir Charles had taken her to seduce her to a house at 65 Warren Street.

Shaw's knowledge of London prostitution came partly from books such as Charles Booth's great study of the London poor and W.T. Stead's sensational articles in the *Pall Mall Gazette* in 1885, "The Maiden Tribute of Modern Babylon". But his personal slant on the subject came from living at 29 Fitzroy Square. Poised precariously on the borders of London's underworld of sex, he lived in the house of a woman who at the age of forty-three found herself needing to support herself and two children on a separation allowance of one pound a week from her alcoholic husband. Lucinda Shaw might have turned to the singing teacher, Vandaleur Lee, whom she had followed to London – most of Dublin supposed she had done so long ago. Instead, she found work teaching singing at the North London Collegiate School for Ladies, supporting herself and her difficult son until he in his forties became rich enough to support her. In later years, Shaw admitted to friends that Mrs Warren was based in some respects on his mother.

Shaw knew that the only dramatic moment in a career of prostitution was the moment of decision, to choose such a life or not. Artfully, *Mrs Warren's Profession*, without bringing a working prostitute onto the stage, presents the moment of decision three times – when Mrs Warren tells the story of her life, when she explains why she still runs her chain of brothels, and when she makes clear to her daughter Vivie that this empire is hers if she wants it. Vivie, too, is partly based on Lucinda Shaw. Rejecting her mother's offer, she rejects the world of carnality that makes that empire possible, family affections and all. One of the fine things about the play is that Shaw makes us see this rejection as tragic. Living at 29 Fitzroy Square, he knew that there was no frontier between vice and virtue. They were both faces of the same city.

Exit the Hero,
Enter the Superman

Programme note for the Shaw Festival's
1994 production of *Arms and The Man*

There's a famous story about the first night of *Arms and The Man*. On April 21, 1894, George Bernard Shaw stepped before the curtain of the Avenue Theatre in response to cries of "Author!" and was met by wild applause and a single loud "Boo!" from the gallery. Raising his eyes toward his invisible critic, Shaw said drily, "My dear fellow, I quite agree with you. But what are we two against so many?"

The rest of the story is not so famous. Shaw meant what he said. The evening had been both triumph and torture for him. He knew it had made his reputation as the most brilliant and ruthless new wit on the London stage. He knew also that this was the wrong reputation for him to make. "I had the curious experience," he wrote to his fellow dramatist Henry Arthur Jones, "of witnessing an apparently insane success, with the actors and actresses almost losing their heads with the intoxication of laugh after laugh, and of going before the curtain to thunderous applause, the only person in the theatre who knew that the whole affair was a ghastly failure."

It was a failure, to Shaw's mind, because the audience in its headlong laughter had failed to recognize the serious argument and emotions on which he had built his comedy. He found it ghastly that this riotous success could saddle him for life with the public image of a heartless joker, a satirist with the smile of a cut-throat razor, in the manner of W.S. Gilbert. To make it ghastlier, that comparison was made by his friend, the critic William Archer, in a review that accused Shaw of draining all the red corpuscles from his characters' veins.

"Gilbert is simply a paradoxically humorous cynic," Shaw wrote furiously to Archer. "He accepts the conventional ideals implicitly, but observes that people do not really live up to them. This he regards as a failure on their part which he mocks bitterly. This position is precisely that of Sergius in the play . . . I do not accept the conventional ideals . . . My whole secret is that I have got clean through the old categories of good and evil, and no longer use them even for dramatic effect. Sergius is ridiculous through the breakdown of his ideals, not odious from his falling short of them." Elsewhere he described Sergius as "a movingly human figure whose tragi-comedy is the true theme of the play."

Shaw was partly to blame for misreadings of his play. Before it opened, he published an imaginary interview with himself in which he pretended to have written it initially as a timeless, placeless comic theorem, then taken the advice of his Fabian friend Sidney Webb to set it during the Serbo-Bulgarian War of 1885-86. The story will not hold water. Shaw's allegedly placeless first draft bore the title *Alps and Balkans*. The whole strategy of the first act depends on the audience discovering that a scene of apparent Dumas romance is happening during Europe's most recent war. In any case, it's impossible to believe that Shaw's start on the play, recorded in his diary on November 26, 1893, owed nothing to the lengthy newspaper reports a week earlier of the death of Alexander of Battenberg, first prince of Bulgaria. The Prince died on November 18, the eighth anniversary of the battle of Slivnitza in which he had led his nation to victory over the Serbs. Sergius' tragi-comedy is, to a great extent, a domestic distillation of that of poor Sandro Battenberg.

The Battenbergs now are better known by the name their English branch adopted during World War I: Mountbatten. They descend from a spirited Grand Duchess of Hesse who, bored with her husband, set up a separate domicile managed for her by her Swiss master-of-horse. There she gave birth to two children, Marie and Alexander, whose good looks bore little resemblance to their Hessian siblings but a marked one to the handsome Switzer.

Marie's Cinderella beauty caught the eye of the Tsarevitch Alexander of Russia, touring the courts of Europe in search of a bride. Her brother accompanied her to Moscow for her wedding, but had to be sent home in disgrace for beguiling an imperial princess and then seducing an imperial lady-in-waiting. As consolation prize for marrying her, he was granted the title Prince of Battenberg, and it was their string of handsome, penniless sons who made the name known and feared in every European palace housing marriageable daughters.

Louis, the eldest, married Queen Victoria's granddaughter and became Britain's First Lord of the Admiralty. Henry, the idlest, outdid him by snaring Victoria's youngest daughter, and never worked again. But Sandro, the handsomest, found himself a throne. His uncle the Tsar Alexander II nominated him as first ruling prince of Bulgaria, wrested by Russia from the Turks in 1878. The Tsar's plan was to establish a Balkan puppet who would help Russia to corner Balkan railway construction and Danube trade. But Sandro, a newly minted Bulgarian, had discovered the pleasures of patriotism. When he turned on his patron to befriend British and German interests, the enraged Tsar recalled the Russian officers who commanded Bulgaria's tiny untrained army, among them Anna Karenina's lover, Count Vronsky. Seizing his chance, the king of neighbouring Serbia ordered three divisions to cross the Bulgarian border.

The Serbo-Bulgarian war was Sandro's finest hour. He led his army, commanded now by inexperienced young Bulgarians, on a forced march from the Turkish border over the Balkan mountains to defend Sofia, the capital. Sandro himself rode at their head to meet the oncoming Serbs before the village of Slivnitza. For two days the battle swayed back and forth. On the third, the Bulgarian cavalry led by Captain Benderev broke the Serbian line, triggering the panic retreat over the Dragoman Pass which opens Shaw's play. With his advance guard, Sandro crossed the Serbian frontier and prepared to march on Belgrade. Before he could do so, Austria's ambassador to Serbia arrived at Sandro's command post. Any further Bulgarian advance, he warned, would be met by Austrian troops and artillery.

Shaw's Heavenly Twins

Programme note for the Shaw Festival's
1995 production of *You Never Can Tell*

Bernard Shaw wrote *You Never Can Tell*, he explained to readers of his *Plays Pleasant* in 1898, in an attempt "to comply with many requests for a play in which the much paragraphed 'brilliancy' of *Arms and The Man* should be tempered by some consideration for the requirements of managers in search of fashionable comedies for West End theatres. I had no difficulty in complying, as I have always cast my plays in the ordinary practical comedy form in use in all the theatres; and far from taking an unsympathetic view of the popular preference for fun, fashionable dresses, a little music, and even an exhibition of eating and drinking by people with an expensive air, attended by an if-possible comic waiter, I was more than willing to shew that the drama can humanize these things as easily as they, in the wrong hands, can dehumanize the drama. But as so often happens, it was easier to do this than to persuade those who had asked for it that they had indeed got it."

What went wrong? Shaw did not exaggerate the rush for his services that followed the riotous opening of *Arms and The Man* in 1894. The New York actor-manager Richard Mansfield snapped up its American rights, asking for more. George Alexander, the handsomest actor-manager in England, expressed interest in any new work from Shaw's pen. Charles Wyndham himself, prince of light comedians, showed flattering eagerness to acquire a Shavian comedy tailored to his talents. Shaw quickly got to work. He dashed off his Napoleonic trifle *The Man of Destiny* for the small, imperious Mansfield. (Unfortunately it was intercepted by Ellen Terry and placed on Henry Irving's desk, where it languished, hated, for two years.) The mellifluous Alexander was offered first refusal of *Candida*, with its golden-voiced Socialist clergyman. (Alexander said he might be interested in playing the adolescent poet Marchbanks instead, if Shaw would blind him to make the role more sympathetic.) But the play in which Shaw invested most hope and effort, from 1895 to 1897, was *You Never Can Tell*, artfully framed to appeal to Charles Wyndham.

The play's plot, hinging on love at first sight in a seaside resort, bears a strong resemblance to the farce-comedy which had launched Wyndham's London career and sustained it with many revivals: *Brighton*, an adaptation for British audiences of Bronson Howard's New York hit *Saratoga*. Valentine, the amorous dentist tossed like a leaf in the wind of passion, is a monogamous twin of *Brighton's* Bob Sackett, who cannot resist proposing to every beautiful woman he meets. But in case Wyndham, now nearing sixty, felt too old for impetuous lovers, Shaw also wrote the part of his waiter William, infinitely wise, experienced, tactful and civilized, in the style of the men-of-the-world Wyndham had taken to playing in the comedies of Henry Arthur Jones. Unfortunately the latest of these, a debonair peer in Jones' *The Liars*, was already on Wyndham's agenda for 1897. Given the choice between playing a lord or a waiter, any nineteenth-century actor felt he owed it to himself to play the lord. Shaw had to look elsewhere.

George Alexander returned the script confessing bafflement: "When I got to the end, I had no more idea what you meant than a tom-cat." However Cyril Maude, an affable young actor who had recently leased the Haymarket Theatre, pursued Shaw for rights to the play. Rehearsals began in April 1897 after a few hiccups – the actor set to play Finch M'Comas walked out, followed by the actress cast as Mrs Clandon, who complained that there were "no laughs and no exits." Winifred Emery, Maude's wife and leading lady, insisted on playing Dolly, until the first reading revealed that Gloria in fact was the play's female lead. But the major problem was the Valentine, Allan Aynesworth, fresh from his success as Algy in *The Importance of Being Earnest*.

An army friend of Maude, Aynesworth was one of the new breed of players from "good" families, sketchily trained as actors but able to present the manners of society with a veracity new to

Piece by piece Sandro saw his victory taken from him. The Powers were not prepared to see him upset their balance of influence in the Balkans. Bismarck and the new Tsar Alexander III, who had never liked his matinee-idol cousin, agreed that Sandro must go. In August 1886 a group of Russian-paid officers, Benderev among them, kidnapped the prince from his palace, bundled him down the Danube in the royal yacht, and handed him over to the Tsar's police at the nearest Russian port. Given the choice of yielding up his throne or seeing Bulgaria disappear, Sandro abdicated. He returned to life as a cavalry officer in the Austrian army, happily married to an attractive commoner. His death in 1893 was caused by a burst appendix. In his deathbed delirium, he believed he was back on the field of Slivnitza, and died crying "Victory! Victory!"

Shaw in *Arms and The Man* pointed the moral of Sandro's war: patriotism and gallantry count for nothing in modern warfare beside armaments, power politics, and political calculation. Does this mean he found Sandro, or his theatrical representative Sergius, ridiculous as well as pitiful? Not, surely, when Sergius recognizes the tragedy into which his inhumanly romantic ideals have led him. But it took forty years for Shaw criticism to reach the insight of Edmund Wilson's essay in *The Triple Thinkers*, which argues that what made the playwright great was his ability to hold two contradictory truths in his mind at the same time. *Arms and The Man* is the first play in which Shaw does this. It is at once a comedy of a perfect rationalist – Shaw's first sketch of a Superman – who points where the world must go, and the tragedy of a heroic romantic who embodies what the world will lose by going there.

For the rest of his life, Shaw harangued actors and managers about the casting of his play; urging Richard Mansfield to play Sergius rather than Bluntschli, begging Firmin Gémier to find for the first Paris production a Sergius as superb, magnetic and handsome as the leading tragedian of the Comédie-Française, Mounet-Sully. It's not clear whether Florence Farr believed Shaw, when he persuaded her to play Louka, the maid who recognizes Sergius as a great Balkan chieftain, that she was abandoning the feminine lead to play the strongest part in the script. But one need only compare the precision of Shaw's details with the fairy tale that Anthony Hope wove around Sandro's kidnapping in *The Prisoner of Zenda* (published some weeks after the play opened) to see that Shaw was interested in human realities, not Balkan romance. Perhaps with a real Balkan war to shed its light on *Arms and The Man* on its hundredth birthday, we may have a better chance to see the play as Shaw intended.

the stage. His love scene with Winifred Emery in Act II, where Valentine and Gloria are seized by the Life Force, defeated him. "It was not that he did it badly, or tamely, or wrongly," Shaw explained later to Mrs Richard Mansfield. "He simply could not do it at all." Shaw, who had been contracted to direct, had to tell Maude gently that the task was impossible and withdraw the play. Six years later, consulted by Maude about how to present the episode in a history of the Haymarket, Shaw scribbled a chapter purporting to be by Maude, laying all blame on the Shavian imp of perversity that willed the rehearsals to fail. It read very funnily. Maude included it in his book.

Shaw was less amused by his play's miscarriage than he pretended. It was the main reason for his decision, a turning point in his career, to offer his plays to the public in print, since no one would offer them in performance. But although it took him time to recognize it, the writing of *You Never Can Tell* embodied a decision even more important. Without intending to, he had written a play impossible for the new generation of actors, reared on naturalism and notions of polite understatement. His creation called for the old breed of theatrical mountebanks he had loved in his youth, trained on Shakespeare, melodrama, and that last refuge of the *commedia dell'arte*, the English pantomime. At some level below consciousness, he had made the decision not to be the apostle of Ibsen and naturalism on the British stage.

How had this reversal come about? It looks like the complicated result of Shaw's admiration for the novel which gave him the germ of his play, Sarah Grand's *The Heavenly Twins*. After reading it in 1895 he pronounced the work touched with genius. (Indeed, his title for the first draft of *You Never Can Tell* was *The Terrestrial Twins*.) Madame Grand was in actuality an Irishwoman named Frances Bellenden-Clark who, having coined the phrase "the New Woman" in 1894, lived up to it by adopting the style of George Sand. She had ridden the wave of Ibsenite scandal provoked by the London premiere of *Ghosts* by publishing a novel, written some years earlier, in which a wife dies of syphilis caught from a dissolute husband – one of three Victorian heroines (the novel owes much to

George Eliot's *Middlemarch* and *Daniel Deronda*) whose lives support the judgment of Gloria in *You Never Can Tell* that the conditions of marriage at present are not such as any self-respecting woman can accept.

Grand's novel is so nearly excellent that the itch to try and improve it is irresistible. Shaw's attempt consisted of taking over its materials and giving them more cheerful outcomes. All of Grand's heroines come to sad or saddish ends: one dead through sexual ignorance, one permanently wounded by learning on her wedding day of her groom's promiscuity, the third – the female twin of the title – cast off by the love of her life when he learns that she is the beautiful boy who has won his friendship on midnight visits in her brother's clothes. Though the novel makes quite moving the man's sense of double loss – both of the boy he has loved and the girl he idealized at a distance – Shaw clearly found something perverse in the notion of rewriting *As You Like It* so as to give it an unhappy ending. No, he rejoined in *You Never Can Tell*, the world is not entirely hopeless, but benign in its insistence on being peopled. Men may be stupid, but not all of them conspire to make women stupider. And where stupidity flies in the face of Nature, Nature can be counted on to enforce common sense.

To make his comic vision prevail over the bleak feminist accusations of Grand's novel, Shaw conjured up the mighty ghost of Shakespeare. The face of his bust in Stratford parish church presides over *You Never Can Tell* on the shoulders of the old waiter whom Dolly has christened "William" because of this resemblance. Like Ephesus in *The Comedy of Errors* or the unnamed capital of Illyria in *Twelfth Night*, Shaw's seaside town is thrown into confusion by the appearance of supernaturally handsome twins from the sea, marvelling at the brave new world unknown to them in their island nursery. Mrs Clandon is a female Prospero who cannot regain her kingdom until she acknowledges that thing of darkness, her furious, wounded husband, as her own. The philosopher Suzanne Langer wrote that tragedy deals with life from the point of view of the individual – all individual lives, one may say, end badly – while comedy perceives it with the eyes of the community or species, recognizing that for every death there is a birth, for every divorce a wedding, for every parting a lover's meeting. Shaw opposes to the severe judgment of minds preoccupied by individual rights the friendlier view – he calls it socialist – of the world of Shakespearian comedy, where spring follows winters, Jack shall have Jill, and all shall be well so long as each generation of society forgets its tragedies in the happiness of its children.

In case the power of Shakespeare is insufficient, the gods of the old Italian comedy take over the stage in the last act. Harlequin, Columbine and Il Dottore drag the older generation out of the melodrama they have made of their lives and into the eternal dance of the seasons and human love. When *You Never Can Tell* finally found its audience in May 1905, during the Vedrenne–Barker seasons at the Court Theatre, the critic Desmond MacCarthy called it a religious farce. He might also have called it the play in which Shaw decided not to be the English Ibsen, but to be Shaw.

A REPUBLICAN HAMLET

Programme note for the Shaw Festival's
1996 production of *The Devil's Disciple*

The play that finally made Shaw a money-earning playwright, *The Devil's Disciple*, happened almost by accident. In February 1896 the actor-manager William Terriss, ringmaster of the Adelphi Theatre's smoky kingdom of melodrama, invited Shaw for a backstage chat while he dressed for a matinee. He was planning a world tour, Terriss confided, and thought it would be fun to include in his repertoire a burlesque of all the stock melodrama situations seen at the Adelphi or the Lyceum Theatre, where he had served twelve years under Henry Irving. He listed them all – the evicted widow, the befriended orphan, the swapped identity, the heroine's swoon, the reprieve from the scaffold. Would it amuse Shaw to string them together for him on a thread of *non sequiturs*, ending each act with the hero dangling from some moral precipice, beginning the next with a shameless equivalent of "with a bound, he was free"?

Shaw hesitated. The burlesque idea, he wrote to Ellen Terry, was "not in my line". Terriss must have read the reviews of *Arms and The Man* which named GBS as heir apparent to W.S. Gilbert. But the thought of writing a real play for Terriss appealed to him. In his *Saturday Review* theatre column, Shaw had often praised the Adelphi company's energetic, heartfelt playing of melodrama, and the masculine dash and sincerity of its leading man. Untainted by the rage for gentility that infected most London stages, the Adelphi fare reminded him of barnstorming heroes of his youth, such as the Shakespearian actor Barry Sullivan. "I seriously think I shall write a play for [Terriss]," he told Ellen Terry. "A good melodrama is a more difficult thing to write than all this clever-clever comedy: one must go straight to the core of humanity to get it, and if it is only good enough, why, there you have Lear or Macbeth." He

wrote Terriss that what the world would want of him was not burlesque but something like *Hamlet*, "on popular lines". The implication was that Shaw would supply it. Terriss did not tell him not
to.

In fact, Shaw found melodrama easier than the clever-clever
comedy then giving him trouble, *You Never Can Tell*. Spending Easter
in the country with his Fabian friend Graham Wallas, he set the
comedy aside and scribbled the outline of a three-act melodrama.
In it a handsome malcontent, dressed in black, rejects the woman
who loves him in order to pursue his destiny, thus saving his country. "An Ishmael better than his people," he jotted in his notebook,
"and therefore rated as worse, and rating himself so." Clearly it was
going to be a play about puritanism.

By December 1896 he had roughed out most of the dialogue, and decided to set the play in New England during the
American Revolution. He wrote Terriss announcing that he was
ready to read it to him. Terriss's plans for a tour had fallen through
and he had no memory of commissioning Shaw to write a play.
But his leading lady, Jessie Millward, insisted on hearing it over tea
at her flat. Terriss composed himself dismally to listen, Shaw told
Ellen Terry, as if dragged into church, but evidently found difficulty following what he heard. "Is this an interior?" he stopped
Shaw to ask about the climax of the first act, and early in the second act repeated the question. Shaw's answer set him "completely
at rest," the author declared; and indeed his next interruption took
the form of a snore. Roused with tea and reproaches by Miss
Millward, Terriss was deeply ashamed, pleading that all literature
except travel books put him to sleep. Shaw assured him that Dr
Johnson shared his disability; at which Miss Millward exclaimed
radiantly, "Oh Willie, I have been doing you an injustice!" There
was no further talk of the play.

Over Christmas 1896, after reading De Fonblanque's life of
General Burgoyne, Shaw put the finishing touches to his creation.
He found in De Fonblanque's book the figures to explain
Burgoyne's defeat at Saratoga – 5000 British troops, plus assorted
Hessian mercenaries and Mohawks, faced 18,000 armed colonists

– and the reason for General Howe's failure to march his army north from New York to join Burgoyne at Albany. George III's Secretary for the Colonies, Lord George Germain, left his office for the weekend without signing the essential papers for Howe, so the order was never sent. But Shaw did not trouble to make his plot conform with history, which as Burgoyne says "will tell lies, as usual." In fact, Burgoyne never set foot in New Hampshire on his march from the St Lawrence to the Hudson, and his defeat at Saratoga occurred early in October, not in winter as Shaw's first stage direction would suggest.

Early in 1897 Shaw sent a copy of the play to Richard Mansfield in New York, hoping its American background might interest the actor who had presented *Arms and The Man* in the United States. He also read it to Johnston Forbes Robertson and his current leading lady, Mrs Patrick Campbell. Mrs Pat disliked the ending, with its implication that Dick Dudgeon would prefer patriotism to a heroine played by her; and though Robertson toured the play round northern England a few years later, Mrs Pat by then had become her own manager. In the end the premiere of *The Devil's Disciple* was staged by Mansfield in New York, at the Fifth Avenue Theatre on October 4, 1897. It ran for 64 performances, then toured the Middle West in 1898, earning Shaw $10,000 in royalties – enough for him to give up his job with the *Saturday Review*.

Shaw hoped its American success might awaken Terriss's interest in the play, and planned an approach to him. But on December 16, 1897, as Terriss let himself into the Adelphi by a private pass-door in an alley off the Strand, he was stabbed by a deranged minor actor named Richard Prince, who had had some small parts in Terriss's productions, and died in Jessie Millward's arms. In his obituary in the *Saturday Review*, Shaw called him "within certain limits, the most efficient actor in London. For art as art he cared nothing, and made no secret of it; for efficiency he cared a good deal."

Was it simply his efficiency that made Shaw so eager for Terriss to play his republican Hamlet? There was also the fact that he had tailored the play to Terriss's specifications. In addition to the evicted widow, befriended orphan, swooning lady and the rest, *The Devil's Disciple* included echoes of several other melodramas: the comic trial of the wrong man borrows from Boucicault's *The Wicklow Wedding*, and Dick Dudgeon's last words on the scaffold recall Sydney Carton's "It is a far, far better thing I do" in *The Only Way*, Martin Harvey's stage version of *A Tale of Two Cities*. But there was a deeper reason why Shaw had jumped at writing a play for Terriss in the first place.

There is a clue to it in the review he wrote of Belasco's *The Girl I Left Behind Me*, starring Terriss, at the Adelphi in 1895. A successful melodrama, Shaw argued, should be "allegorical, idealistic, full of generalizations and moral lessons and it must represent conduct as producing swiftly and certainly on the individual the results which in actual life it only produces on the race in the course of many centuries." He identified melodrama as a way of expressing theatrically his belief in Creative Evolution, and Terriss as an actor who could display the process by which the Nietzschean superman changes history, translating deep conviction into willpower, and will-power into heroic action. Dick Dudgeon is the first of the line of heroes of conviction that includes John Tanner in *Man and Superman*, Lavinia and Ferrovius in *Androcles and the Lion* and, eventually, Saint Joan.

The secret, Shaw realized, lay in the quality of the acting. We recognize the superiority of Saint Joan's truths to those of her judges not by their superior logic, but by the fact that they are the product of her whole nature and personality – rising from her boots to her lips with the unflawed conviction of an entire life, as the names "Brighton" or "Ramsgate" run all the way through a stick of British seaside rock candy. It takes an actor to show to an audience that kind of conviction. "All you need for great acting," said the late Fred Allen, "is absolute sincerity. If you can fake that, you've got it made."

A VISITOR FROM THE FUTURE

Programme note for the Shaw Festival's
2002 production of *Caesar and Cleopatra*

On his last tour of North America, in the autumn of 1914, Johnston Forbes Robertson decided not to take *Caesar and Cleopatra* to Canada. He had played it in major cities on earlier visits. This trip was his farewell to the "split week" dates – three nights in this town, three in the next – so would need only three of the four productions he had brought across America. Small places like these would want to see his Shakespearian showpieces, *Hamlet* and *Othello*, and Jerome K. Jerome's sanctimonious, horribly popular fantasy *The Passing of the Third Floor Back*. To drop *Caesar and Cleopatra*, his heaviest show, would be an enormous saving. Of the ten railway cars with which he had left New York the year before, its scenery and properties had filled three.

Customs regulations forbade selling the production or giving it away. So at the end of its San Francisco run, Robertson got permission from the local authorities to burn it on a waste site by the Pacific. Early one morning after the play's last performance, its sets and furnishings were piled on the shore around Cleopatra's Sphinx, a fifteen-foot structure designed by the sculptor Lucchesi, and set alight. Robertson's stage carpenter and crew, who had built and handled the show across the continent, watched sadly as smoke rose around the Sphinx, her face above its clouds staring with timeless inscrutability into the rising sun. Then flames engulfed her, and her ashes floated up on the sea wind into the Pacific morning.

If you like symbolism, you can interpret the incident as the Gotterdammerung of the great actor-managers – by 1918 they were all dead or retired – set by fate on the California coast so that its fiery seeds might drift south and engender the age of their heirs, D.W. Griffith and Cecil B. De Mille. For Shaw scholars, the story has a simpler point. It demonstrates that, from the play's first staging, producers have dealt with the problems raised by one of Shaw's most problem-rich works by burying them under spectacle. Nothing silences questions like a ton of scenery. If you worry about your audience believing that Cinderella's coach turns back into a pumpkin, stage the transformation with whatever smoke, mirrors and trap-doors you can muster, but be sure to do so before a life-size, three-dimensional replica of the grand front staircase of the palace of Fontainebleau.

This was the strategy employed by Gabriel Pascal when he directed his film of *Caesar and Cleopatra* in 1945. With over seven million dollars of J. Arthur Rank's flour-mill fortune, he bought Vivien Leigh out of her contract with David O. Selznick to play the Egyptian queen to Claude Rains' Caesar; built the harbour of Alexandria and palace of the Ptolemies at Denham studios west of London; and rented a battalion of the Egyptian army to gallop about the desert outside Cairo wearing helmets and breastplates. The only question raised by the finished film was how so much money could have translated into so much tedium.

Producers shovel on the spectacle because they discover early in rehearsal that, while undoubtedly the first of Shaw's really great plays, *Caesar and Cleopatra* is also one of his oddest. Crammed with authentic historical detail mined from Theodor Mommsen's five-volume history of Rome, it then plays frivolously with his facts. Caesar's soldiery are made to talk like members of the army that occupied Egypt in 1882 to protect Britain's investment in the Suez Canal. Caesar's secretary Britannus explains why all British men of social standing regard blue as the only respectable colour to wear, in peace and war. Again and again in the course of the play, at its most spectacular moments, Shaw throws some anachronistic joke at the audience, as if to say with a wink, "Don't believe a word of it!" Most drastically, he presents the young Cleopatra, nearly twenty-one when she first met Caesar, as a schoolgirl of only sixteen.

Scholars have supposed that Shaw must have garbled the dates Mommsen gave in his history for Cleopatra's ascent to her father's throne in 53 BC and for Caesar's arrival in Egypt in 48 BC.

(Mommsen makes it easy to do so by using throughout the Romans' system of dating events from the founding of their republic.) I think it likelier that Shaw swallowed the dismissal of Caesar's liaison with the queen of Egypt in the short life of Caesar published in 1886 by J.A. Froude, a slapdash and opinionated historian held in mysteriously high regard by Victorians. Froude conceded in a footnote that it's possible that Caesar had an affair with Cleopatra, but declared that only a frivolous, scandal-loving mind could believe that the master of the world would let his public conduct be affected by "a connection with a loose girl of sixteen". The tone is close to the one Shaw adopted when talking about his play and people's expectations of it, and Shaw repeated Froude's mistake about Cleopatra's age.

But more important than either of these possible sources, I'd say, was the comment Shaw made in January 1895 when reviewing Oscar Wilde's *An Ideal Husband*. "Mr Wilde is to me," he wrote, "our only thorough playwright. He plays with everything: with wit, with philosophy, with drama, with actors and audience, with the whole theatre." Shaw was deliberately playing with history when he sat down to write *Caesar and Cleopatra* three years later. During his years as theatre critic for the *Saturday Review*, he had come to the conclusion that the pictorial theatre of the painted, gaslit nineteenth-century stage was a force for stasis, a stumbling block in the path of progress. With its aesthetic of picture-making before everything else, it created a discipline of obedience to the picture's decorum, of acting in accordance with the style of the picture. The only way of escaping the tyranny of the picture was to walk out of it, slamming the door like Nora in *A Doll's House*. The only way of showing on stage a world capable of change was to subvert the picture from within – writing a scene, for instance, like the opening of *Arms and The Man*, about a fleeing soldier hiding in a lady's moonlit Balkan bedroom, in which he shows no interest in making love to her but only in food, sleep and escape. By doing so, he demonstrates that he is a part not of the picture, but of reality.

Much of Shaw's mock rivalry with Shakespeare – the part that was not clowning self-promotion – had to do with the fact that Shakespeare was the main pillar of the pictorial theatre of the actor-managers. In the world of Shakespeare as depicted on the stages of Henry Irving, Beerbohm Tree and Augustin Daly, splendid with Gothic cornices, painted marble and live rabbits hopping through the woods near Athens, nothing could change except the seasons and the names of the kings. *Caesar and Cleopatra* was written in angry reaction against two recent spectacular revivals: *Julius Caesar*, produced by Tree in January 1898 with superb vistas of ancient Rome by the painter Alma Tadema, and *Antony and Cleopatra*, brought south from Manchester by Louis Calvert and Janet Achurch in May the previous year. To Shaw, Tree's *Caesar* was an overblown libel on the man Mommsen called the last great creative mind of the classical world, giving him no line worthy of "an average Tammany boss". *Antony and Cleopatra* he found emptily rhetorical, a display of scenery for the sake of chewing it. "An afternoon of lacerating anguish," he called it, "spent partly in contemplating Miss Achurch's overpowering experiments in rhetoric, and partly in wishing I had never been born."

The one exception he made in his dismissal of picture-stage Shakespeare was *Hamlet* as produced by Forbes Robertson at the Lyceum in October 1897. Robertson made it seem a genuine political tragedy: had his Hamlet succeeded to its throne, Denmark would obviously have become a better, less rotten place. This, Shaw argued, was because Forbes Robertson was "essentially a classical actor, the only one ... now established in London management. What I mean by classical is that he can present a dramatic hero as a man whose passions are those which have produced the philosophy, the poetry, the art and the statecraft of the world, and not merely those which have produced its weddings, coroners' inquests and executions." Robertson's Ophelia in this production was Mrs Patrick Campbell, with whom he was painfully in love. He was looking for more plays in which they could appear together. Shaw suggested *Caesar and Cleopatra*, but by the time he finished it the lovers had gone their separate ways, Robertson to a nervous breakdown. He did not produce the play until 1906.

By then, *Caesar and Cleopatra* had lost some of the novelty it might have had in 1899. It was Shaw's first full-dress attempt to put his idea of the Superman on the stage, and his first use of the playful anachronism necessary to do so. Shaw's notion of the Superman is of a kind of visitor from the future: a representative of the next stage of human evolution appearing on earth before his time. For an audience to feel his significance, he needed to appear in a society the audience could think of as primitive but also just like themselves; to strike contemporary listeners as one of us battling an ignorant past, but also as a superior being from a time yet unborn showing us how to become Supermen ourselves.

Shaw knew little about Egypt when he wrote *Caesar and Cleopatra*. What he knew, he had learned chiefly in the Egyptian gallery of the British Museum, where he took breaks from study in the Reading Room to flirt with the writer Edith Nesbit. The principal lesson he learned from that great hall of stone gods with animal heads, giant obelisks and black marble cats was that human nature was many centuries older and more primitive than most Victorians supposed. The corollary of this was that it might go on evolving for centuries more, until what passed for civilization in nineteenth-century Europe might seem as barbarous as ancient Egypt.

From this Shaw reasoned that the highest form of human intelligence is one that feels its unity with this immense river of time, at home at once with Socrates, Shakespeare and Darwin; capable of stretching back in imagination to the dawn of history and forward to a world fit for supermen and superwomen. That is the state of mind into which he tries to manoeuvre us.

If he succeeds, we come to recognize that *Caesar and Cleopatra* is a comedy about a tragedy, whose full meaning we grasp only if we carry *Antony and Cleopatra* in our heads. Their heroines are the same unteachable woman. As usual, the visitor from the future comes to alter the course of history if he can, to try to avert Shakespeare's tragedy. For a moment, when she rises to his vision of a kingdom of the future at the source of the Nile, Caesar hopes he can give Cleopatra the mind of a great ruler. But a moment later, she proves herself a woman who lives only in the present, addicted to such instant gratifications as cruelty and revenge. She sees no value in futures. When her bright day is done, she will choose the dark.

WHITE WITCH OF THE WEST

Note for the Shaw Festival's 1979 production of
Captain Brassbound's Conversion, from the
souvenir book for that season

The origin of *Captain Brassbound's Conversion*, Shaw told his biographer Hesketh Pearson, was a remark Ellen Terry made on the birth of Gordon Craig's eldest daughter. "Now that I am a grandmother," she said, "nobody will ever write a play for me." He immediately wrote *Brassbound* for her, "out of a natural desire to contradict," as she said. It is a good story. Unfortunately the facts don't fit. Rosemary Craig was born in April 1894, Shaw and Ellen Terry didn't become intimates-by-letter until a year later, and *Brassbound* was not written until 1899. Shaw invented his tale to conceal a better, more complex and personal one which began with two accidents on a night in 1896.

In the early hours of December 20 that year, after a triumphant revival at the Lyceum Theatre of his celebrated *Richard III*, Henry Irving stumbled on the stairs of his apartments in Grafton Street, Mayfair, and injured his knee. The fall tore the ligatures of his kneecap, keeping him off the stage for ten weeks, but it did even greater damage to a conspiracy which had been hatching under his nose for over a year. Since the previous autumn his leading lady, Ellen Terry, had been secretly corresponding with his fiercest critic, Shaw. Not very seriously, they pretended the object of their correspondence was courtship, the seduction of England's most adored actress by its most hated weekly reviewer. Really, both knew, its aim was seduction of another kind: the conversion of Irving to the new drama of Ibsen and Shaw himself.

Fabian that he was, Shaw knew the best hope for theatrical revolution was to infiltrate the citadel of tradition, the Lyceum. If Irving would accept the new drama, so would the British public. To this end, he sent Ellen Terry a comedy, *The Man of Destiny*, baited with a sparkling role for herself and an even more alluring one for Irving – the young Napoleon.

For her part, Ellen Terry knew such infiltration was necessary. Both her children were involved in the new movement. She did not need them to tell her that, in the London of Wilde's comedies and *The Second Mrs Tanqueray*, the Lyceum had grown old-fashioned. Besides, she had played all the good women's roles in the old repertoire. The new drama offered a new lease on her waning career – Ibsen's Lady from the Sea, Rebecca West, Mrs Alving, Shaw's Candida and the lady in *Man of Destiny* – if Irving would countenance it.

She talked Irving into accepting *The Man of Destiny*. While he was chairbound by his accident, she forcibly read him *John Gabriel Borkman.* ("Threadworms and leeches," he wrote savagely in his diary). She could not know there had been another accident that December night, a verbal one. In his review of *Richard III*, Shaw remarked innocently that Irving seemed "tired . . . not to be answering his helm satisfactorily"; that in the last scenes, "his exhaustion was too genuine to be quite acceptable as part of the play." By the time the review appeared, news of Irving's accident was out. Put together, their implication seemed obvious: Sir Henry had been drunk on stage and gone drunk up to bed.

It took Shaw six months to realize what had happened. He found out only the following May, when Irving returned *The Man of Destiny* with a curt message that he had changed his mind. It took Ellen Terry even longer to grasp the extent to which she had forfeited her partner's trust. She saw only that he was reserved, even furtive with her; that he gave his affection now to a journalist, Mrs Aria, whom he met that summer. She saw him now only before others. "I feel so certain Henry just hates me," she wrote Shaw despairingly. "I can only guess at it, for he is exactly the same sweet-mannered person he was when 'I felt so certain' Henry loved me." But although she thought of ending their Lyceum partnership, it was too late.

From the night of Irving's fall, the Lyceum's fortunes declined. His absence from the stage caused a heavy loss that season. The next brought a more crippling blow: all his scenery, sets for forty-four productions, was destroyed in a fire. Panicked, he put his theatre in the hands of a group of businessmen for whom he worked on ruinously unfavourable terms. So placed, there was no way Ellen Terry could desert him honourably, though the roles he offered insulted her talents.

Meanwhile her paper suitor also deserted her. In 1898, another accident threw Shaw into the arms of an Irish heiress, Charlotte Payne-Townshend. Lacing a boot too tightly, he caused an abscess which infected his foot bone. Charlotte, who had gone to Rome to forget him, returned to find him helpless in the house he shared with his mother, up to his necrosed ankle in books, squalor and dirty dishes. Raging at his mother's neglect, she married him and bore him off to the country, where it took a year to nurse him back to health. At the end of that year, guiltily aware of the lurch in which he had left Ellen, Shaw began a play for her.

In their days of paper flirtation, she had given one specification for it. "Don't write plays to be acted in a scene of four walls. Oh, the Open, the Open! Let mine (!) be in the open." That chimed with his convalescent reading. Influenced by Charlotte, an indefatigable tourist, he had been devouring travel books – Stanley's Congo journal, Mary Kingsley's *Travels in West Africa*, R.B. Cunninghame Graham's *Mogreb-el-Acksa: A Journey in Morocco*. Though leisure reading, they bore on his political interests. The Fabian Society was wrestling with the question of imperialism: march of civilization or simply the march of capital? West Africa, the Congo and Morocco were leading prizes in the current European grab for Africa. Britain, having grabbed back the Sudan from the Mahdi, was about to grab the two Boer republics. The United States was girding to grab Cuba and the Philippines from Spain. A play took shape in Shaw's mind contrasting travellers with conquerors, Europe's *mission civilisatrice* with her aggressive acquisitiveness.

Another specification was implicit. Ellen Terry must be able to do the play with Irving if she stayed by him, without him if her position at the Lyceum became untenable. That meant a "modern" heroine for her, a traditional romantic hero for him. A plot began to crystallize. Why not stage Shaw's own contest with Irving, the tug-of-war between traditional theatrical morality and the new drama, the conversion of a melodrama hero to Ibsenite enlightenment? And what better setting than Peer Gynt's first landfall: the Morocco of Cunninghame Graham, that bizarre mixture of radical socialist and Byronic corsair?

One more ingredient went into the broth. Dashing off his long essay on Wagner during his convalescence, Shaw re-read Shelley to compare *Prometheus Unbound* with the *Ring Cycle*. Another poem caught his eye: *The Witch of Atlas*, Shelley's platonic dream of a white goddess who tames all savage natures, quenching "the earth-consuming rage/ Of gold and blood – 'til men should live and move/ Harmonious as the sacred stars above." It gave him his working title and his heroine. "*The Witch of Atlas...* represents you travelling in the Atlas mountains," he wrote Ellen Terry on June 1, 1899.

To his chagrin, she found it "not the sort of play for me in the least." She could not see herself in the role of Lady Cicely Waynflete, the all-conquering charmer who "walked across Africa accompanied only by her little dog," until she caught her maid laughing to herself while watching her open a bazaar. "I'm so sorry," the girl blurted, "but Lady Cicely is so like you! She gets her way in *everything – just like you!*" She showed it hopefully to Irving, but he choked on the scene where Brassbound appears in frock coat and silk hat. "Shaw wrote it to make them laugh at me," he exploded, and Shaw admitted he was right.

In the end the play was produced by the Stage Society in 1901 with neither star. Janet Achurch played Lady Cicely, Irving's son Laurence was Brassbound. Not until a year after Irving's death in 1905 would Ellen Terry betray her old partner by playing in it for Vedrenne and Barker at the Court Theatre. Even then she felt uneasy in it, convinced that Shaw was unsatisfied by her incarnation of his white goddess.

She may have been right. Hidden behind his play for her was one he wrote for himself: a play not only about imperialism but also about his ideal of womanhood. In the flesh, even Ellen Terry may not have lived up to it. As it turned out, she was not quite Shelley's sexless Witch. During rehearsal, she tucked the American actor who played Captain Kearney, James Carew, under her arm and made him her third husband.

"Before you can play Lady Cicely perfectly," Shaw had told Janet Achurch, who also dissatisfied him, "you will have to make a careful study of the English lady." It was not a word he used with approval except of one woman – his wife. The travelling Lady Cicely is an idealized portrait not only of Ellen Terry but also of Charlotte Shaw, the woman who taught her husband that not all her sex were theatrical egotists like the mother too busy with her own musical career to care for his crippled foot. *Captain Brassbound* is not only about the conversion of a romantic to Ibsenite good sense. It is also about the conversion of a neglected, emotionally wounded son to romance. It has often been dismissed as lesser, occasional Shaw, a play written to discharge an obligation, into which Shaw put too little of himself. Looked at closely, it becomes one of the most personal things he ever wrote – too personal to tell the truth about its origin and inspiration.

A PLAY WITH DYNAMITE

Programme note for the Shaw Festival's
1998 production of *Major Barbara*

Bernard Shaw's friendship with H.G. Wells lasted, with intermittent strains and wobbles, for fifty years, from their meeting at a theatre in 1895 (both were reviewing the disastrous first night of Henry James' *Guy Domville*) until Wells' death in 1946. It was a fragile, prickly relationship, made up of rivalry, admiration, mutual pie-throwing, affection and irritation. But it tells something that, of the many contemporaries who irritated Shaw, Wells was the only one to serve him as sand serves an oyster. From the irritation that Wells caused him grew two of Shaw's greatest pearls. One was *Heartbreak House*, in which Shaw caricatured Wells' habit of seducing young socialist ladies with his tales of anthropophagi and Martians with heads beneath their shoulders. The other was *Major Barbara*.

The irritation that caused *Major Barbara* began in 1903. In that year Shaw and his friends Sidney and Beatrice Webb persuaded Wells to join the Fabian Society. They had admired his book *Anticipations*, with its vision of a future federation of the world run by superbly intelligent trained technicians. This was much the same future the Fabians dreamed of and much the role they imagined themselves playing in it. By adding Wells to their number they hoped to bring both future and role nearer.

The older Fabians knew that their society was in the doldrums. They had founded it twenty years earlier, when they were young and unheard of, as a club for middle-class people to discuss socialist ideas. Those twenty years had made them famous – their *Fabian Essays* were a best-seller, Shaw was always in the papers, the Webbs dined with leaders of both great political parties. But the more famous they became, the more ineffectual they seemed. After twenty years, they were still just talking. Children of John Stuart

Mill, they had grown up believing that in a free market of free speech, the best ideas were bound to win. In a new century, an age no longer Victorian, of penny newspapers, publishing wars, advertising, dreadnoughts and jingoism, the triumph of the best ideas no longer seemed inevitable. Wells was a consummate man of the new age. Perhaps he could lead the Fabians into it.

A year into the Society, Wells tried to resign. It was in worse shape than he had imagined. He put his finger at once on the Fabians' major weakness: they were afraid to compromise themselves by acting. They said their aim was to convert Britain to collectivism. Now that there was an Independent Labour Party, created by Keir Hardie and other trade union leaders for that purpose, they dithered over supporting it for fear of losing influence over Liberals or Tories. They had almost split apart over the Boer War. Half of them felt it their socialist duty to oppose war and support South Africa's brave little farmers against capitalist imperialism. The other half, Shaw among them, thought it foolish to resist the march of history, spreading technology around the globe in ever larger economic units. Many, like the Webbs, found the whole thing distasteful, a greedy, ill-bred business, and would rather have ignored it as irrelevant to socialism. Inverting Lord Acton's saying that power corrupts, they had come to regard powerlessness as a form of virtue.

Shaw knew Wells was right. That was why he wanted him in the Society. Since his Fabian youth, Shaw had discovered Schopenhauer and come to believe that the world is created by will. To will an end without willing the means to achieve it, he now recognized, was not really to will it at all. Like Wells, he wanted the Fabians to imitate the Roman general for whom they named themselves, Fabius Cunctator: having saved up their strength for the moment to strike, they should now strike with all their force. But he did not wish to be the man to demolish the talking shop where he and his friends had been happy. He wanted a new generation to take over the Society and remake it in their image. He persuaded the Fabians to strike a committee to review their entire enterprise, from top to bottom, with Wells as its moving spirit. Then, nominating his wife Charlotte to keep an eye on things, like a good dramatist he left his characters to spin their plot and went off to write a play.

For suddenly his career had taken off. Harley Granville Barker and John Vedrenne, manager of the Court Theatre, had launched a repertory whose mainstay was the plays of Shaw. *John Bull's Other Island* had been the hit of 1904, seen five times by the prime minister, Arthur Balfour, and once by Edward VII, who broke his chair laughing. A new play was needed for 1905, preferably one that dealt with the condition of England as *John Bull* had treated Ireland. Shaw fell back on a suggestion Beatrice Webb had made ten years earlier, trying to head him off writing *Mrs Warren's Profession*. Put on the stage, she had urged him, "a real modern lady of the governing class – not the sort of thing theatrical and critical authorities imagine such a lady to be." He had pretended to do so in Vivie Warren, but he knew what Beatrice really meant, and now acted on it. He put on the stage Beatrice herself, disguised in a Salvation Army uniform.

Beatrice was a Potter, daughter of one of the Midland dynasties created by steam, iron and cotton. Her grandfather had sat in Parliament with John Bright, the reformer. Her father promoted railways and was friends with Herbert Spencer, the Positivist philosopher. He put Beatrice and her eight sisters on the London marriage market, but after falling painfully in love with the rising statesman Joseph Chamberlain and discovering he only liked women who agreed with him, she turned her back on society and its small talk. She went to work for the shipping magnate Charles Booth, a cousin by marriage, who was devoting his fortune to a study of poverty in east London. Dressed as a poor seamstress, Beatrice toiled in an East End sweatshop sewing trousers. Her account of her experiences made a chapter in Booth's first volume of *Life and Labour of the People in London*. Sidney Webb, reviewing it in the *Star*, pronounced Miss Potter "the only contributor with any literary talent." They married in 1892.

Beatrice's years in the East End convinced her that poverty was not a disease curable by charity. It was an entire culture, she determined, shaping the lives of both its victims and their victimizers, whose only remedy was to remake the society that had spawned it. With Sidney she spent her life drawing the blueprints for the Welfare State their pupil William Beveridge would erect for the Labour Government of 1945. Her idea is the one translated into Andrew Undershaft's declaration in *Major Barbara* that poverty is the greatest of all crimes. Shaw's notion of presenting Beatrice as a Salvation Army major may have come from the coincidence of Charles Booth's name with that of the Army's founder, William Booth, the other great voice crying "Shame!" from the East End in the 1880s. But it also fitted the debate Shaw wanted to dramatize about ends and means. The Salvation Army set out to win the world with weapons of the spirit. It deliberately contrasted itself with the other dealers in arms, increasingly conspicuous in Europe since the bombardment of Paris in 1870, whose weapons were those of war.

The Franco-Prussian War had been won by the guns of Krupp, now the largest commercial enterprise in Europe. The Boer War and several small African wars before it had been won by the Maxim gun, manufactured by Vickers of Newcastle. Armaments had changed more in the forty years since the American Civil War than in the five centuries since Marco Polo brought gunpowder out of China, and their makers were a new kind of mysterious international royalty. Alfred Nobel, inventor of dynamite, made headlines with his prizes for the arts of peace, set up in 1900. So did Friedrich Krupp's death in 1902 and the bequest of his works in Essen to his daughter Bertha. A small number of people knew of the exploits of Basil Zaharoff, Vickers' overseas salesman, who spoke so many languages like a native no one knew which was his own. Having sold one of the earliest submarines to the kingdom of Greece, he persuaded the Emperor of Turkey to buy two to protect his realms from his old enemy across the Aegean.

There was a smell of cordite in the air. The long Victorian peace was breaking down. There had been no major revolutions in Europe, if you discounted the Paris Commune, since 1848; no blood in European streets since the days of Garibaldi and Kossuth. Then on January 22, 1905, a huge procession of workers and their families converged on the Winter Palace in St Petersburg to beg the Tsar to give them a democratic assembly. They were a peaceful, hymn-singing crowd, confident that the little Father of all the Russias would hear his children's pleas. Instead a company of mounted Cossacks drew their sabres and charged into the crowd, slashing indiscriminately. When the Cossacks were out of range, foot-soldiers fired into the shambles they had made. Five hundred people were killed, thousands wounded, and the Russian Revolution of 1905 had begun. The age of peaceful persuasion and asking nicely was over.

"Nothing is done in this world," Shaw's armament maker Andrew Undershaft quotes one of his predecessors as saying, "until men are prepared to kill if it is not done." Shaw himself was not preaching revolution, but he wished to remind middle-class liberals like the Fabians that power need not be a monopoly of tyrants and exploiters. The arms industry, as Undershaft tells his daughter and future son-in-law, is as neutral as money – it sells its wares to all customers. Shaw did not have to offer the first audiences for his play an example of what Undershaft says. They had all heard, five months before *Major Barbara* opened, of the battle of Tsushima.

The Russian Revolution of 1905 was partly a protest against Russia's bungling of its war with Japan, aimed at annexing a warm-water gate to the Pacific at Port Arthur. In January 1905, a week before the Petersburg massacre, the Japanese had captured the port and its Russian garrison. Two months earlier, Russia's Baltic fleet had been dispatched around the globe to cut the Japanese army's supply lines from home and end the war. On May 26, it steamed into the misty strait of Tsushima between Japan and Korea, bound for Vladivostok. Out of the mist swooped a fleet of Japanese warships bought from the shipyards of Britain, France and Germany, the last word in modern naval armament. By noon the next day, 33 of the 38 Russian ships that entered the battle were sunk or captured. Five thousand Russian sailors were drowned, 6000 taken prisoner, and 150,000 tons of Russian armourplate lay on the bed of the Sea of Japan. For the first time, a "backward" country of the kind normally carved up to fatten Western empires had defeated a major European power, changing the course of history.

Unfortunately, the keenest recipient of *Major Barbara*'s message was already a convert. When H.G. Wells presented the report of his review committee, three years late, it proposed a Fabian Thermidor, revolution by bloodbath. The Old Gang were to be swept away, and replaced by Wells and selected New Republicans. Shaw was summoned to exorcize the devil he had raised. He did so at a crowded meeting of the Society. First, he said, he must explain the delay of Wells' report. During his committee's deliberations, he said, Wells had written a book on America. "And a very good book too. But whilst I was drafting our reply I produced a play." Shaw paused. Silence fell. He seemed to have lost his thread, and gazed at the ceiling. Then his eyes returned to the audience. "I paused there," he resumed, "to enable Mr Wells to say 'And a very good play too!'" The hall rocked with laughter. Wells' *coup d'état* was over, felled by the sabre of Shaw's wit. "It was an altogether horrid business," Beatrice Webb wrote in her diary. The Fabians' flirtation with the use of power was over too.

APOCALYPSE THEN

Programme note for the Shaw Festival's 1999 production of
Heartbreak House. Excerpted from a longer essay,
"The Roads to Heartbreak House," in *The Cambridge
Companion to George Bernard Shaw* (1998)

Heartbreak House gave Shaw more trouble coming to birth than
any of his previous plays. He had started to write it in March 1916,
but three months later still had no clear idea where it was going.
"I, who once wrote plays *d'un seul trait*," he wrote to Mrs Patrick
Campbell in May, "am creeping through a new one (to prevent
myself crying) at odd moments, two or three speeches at a time. I
don't know what it is about." In November he read the first act to
Lady Gregory, but told her he did not know how to go on, what he
had written was so wild. In December he confessed to William
Archer that he still had only one act, and was stuck.

Something broke the log-jam for him early in 1917. It may
have been his visit to the Western Front at the invitation of Douglas Haig, the British commander-in-chief. Shaw told the *Daily
Chronicle* that he found the nightly bombardments finer than
Tchaikovsky's 1812 overture. Twenty-three years later, during another World War, he told Virginia Woolf in a letter that the conception of *Heartbreak House* came in June 1916, when the Shaws, Webbs,
and Woolfs found themselves at a weekend house-party at Wyndham
Croft in Sussex. Sitting on the terrace after dinner, they heard the
distant thunder of artillery launching the Allied offensive on the
Somme. Evidently his tour of Flanders the following year linked
with that experience, and with his memory of watching a German
zeppelin sail over his house in Ayot St Lawrence and fall "like a
burning newspaper" near Potters Bar, brought down by fighter
planes in October 1916. These incidents crystallized into Ellie
Dunn's line in the last scene of *Heartbreak House*, as the sound of
falling bombs grows nearer: "By thunder, Hesione, it *is* Beethoven."

Stanley Weintraub's chronicle of Shaw's activities between
1914 and 1918, *Journey to Heartbreak* (1971), suggests how these

wartime experiences combined in the play. But some of the concerns treated in *Heartbreak House* reach further back into Shaw's past. Working without a developed plot line in his head, he drew more than ever before on personal emotions and memories, conscious and semiconscious. Much of the power and richness of the play comes from the sense of emotions at work behind it too large to be expressed in its characters and situations. Much of its density and mystery comes from the shadowy movement below its surface of deeper, drowned patterns of meaning, the shapes of other plays it might have become lying like submerged mountain ranges beneath the play it is.

One of these plays was to be a variation on the manner of Chekhov. Shaw acknowledged this intention in his subtitle for the play, "A Fantasia in the Russian Manner on English Themes," but in the finished play his intention is clearer than Chekhov's direct influence. Shaw had first heard of Chekhov in 1905, possibly from his German translator Siegfried Trebitsch when the Moscow Art Theatre made its first foreign tour to Berlin. He wrote to ask Henry Irving's son Laurence, who read Russian, whether any of Chekhov's plays might suit the Stage Society, short of playwrights now that Shaw and Granville Barker were succeeding commercially at the Court Theatre. It was probably Shaw's advocacy that led the Society to stage *The Cherry Orchard* in May 1911, in an under-rehearsed and much derided production. The Stage Society then mounted *Uncle Vanya* in May 1914. Coming out of its first performance, Shaw said to a friend: "When I hear a play of Chekhov's, I want to tear my own up."

Because *The Cherry Orchard* is the Chekhov play invoked most specifically in Shaw's preface, and because of a few obvious parallels – bankrupt house, undisciplined servants, impending disaster – it is the work by Chekhov to which *Heartbreak House* has been most frequently compared. But in its concern for what one generation passes to the next, what values parents raise their children to honour and pursue, *Heartbreak House* is much closer to *The Seagull*. The miasma of romantic bohemianism that hangs over the Shotovers' stranded ship of fools comes much closer to the atmosphere of the Sorins' love-infested house by the magic lake than to that of Madame Ranevskaya's fading mansion among its cherry trees, and what he says has far more in common with Nina, walking into the storm to pursue her vocation as an actress, than it does with the muted, relieved farewells that Gayev, his sister and family say to their old lives.

In the end, the unique brilliance of *Heartbreak House*, which makes it unlike any play written before it, was the result of Shaw's recognition that there was no narrative connection to be made between the play's beginning and ending. Its action consists of the unmooring of the play from the reality in which it begins, floating it above and beyond that reality like an airship, and bringing it home on target to the reality of wartime. Had the play been staged then, the audience would have watched the curtain go up on a country-house weekend of the kind that provided the matter of innumerable Edwardian comedies, and they might have supposed that the reality in which the play is set is the unreality of any upper-class Edwardian play of wit, flirtation, and snobbish class warfare. But gradually that unreal reality becomes more and more unreal, its characters protesting that normal people do not behave as they do. And suddenly an aimless, typically Edwardian discussion about the frequency of local night trains ushers in the ominous, barely audible noise of zeppelins overhead, and the time is clearly 1917.

The real action of the play is the artifice with which Shaw brings about this passage from an illusion of unreality to an illusion of reality. He uses two main devices. The first is presenting the Shotovers' house on the Downs as a palace of sleep, where everything may have been asleep for a hundred years, or alternatively may just have dropped off, to dream uneasily of a nightmare future. The play begins with Ellie nodding off to sleep over her copy of *Othello*, while her hostess has drowsed off upstairs arranging flowers (poppies and mandragora, no doubt) in a guest room. In the second act, Ellie puts Boss Mangan to sleep in a hypnotic trance, and Ariadne tongue-lashes Randall to tears, like a fractious child, to make him drowsy for bed. In the third act, Mazzini Dunn comes down to join the dreamers on the terrace in pyjamas and a flamboyant dressing-gown, declaring that he feels perfectly at home so dressed at Heartbreak House. Meanwhile, Captain Shotover, deprived of the rum that keeps him awake, has drifted off to sleep in Ellie's arms. After the initial sound of a clock striking six at the opening of the play, the audience never knows the time. The night takes on the endlessness and formlessness of the small hours, while the watchers in the house sit entranced by moonlight that reminds Hesione of the night in *Tristan and Isolde*. Part of the sense that the house has drifted away from its moorings in reality comes from this carefully created illusion that time has stopped, and the mundane reality of daytime receded.

Shaw's other device is an equivalent unmooring of the Shotovers' house from the here and now. Mostly this is achieved by letting Captain Shotover expand the world of the play into the world of his memory and ancient perspective on life. The means by which he does this varies from details as small as asking Ellie to "favour me with your name," a usage with the period courtliness of his Regency youth, to his refusal at his age "to make distinctions between one fellow creature and another." There are also of course the hundred small ways in which he treats the house as if it were a ship, blowing his captain's whistle and shouting nautical commands. Above all, he makes the house feel as if it were a flimsy, impermanent structure. "I came here on your daughter's invitation," protests Mangan, when the captain upbraids him for wanting to marry a young girl. "Am I in her house or yours?" "You are beneath the dome of heaven, in the house of God," Shotover replies. "What is true within these walls is true outside them. Go out on the seas; climb the mountains; wander through the valleys. She is still too young."

Much of the difficulty critics encountered in *Heartbreak House* in its early productions was surely the result of the fact that it was never played as it was designed to be played – in wartime. Its world premiere was staged by the Theatre Guild in New York in 1920, its first London production by J.B. Fagan the following year. Shaw says in his preface that he withheld the play from production in 1917 because he recognized that national morale must come first in time of war, and *Heartbreak House* might have lowered morale. He may also have recognized that no management was likely to take a chance on it while theatres were filled by such things as *Chu Chin Chow* and *The Maid of the Mountains*.

As a result, *Heartbreak House* had to wait for real success in the theatre until the Second World War, when Robert Donat staged it at the Cambridge Theatre in London in March 1943. Donat himself played Captain Shotover; Deborah Kerr, then twenty-two, played Ellie Dunn. By then, the worst German air raids on London were over and the V-1 rocket raids had not yet begun. Still, audiences seeing the play could experience directly the unique effect Shaw had designed it to produce. What begins as an Edwardian comedy lifted out of its period, to float in a timeless twentieth-century mixture of disillusion and presentiments of disaster, ends in the present with bombs raining down on England. There has scarcely been a year since 1917 in which Shaw's extraordinary theatre poem, as authentic a myth for imperial Britain as Blake's prophetic books, has not seemed uncannily relevant to the civilization whose end it foresaw.

A MASQUE AT MALVERN

Programme note for the Shaw Festival's
2000 production of *The Apple Cart*

Bernard Shaw's comedy *The Apple Cart* was the first of six plays he wrote after turning seventy which had their British premieres at the Malvern Festival. The festival was the creation of Sir Barry Jackson, founder of the Birmingham Repertory Theatre, who had endeared himself to Shaw by staging the first production in Britain of Shaw's "metabiological pentateuch," *Back to Methuselah*, in 1923. Discovering on that and subsequent occasions that he had overestimated the Birmingham audience, Jackson retired to the countryside to dream of a summer festival like the one presided over by Max Reinhardt at Salzburg – pastoral, perfect, with a self-selected audience of lovers of excellence.

Another model closer to hand was the Three Choirs Festival at Gloucester, whose animating spirit was the greatest living English composer, Sir Edward Elgar. Letting his eyes rove past Gloucester along the green plain stretching from the Severn River to the Welsh border, Jackson's gaze fell on Malvern, a nineteenth-century spa curled round the feet of a bare range of hills crowned with the remains of a Stone Age fort. For his genius of the place, he turned to the greatest playwright working in English. Shaw was delighted. He was feeling out of fashion in the West End of Noel Coward, Frederick Lonsdale and Somerset Maugham. Besides, he liked to spend his summers working. His wife Charlotte preferred to spend hers in country hotels. In Malvern, both would be possible.

It comes as a shock to realize that Shaw's association with Barry Jackson and Malvern produced as many plays as his more famous partnership before the Great War with Harley Granville Barker, perhaps more. This is not to say the Malvern plays – *The Apple Cart, Too True To Be Good, The Simpleton of the Unexpected*

Isles, In Good King Charles's Golden Days, Geneva, Buoyant Billions
– compare in quality with the plays staged under Barker's management: *John Bull's Other Island, Major Barbara, The Doctor's Dilemma,
Getting Married, Androcles and the Lion*. Barry Jackson never held the
kind of place in Shaw's life that Granville Barker, adoptive son in
art, had taken. But while the earlier plays have been studied closely
in the light of Shaw's friendship with Barker, less attention has been
paid to the Malvern plays as a group, or to the common characteristics they may have owed to their place of conception or to Barry
Jackson's personality. They bear marks of both.

Probably because it was one of the models they imitated,
Malvern bears a curious resemblance to the Indian hill stations –
Simla, Darjeeling, Mussoorie – that the British Raj left behind in
the foothills of the Himalayas. Its Victorian terraces wind about
the sharp slopes of its hills in hairpin turns designed for horse-
drawn carriages. The only industry, clearly, is catering for visitors:
guest houses, tea rooms, lending libraries, chemists and gift shops
cluster round the Assembly Rooms, which became the theatre,
and the Winter Garden. The green levels of the Severn plain, re-
ceding in summer haze, heighten the sense of altitude and remote-
ness. It is easy to imagine people in evening dress and decorations
sitting round candlelit tables pondering the future of toiling millions in faraway, dusty cities.

The ruling presence of Barry Jackson increased Malvern's vice-
regal tone. Tall, fresh-faced and high-coloured, the son of the founder
of Maypole Dairies which supplied the Midlands' milk, Jackson
was known as the Butter King and had spent a hundred thousand
pounds of his own money on the Birmingham Repertory Theatre.
"I asked him if he was mad," Shaw wrote, recalling how this stiff, imposing young man had requested the rights to *Back to Methuselah* as if
Shaw owed them to him. "I demanded whether he wished his wife
and children to die in the workhouse. He replied that he was not married." Shaw pointed out that, for the sums he was spending on his
theatre, he could have run a yacht. Jackson replied that running a
theatre was more fun than running a yacht.

Every summer Jackson rented a local girls' boarding school, Lawnside, to put up guests and visitors. Garden parties were given there, lectures and concerts in the Winter Garden, at all of which Jackson presided with royal shyness (he sometimes experimented with a monocle), towing flotillas of young male secretaries in his wake carrying things for him. In his last festival programme he wrote that he hoped the combination of theatre and countryside, beauty and civilization, might produce the atmosphere of "a large and happily constituted country-house party."

It was fitting, therefore, that the first audience to which Shaw read *The Apple Cart* were the guests of Nancy and Waldorf Astor, spending the New Year of 1929 at Lord Astor's country house, Cliveden. The Astors became the main providers of Shaw's political social life in the late 1920s. Granville Barker had withdrawn himself into his second marriage, and the old Fabian friends met less often. (Beatrice Webb could not stand Charlotte's Anglo-Irish self-satisfaction, and Sydney Olivier had a mentally disturbed daughter.) As a result, Shaw's perspective on politics changed. At Cliveden, the Astors' Italianate palazzo on its bluff above the Thames, there was little talk of the slum conditions and parish issues that had preoccupied Shaw in his days as a St Pancras vestryman. Instead of trade union leaders and East End socialists, the Astors' guests were T.E. Lawrence, Charlie Chaplin, Lindbergh and von Ribbentrop. Cliveden's French windows opened onto not only the finest lawn in Europe, but also the great world of celebrity and international affairs.

Accidentally or deliberately, all Shaw's Malvern plays contain elements of that archetype of courtly entertainments, the masque. In its commonest form, as seen at the courts of James I and Louis XIV, the masque is usually an imaginary embassy from one plane of reality to another. Gods and goddesses, figures from myth and legend, nymphs and satyrs or noble savages from the New World, arrive with festive trains of followers, bringing gifts and blessings. They dance with their earthly equivalents, mingle their courtiers with those visited, then withdraw to wherever beyond time they came from. In Shakespeare's *Tempest*, Juno, Ceres and Iris, goddess of the rainbow, descend to bless the betrothal of Ferdinand and Miranda. In his *Love's Labour's Lost*, after a mock visitation by Cossacks from Muscovy, the heroes of antiquity come to do honour to the young Renaissance courtiers who have gathered to study them.

Shaw's *Too True To Be Good* opens with a man-sized influenza germ visiting the bed of a young lady. Cured, she takes off for the Middle East, to find history's latest Superman, T.E. Lawrence, disguised as a common soldier. In *The Simpleton of the Unexpected Isles*, an angel descends to announce the Day of Judgment. In *Good King Charles's Golden Days*, the Merry Monarch arrives with a retinue of spaniels and mistresses to visit the academic cloister where Isaac Newton voyages through strange seas of thought alone. In *Geneva* the Fascist dictators arrive like beings from another reality to mock the intellectuals of the League of Nations. In *Buoyant Billions*, an Oxford idealist in the Panamanian jungle stumbles on a "holy woman," a cross between the Shell heiress Olga Deterding and W.H. Hudson's Rima the Bird Girl, who can charm snakes and alligators with a soprano saxophone.

Shaw's first Malvern entertainment, *The Apple Cart*, hides a masque within a masque. To that first audience in the spa's converted Assembly Rooms appeared a court of beings from the future – a King of England from some period in the late twentieth century, with his secretaries and cabinet. Gracefully, even musically, they debate the perennial problem of politics – how to reconcile the desirable with the art of the possible. Then in a break for lunch and inspiration, King Magnus visits his resident muse, goddess and window on the impossible, his official mistress the Divine Orinthia, modelled by Shaw on the most impossible woman he had known, Mrs Patrick Campbell. Orinthia would teach Magnus how to be a real king – an absolute monarch, pursuing Utopia without compromise – if only he would marry her and make her his real Queen. But he knows that if he deserts politics to pursue the art of the impossible, he will become nothing but an icon. That is why his relationship with the Divine One can consist only of ceremonial visits: tiny masques for two players.

Its first audiences welcomed *The Apple Cart* for its extravagant wit, its reminder of the Shaw who in the days before *Heartbreak House* and *Saint Joan* had written *Misalliance*, *Androcles* and
Pygmalion. But hidden within the glittering double-masque of his
courtly entertainment was a private, heartbroken personal message. *The Apple Cart* was Shaw's secret reply, hidden in public
display, to Granville Barker's last play *His Majesty*, published in 1928.
As Shaw embarked on his new partnership, his heart was still rav-
elled in the old one.

Barker's play is about a king who abdicates. Henry of Carpathia
flies back to his central European kingdom, torn from him by revolution after the Great War, when a royalist counter-revolution breaks
out. If it succeeds, that will mean he is a real king – his people want
him back. If it does not, as a real king he must try to prevent his
people from killing each other in his name. In the end, he has to
choose the second course. He prevents a civil war by abdicating.
There are times, Barker seems to say, when history carries you past
the possibility of public usefulness; when the only thing to do is to
withdraw and leave the field to others.

It is a moving play. In it you can read Barker's disillusionment
with the theatre that he had hoped to turn into one of the great
national institutions of British life. Failing to do so, he abdicated his
position as Shaw's heir apparent. Behind the raging high spirits of
The Apple Cart burns the rage of Shaw's disappointment and sense
of desertion. There is only one medium in which you can build a
better world, he hisses at Barker through the lips of King Magnus –
the present, the possible, the world we live in. There can be no such
thing as abdication if your job is to build the Just City in England's
green and pleasant land. Even if you know that the Just City is
doomed to become a dormitory suburb of New York.

THE SORROWS OF SUPERWOMAN

Programme note for the Shaw Festival's
2001 production of *The Millionairess*

In their seventies, after thirty years of marriage, Charlotte and Bernard Shaw finally reconciled the profound difference that had made their lives together a tug-of-war. Simply, Charlotte loved to travel and Shaw could not bear it. Like most writers, Shaw could have lived at his desk, interrupting his work only for three meals a day at regular hours. Charlotte, born in the leisure class but doing her duty in the station of life to which she had been called with the fervour of a convert, hated housekeeping and domestic routine. Her idea of a perfect life was moving from one luxury hotel to another, enjoying the ministrations of head waiters and master chefs. The compromise they hit on late in life was ocean cruising. So long as she was on a luxury liner steaming purposefully from continent to continent, with stewards in white drill bringing beef tea to her deck chair, Charlotte was perfectly happy. So long as the continents were separated by days of blue stasis between empty horizons, with no letters or telephone calls to damage his concentration, Shaw was absolutely content. It was on the longest and least eventful of their cruises together, to New Zealand and back in 1934, that Shaw drafted his comedy *The Millionairess*, one of whose subjects is marital happiness.

It set out originally to address other matters. Shaw wanted to clarify his attitude, much criticized, to the rising European dictators Mussolini and Hitler. He had made himself unpopular by pointing out that it made little sense to upbraid them for being undemocratic when they so obviously represented the wishes of enormous majorities in their respective countries. He also wanted to show sympathy for the troubles of his friend Nancy, Lady Astor, whose country house on the Thames, Cliveden, was a meeting place for the few people in British public life who recognized that the botched, vengeful Treaty of Versailles which ended the First World War was less likely to bring Europe peace than to cause a second global conflict. Finally, in addition to these concerns, Shaw wanted to do a good turn for one of his favourite actresses, Edith Evans.

Edith Evans had played Ariadne Utterword in the British premiere of *Heartbreak House*. She had been the Serpent and She-Ancient in the first British production, at the Birmingham Rep, of *Back to Methuselah*. She had created brilliantly the role of Orinthia, the royal mistress in *The Apple Cart*. Helped by these memorable creations, she had gone on to play most of the great comic heroines in British drama: Millamant in Congreve's *The Way of the World*, Rosalind in *As You Like It*, Katherina in *The Taming of the Shrew* and (more comically than tragically) *Cleopatra*. Now 46, she seemed to have reached a point in her career where managers no longer considered her for starring roles. She had wasted most of 1933 playing a plain housekeeper, modeled on the kitchen maid Rembrandt made his second wife, in an arty middlebrow item called *The Late Christopher Bean*. For 1934, she had accepted the role of the Nurse in Katharine Cornell's New York production of *Romeo and Juliet*. Shaw determined to write her a great, fizzing firecracker of a star part in a comedy "such as Ben Jonson might write". He was astonished when she turned it down, saying she found the role unsympathetic and the kind of playing it demanded old-fashioned.

Edith Evans had smelled a rat. Shaw had pushed himself into the bombastic larger-than-life manner of Ben Jonson by deciding to treat the question of the dictators in the character of a forceful woman. In effect, he was asking her to play Hitler and Mussolini, but to make them attractive by her bottomless technique and siren charm. By doing this, he hoped to show that the problem the dictators posed was not a matter of political fashion nor militarized testosterone, but a question of evolution. The world moves forward, he believed, by casting up in every generation natural leaders of both sexes, born with the energy, will and charisma that draw others to follow them. Such leaders advance mankind by showing the rest of us what we should like to be if we had their pride and courage. When Mussolini, he wrote in his preface to the play, "deliberately spat in the face of the League of Nations . . . and defiantly asked the Powers if they had anything to say about it, he was delighting his own people by the spectacle of a great Italian bullying the world, and getting away with it triumphantly."

The problem with born leaders, Shaw wanted to show, is not that they exist, but what to do with them. Forces of nature, they challenge us to discover how Nature wants them to be used. This is easier to recognize if we assume that the qualities of leadership may be found as readily in a woman as in a man. "In the humblest cabin that contains a family," argues Shaw's preface, "you may find a *maîtresse femme* who rules in the household by a sort of divine right. She may rule amiably by being able to think more quickly and see further than the others, or she may be a tyrant ruling violently by intensity of will and ruthless egotism. She may be a grandmother or she may be a girl. But the others find that they are unable to resist her." Shaw wanted to suggest to women that a new career was open to them, one that did not require them to marry like Candida, nor burn like Saint Joan, nor improve their vowels like Eliza Doolittle nor turn themselves into cigar-smoking surrogate males like Vivie Warren. One of the solutions to the problem of the dictators might be to make the dictator a woman. A model for her might be found in the first woman to occupy a seat in the British House of Commons, Nancy Astor.

The simplest reason why Shaw and Nancy Astor became such good friends, as he moved from his seventies into his eighties, may have been that she was one of the few people outside of his elderly contemporaries who treated him without deference. Like Henry Higgins in *Pygmalion*, she treated everyone alike, duchesses and flower girls, as if they were all equals. This probably had less to do with the fact that she was married to one of the richest men in the world than with her origin as one of the Langhorne sisters of Virginia. Like all Virginians, the Langhornes considered themselves aristocrats, even if during the lean years after the Civil War Nancy's father had been driven to earn a living as a tobacco auctioneer. But more than that, they had become famous as "the last of the Southern belles," as each in turn made her debut in the New York society of the 1890s and married brilliantly into the Gilded Age of the railway tycoons. The second of them, Irene, married the artist Charles Dana Gibson, and she and her sisters lent their fine profiles and upswept hair as models for his icon of American beauty, the Gibson Girl.

Nancy's first marriage, to a brutal, alcoholic son of a Boston copper fortune, ended in a quick divorce, but her second, the most brilliant of all, was to Waldorf Astor, son of the man who owned all the most valuable real estate in Manhattan. As a wedding present her father-in-law, who had moved his family to Britain to show his distaste for the American electors who refused his services, gave his son and daughter-in-law Cliveden House, an Italianate palace built by Charles Barry on the Thames near Marlowe. To help with its running expenses, he added a few years later, as a birthday present, the Waldorf Astoria Hotel in New York, whose revenues yielded $200,000 a year. With such an endowment, Nancy rapidly turned Cliveden into a showplace, whose weekend house-parties of forty or more included royalty, cabinet ministers, famous writers, film stars and other international celebrities. When Waldorf reluctantly took his father's place in the House of Lords after the old man's death, he put forward Nancy as his successor in the Plymouth constituency he had represented in the House of Commons. As the first woman MP, beautiful, witty and outspoken, Nancy rapidly became a celebrity in her own right.

She lured Shaw and Charlotte to Cliveden for Christmas in 1927. A blizzard snowed them in for 18 days, at the end of which they were bosom friends. In 1931 Charlotte entrusted Shaw to Nancy for a tour of the Soviet Union, in the course of which Nancy washed Shaw's hair with the soap flakes she had brought for her stockings in preparation for a meeting with Stalin in the Kremlin. In return, Shaw tried to console her for the discovery, just before they left London, that the son of her first marriage, Bobbie Shaw, had been kicked out of the Guards for homosexuality. Nancy, a convert to Christian Science, was convinced he was steeped in sin. Shaw explained to her gently that Bobbie had no more control over his sexual orientation than over, say, being colour-blind. He was equally supportive when her Astor children, one by one, defied her will to control them. David, the most brilliant, had a breakdown at Oxford, and then left home in 1933. Guests could seldom resist Nancy's wit and charm, but her family found it hard to live with her.

"People will say you are the millionairess," Shaw wrote to Nancy after finishing the play, but implied that this would be an absurd mistake — his heroine was "an awful, impossible woman." Had Nancy known him longer, she might have noticed that this was not exactly a denial. Shaw camouflaged his millionairess with traits that distinguished her from Nancy — she is Italian, humourless, and inherited her money rather than marrying it — but he could not resist one detail that identified her as his model. The one achievement that shows Epifania Ognisanti di Parerga's compulsion to better the world is her conversion of a shabby Thameside pub into a gleaming luxury resort for weekend visitors. Everyone knew how Nancy had swept Cliveden clean of her father-in-law's gloomy German bronzes and dark panelling, filling it with sunlight, cheerful chintzes and huge bowls of flowers.

But above all Epifania resembles Nancy in her driving will and impatient energy, and the pathos of the fact that no one can live with her. One of Nature's dictators, she is a destructive force until Nature finds a use for her. The way to deal with dictators, Shaw indicates slyly, is to put them into a play where, as in real life, they have to learn to negotiate with other people. He himself had celebrated marriage to Charlotte by writing *Man and Superman*, in which the invincible John Tanner is ensnared by a girl who always agrees with him. Thirty years of marriage had taught Shaw that every time a spouse wins an argument, the marriage loses. His solution to the problem of dictators, as to all problems in comedy, is a happy marriage. Unfortunately, the drama playing itself out in Europe in the 1930s was not a comedy.

SHAW'S SHYNESS

Review of *The Collected Letters of Bernard Shaw*,
edited by Dan H. Laurence. Originally published in
the *Spectator*, October 1965

It was Edith Nesbit who saw to the bottom of Shaw's secret. She fell briefly in love with him during the 1880s (her husband, Hubert Bland, had just brought home the first of his by-blows for her to adopt) and she was always perceptive about adolescent psychology, if not specially good with adolescents. "Kind," she wrote him down after his first appearance at a Fabian meeting, "unattractive and shy."

Shy? Suddenly, everything makes sense. Who but a desperately shy man would force himself to become a public spectacle? Who would strain every nerve to appear unabashable but a man to whom the central fact of life is bashfulness? What else could account for the elaborately studied rhetoric, going through every motion of charming, flattering and persuading, save the fundamental gesture of showing the smallest confidence that anyone might be persuaded, flattered or charmed? His prose has the perfection of book-learned French, flawlessly correct, syntactically dazzling, but never at any point expecting an answer. Who but a tragically insecure man would have turned himself into the most bristlingly golden male lion in London, and remained a virgin until he was nearly 30? Who else would have written plays whose basic gambit was sardonically to parody the most up-to-the-minute theatrical fashion, demonstrating as he demolished each that he had been with-it before he turned against it?

All most of us saw of him was the brilliant old mask. The defensiveness it was so artfully moulded to shield had long shrivelled inside it, as the people whose opinions really mattered to him died out one by one. The fascination of Dan Laurence's first volume of Shaw's collected letters is that it stops just before success closed in on him, with Richard Mansfield playing *The Devil's Disciple* in America, *Candida* touring the provinces, and marriage to Charlotte Payne-Townshend – whose wealth finally rescued him from Grub Street and dependence on others – around the corner. This was the period when the mask was made and fixed. These were the years when other people really mattered to him. The volume opens with him working out the tone in which to address a mother who had deserted her drunken husband and their son in Dublin in order to go off to London with her music teacher cum lodger. It ends with him working out the tone with which to let Ellen Terry realize that it no longer means life or death to him whether Irving decides to play *The Man of Destiny*. Between them the style of his life and work laid itself down. It is that of a man who cared what others thought of him, but was too insecure to let this crack his sedulously fostered indifference.

For all its bulk (the volume runs to 850 pages, and is only the first of four), Mr Laurence's catch contains more sprats than mackerel. There is only that single letter to his mother; only one, a cryptic little note ending "I am, Madam, your obedient servant," to her plump, passionate friend Jenny Patterson who, herself a widow rising 45, helped him celebrate his twenty-ninth birthday by relieving him of his chastity, and clung on for eight years tempestuously enough to inspire the character of Julia in *The Philanderer*. There are not many more to Florence Farr, the actress to whose arms he graduated from Mrs Patterson's, only two to his sister Lucy, and none whatever to his father – only a note announcing the latter's death to a friend: "Telegram just received to say that the governor has left the universe on rather particular business and set me up as – An Orphan." The rarity of his really personal communications is emphasized by the acreage of business correspondence in which they're embedded – applications to publishers, solicitations to editors, compulsive pages of Fabian and St Pancras parish business, but even these are eloquent in their way. The youthful letters to prospective publishers are too long, too garrulous and cocksure – and usually end with a painful flourish of deprecation: "I fear the story is too preposterous to be worth publishing."

But there's at least one major haul in the correspondence with Alice Lockett, a nervously "modern" young woman who lived with a sister and bed-ridden mother at Walthamstow, with whom Shaw fell in love in 1881. For four years they conducted a wrangling, passionate, unconsummated relationship, with Shaw constantly goading her to live up to the intellectual pretensions which drew her to him, and Alice retreating to upbraid him for his vanity, egoism and cerebral inhumanity. Obviously he found her attractive but maddeningly stupid; equally obviously, she found him fascinating but unattractive sexually, and with these weapons they fought, working their mutual revenges deeper and deeper under each other's skins. Their letters are adolescent in their rudeness, spirited and anguished. Clearly the relationship behind them was the basis for many of Shaw's sex-duels between his New Women and Supermen, which read so implausibly today. The relationship they describe was real enough. Unfortunately, like most men, Shaw never realized that his own experience was too singular to generalize into a philosophy of sex.

"When I return I will make you fall in love with me, merely to shew you how clever I am . . . I will make love to you, to relieve the enormous solitude which I carry about with me." These were Shaw's formative years, and both the solitude and the defensive cleverness were to harden into the immensely elaborate courtship -and-withdrawal display of his theatrical strategy. It's fascinating, in the same week as Mr Laurence's splendidly meticulous compilation, to come on both motives at work, forty-five years later, in the 1932 comedy *Too True To Be Good*, revived with knock-your-eye-out cast at the Strand. Even at seventy-five Shaw was still showing off to audiences, blandishing them with superb wit, grace and the flattering rudeness of equals, then turning away with an indifference not softened by his cry of loneliness as he turned.

He liked to exploit theatrical fashion while debunking it. *Arms and The Man* anticipated the Balkan vogue of Zenda and Graustark, *Major Barbara* pillaged the plot of *The Belle of New York*, *Heartbreak House* was meant to be a pastiche of Chekhov. *Too True To Be Good*, coming in the age of Cochran and Coward, is a revue: a series of turns based on newspaper topicalities of the day – millionaires, flappers, the promiscuity of the young, the career of T.E. Lawrence as Aircraftsman Shaw, nudism, the Oxford Movement, the romance of gangsterism. Shaw is eager as ever to show he has kept up, not merely with the papers but with the theatre, so the curtain rises on a debutante in bed with a germ her own size (when was the first production of Capek's *Insect Play*?), rises again on the T.E. Lawrence skit and its *Desert Song* scenery, rises a third time on a tart on a tropical beach endeavouring to seduce a man of God. (*Rain*, anyone?) She is also a bogus French countess, in league with an unfrocked Air Corps padre who has turned to burglary, the son of a militant atheist who has lost his lack of faith. "They are too absurd to be believed in," declares this prodigal in a final parabasis, "yet they are not fictions: the newspapers are full of them." They are the Signs of the Times: like a true Victorian prophet, the last heir of Carlyle, Shaw shuffles them to cast a horoscope for history, part divination, part fairground entertainment, like an Arab fortune-teller reading futures in his sandbox.

It isn't one of his great plays, but I prefer it to the ones in which he wrenched episodes from history, in Carlylean style, to make a sermon for our latter days. Probably the test for a great Shaw play should be that it does not meddle with Caesar, Saint Joan, or other historical hero still capable of maintaining that anything is possible with miracle-working Creative Evolution. It should be about modern men, aware that nineteenth-century Europe has come to the end of its tether, not knowing where to go next, but sure this danger intensifies living, and that intensity of living is the only ultimate value. In other words, it should be *Heartbreak House*, or as near it as possible: the impressiveness of Shaw, surely, rests in that period when he himself embodied the close of the great historical arc of confidence from Rousseau and Shelley through Hegel, Ruskin, Bergson. His own life shows the Romantic trajectory from a faith in perfectibility to Existentialism. He spent his youth collecting ideas in order not to be alone. Only when he began to discard them in old age did the fundamental Shaw enter the plays.

Too True To Be Good does not fail the test by much. Less scrambled together than it looks, it heralds Shaw's best second-act turn – the clever, factual mind (Private Lawrence/Meek's) coolly demonstrating to a typical Englishman that his real motives are not those he admits or imagines – with one almost as cunning: preparing the audience for an intellectual demonstration by winning their assent to the proposition that it is more fun to be braced than entertained.

But the imposing act is the third, in which Shaw's own mind reaches the rocks on which, he preaches once more, life is most alive. As the darkness gathers on stage, Shaw turns away from his audience, the burglar-padre's voice rises: "I am ignorant . . . all I know is that I must find the way of life, for myself and all of us, or we shall surely perish. And meanwhile my gift has possession of me: I must preach and preach and preach no matter how late the hour and how short the day, no matter whether I have nothing to say . . ." Shaw never came much closer to himself than that.

Frank Dunlop's production is good enough to become a text-book example for playing Shaw. Or perhaps it would be simpler to say for casting him. The cast Mr Dunlop has rounded up consists, more or less, of the best comic actors available – Alastair Sim, Dora Bryan, George Cole, Athene Seyler, with Kenneth Haigh to carry what straight acting there is. The style they create together is broad, extroverted, never for a moment credible – they are there to make the most of lines, not to evoke reality. For the reality a Shaw play is directed toward, which it constructs and confronts you with, is Shaw's own intelligence. That moment of confrontation is still one of the most exciting in drama. To me, at least, it's part of the rarity of the moment that this seems to have been the only form of companionship the shy man in the comic mask allowed himself.

DRAGGING SHAW
OUT OF THE CLOSET

Review of *Bernard Shaw: The Ascent of the
Superman* by Sally Peters. Originally published
in *The Globe and Mail*, June 1996

It's a dirty job, but I suppose someone had to do it. The sex life of
George Bernard Shaw clearly was a problem of some kind to him,
and has been one to his biographers. A virgin until his twenty-
ninth birthday, he spent twelve years furiously paying court to every
good-looking actress and liberated woman in London, then contracted a "white" marriage – unconsummated by the wish of his
wife – with the Irish heiress Charlotte Payne-Townshend.

Thereafter, apart from his famous flirtation with Mrs Patrick
Campbell and various discreet crushes on young actresses in his
plays, he apparently remained celibate until his death at 94. Someone was bound to ask someday whether these dramatic leaps in
and out of the sexual frying pan might not indicate some amb-
ivalence. Could the hesitant wooer behind Don Juan's philander-
ing mask perhaps have been sexually unattracted to women?

This nettle has been grasped with both hands by Sally Peters,
a visiting lecturer at Wesleyan University in Connecticut in liberal
studies, an academic field that presumably encompasses such re-
search. She has spent twenty years, she says, sifting through Shaw's
writings and the literature about him, trying to make sense of the
kiss-and-run record of this reluctant amorist. Her conclusion is that,
like his Caesar in *Caesar and Cleopatra*, his genius was rooted in
androgyny; that his secret, shared with the Sphinx, was a divided
nature, "part brute, part woman, part god." In other words, she argues, Shaw was a homosexual who spent his life in the closet.

"To probe the mystery of man and artist," says Dr Peters,
"I have forged my own method, using everything from existential
phenomenology to popular culture to track down clues." Her
method has no difficulty demonstrating the closet part of her the-

sis. So there is no evidence of Shaw ever laying a finger on another male? Well, naturally: he took care to cover his traces, Dr Peters deduces. So he told friends and biographers that, while he sympathized with Oscar Wilde and opposed his imprisonment, he did not share his sexual tastes? An obvious case of denial, she reasons. So he took up the manly art of boxing, and wrote a novel and play about it? Clearly a disguise for his innate effeminacy.

Dr Peters becomes less confident when trying to demonstrate Shaw's homosexuality. This may be because she never defines precisely what she thinks homosexuality is, or how one would recognize it. Sometimes she seems to argue that Shaw had a feminine sensibility housed in a male body – that there are essentially female ways of walking, talking and thinking which Shaw shared. She finds his pose in a well-known photograph on William Morris's balcony unmistakably feminine, including a "feminine positioning" of his hands on his hips. I'm reminded of the belief at my boys' school that straight men make fists to look at their fingernails, while gay men flatten their hands at arm's length. Such superstitions abounded in the days of McCarthy's witch hunts, when reds and queers were thought to lurk, probably holding hands, under every bed.

At other moments, Dr Peters seems to think of homosexuality as a product of culture rather than genes, the result of experiences which jangle our sense of gender. Thus, she points ominously to the facts that, until he was three or four, Shaw wore skirts, and that his first theatrical memories included seeing girls dressed up as boys and men dressed as women in Dublin pantomimes. She doesn't discuss the effect the same experiences must have had on the millions of other infant British males who shared them. She may secretly believe all British islanders are sexually confused – she is obviously well read in the annals of Bloomsbury and its campfollowers – but if so, it's hard to understand why she singled out Shaw.

Her most sensational evidence is a batch of photographs Shaw and the young Harley Granville Barker took of each other frolicking in various stages of undress on a beach in Dorset. She passes over the fact that the batch includes a photograph of Charlotte Shaw on the same sands the same day, looking unusually youthful and happy. Clearly no one has informed Dr Peters how late in cultural history swimsuits for men made their appearance. Well after the turn of the century, men were still skinny-dipping in the Isis and Cam outside Oxford and Cambridge, and there's a charming snapshot of the last tsar of all the Russias wading into the Black Sea with some courtiers, all naked as jaybirds. Shaw undoubtedly loved Barker, the brilliant son he never had, but nothing in their busy, affectionate correspondence hints at lust.

The pity is that, behind Dr Peters' divorce-court sniffing through dirty linen and her maddening enthusiasm for the wilder shores of post-modern gender theory, lies a benign purpose. She wants to show how Shaw's uncertain sexuality made him a friend to women's liberation, a male with a feminine mind. Unfortunately, her obsession with proving him gay blinds her to Shaw's more important contribution to the liberation of both sexes – his lifelong attack on Victorian ideas of manliness. In Shaw's plays, men are always bursting into tears, fleeing from women, and confessing their fears and insecurities.

If ever a culture created homosexuality where it didn't pre-exist in nature, it was surely that of Victorian imperialism. The Victorian empire was infatuated with exaggerated masculinity and built on the Kiplingesque belief in male bonding. In a wickedly brilliant review, Max Beerbohm argued that the stage version of Kipling's *The Light That Failed* must be a woman's work – only a woman could fall so madly in love with male muscularity, the odours and secrecy of masculinity, the whole cult of the manly. Beerbohm, Shaw's heir in dramatic criticism, also followed his diagnosis of their sick society: that it could only cure itself by admitting that real males are just as capable as women of weakness, tears, timidity and sensitivity. What Dr Peters points to as Shaw's lack of manliness was his deliberate demonstration that the only natural relation between the sexes is one in which they behave as much like each other as possible.

SHAW TESTS THE ICE

Review of *Bernard Shaw: The Diaries*, edited by
Stanley Weintraub. Originally published in the
London Review of Books, December 1986

In his last will, made the year before he died, Shaw let his modesty
hang out for once. He left his diaries, with his account books, cheque
stubs, box-office statements and business records, to the London
School of Economics. Their only interest, he said, would be to economic and legal historians, and occasional biographers, "seeking
documentary evidence as to prices and practices during the period covered by my life." He was not, he recognized, one of nature's
diarists. He lacked the confessional itch of a Boswell, the bureaucrat's
recording instinct of a Pepys. Only once, during the dark years of
the Great War, did he turn the scrutiny of his art, like Virginia Woolf,
upon himself. In January 1917 he started a detailed journal of his
life at Ayot St Lawrence with his wife Charlotte. On 9 January he
had to record a difference between them. He tried to amuse Charlotte with news of a marital scandal in provincial musical circles.
She was unamused and offended by his levity: she took his bohemian tolerance of such things as sign of "a deplorable looseness in
my own character". He abandoned the subject and, the following
day, the diary. Clearly he could not keep it truthfully without some
betrayal of his wife. He had not the first loyalty to self of which
great diarists are made.

He used diaries in the stationer's sense: to keep track of engagements and weekly expenses. His first, kept for six months in
1880 while working for Edison Telephone, records little but shillings and pence spent in the company's service, on stamps, bus fares,
advances to colleagues, haircuts and boot-cleaning. (A kind of salesman, soliciting "way-leaves" to run wires over premises, he had to
look spruce.) When Edison sold out to Bell, he gladly gave up both
job and journal. When he resumed diary-keeping in 1885, his cir-

cumstances had changed, but not his motives. After nine lonely years studying and writing novels in the British Museum, he had acquired a bustling social life as a result of his conversion to socialism. Suddenly, his days were filled with more speaking engagements, committee meetings, deadlines, and advanced ladies misled by his serio-comic Irish gallantries, than he could keep straight any longer in his head.

In an effort to reduce this chaos to order, he kept diaries from 1885, when he turned twenty-nine, until 1897. In the space for each day, he would jot down forthcoming lectures, concerts and social arrangements. Later, he would record in shorthand how in fact he had spent the day. Each entry would end up with a short account of receipts and expenditures: "Dinner 10d. Stamp 1d. Pall Mall Gazette 1d. Train to Hampstead Heath 3d. Haircut etc 9d. Rec'd: Mother 3/6." As he grew busier, conscientiousness about both engagements and entries waned. Sometimes he made entries weeks after the event, admitting that he no longer remembered clearly. Then in 1897 Charlotte Payne-Townshend, with her private fortune, burden of leisure, and passionate need for a cause to offer them to, appointed herself his unpaid secretary and, in due course, put in order his dishevelled social and sexual lives for good. The year before they married, the diaries peter out.

Stanley Weintraub, who has edited all twelve diaries and the fragments from 1880 and 1917 into two stout volumes, gives the game away in his lively account of their provenance. When Shaw married Charlotte, he left his papers at his mother's house in Fitzroy Square, where they lay neglected until Virginia Woolf and her brother Adrian took over the lease in 1907. A bookseller brought in to pick through the rubbish found the 1892 diary and returned it to Shaw, who put it on a shelf and forgot it. He made no effort to retrieve the others, which moved with his mother, passed at her death in 1913 to his sister Lucy, and on Lucy's death to their aunt Arabella Gillmore, who took over Lucy's house on Denmark Hill. When the house was bombed in the Blitz, Shaw's cousin Georgina Musters dumped the contents in a warehouse to sort after the war. Only then were the diaries discovered and handed over to Shaw's secretary, Blanche Patch, who spend her post-war leisure deciphering them. If she mentioned them to Shaw (she may not have), he appears to have shown no interest. Nor has anyone else, much, in the thirty-six years since Shaw's death, except the predicted biographers. St John Ervine skimmed their scandalous cream in his ill-tempered centenary life in 1956. Other scholars have browsed them for background material, notably Norman and Jeanne MacKenzie in their book *The Fabians*. But it has taken until now for any publisher to be persuaded that a public wider than that of economic historians has been waiting to learn what Shaw paid for boot dubbing (threepence) and boots (nineteen-and-ninepence) a century ago.

Presumably Professor Weintraub persuaded the press of his own university to take the risk of publication by dint of the astonishing industry with which he and a platoon of helpers have managed to flesh out Shaw's skeletal jottings with the context of late Victorian London and its half-worlds of politics, music and journalism in which Shaw moved. Weintraub is not as immaculate an editor as Rupert Hart-Davis, nor his match as a stylist (in one footnote he refers to Shaw's "massive disinterest in Scottish music"), but he comes close to rivalling Hart-Davis's superb annotation of Oscar Wilde's letters, tracking down and identifying a supporting cast of thousands. Did Shaw covertly admire a young Scandinavian lady at a tea-party given by one of his advanced admirers, Bertha Newcombe? Weintraub can tell us that Nellie Erichsen lived at 6 Trafalgar Studios, Manresa Road, Chelsea, illustrated several volumes of the "Highways and Byways" series and translated a number of Strindberg's plays with Edwin Bjöorkman. Does Shaw dine with his neighbour George Wardle, manager of William Morris's Merton works, in April 1887? Weintraub reminds us that Mrs Wardle, twenty-six years earlier, was acquitted in a sensational trial of the charge of murdering her lover. As Shaw grows more cavalier about keeping up the entries, Weintraub grows more assiduous, eking out Shaw's bare notes of forward engagements with backward looks at the days in question from his letters or notices in the *Saturday Review*. At times the final diaries seem almost as much his work as

Shaw's, like the "autobiography" pasted together from similar fragments which he redacted for Shaw some years ago.

His work has been prodigious. Nevertheless, readers faced with the customary princelet's ransom now demanded for academic books on this scale are entitled to ask whether the results are worth the effort. After all, half a dozen biographers have already been over the ground for us. Without one of their volumes at one elbow, and Dan Laurence's edition of Shaw's letters at the other, the diaries themselves, however well annotated, will not yield a full picture of Shaw in his prime. It is true, as the books' jackets claim, that we can learn the cost a hundred years ago of visiting Madame Tussaud's, crossing the Channel, moving a piano, buying a typewriter ribbon and weighing yourself at a railway station. Apart from that, will the diaries tell anything new that we really want to know about Shaw?

The answer, after all cavils, is yes, they will. A microscope picture of facial skin is less interesting than a portrait, but it conveys information a portrait can't. It's one thing to be told by biographers that the grinning old prophet who survives in newsreels was once a shy and cunning young Dubliner in exile. It's another to track him down on his daily courses through the London of music halls, pea-soup fogs and the dock strike, counting his pennies, spending one on a crossing-sweeper to save those new boots from mud and horse-droppings (even on nothing a year, he remains a member of the sweeper-tipping class), suddenly squandering seven on a piano arrangement of Rossini's *Semiramide*. To save money, he walks everywhere, resorting to public conveniences ("Lavatory man 1/") to wash and brush up before engagements. He tramps so vigorously from Bloomsbury to Hampstead, Hammersmith and Blackheath that it comes as a shock to learn that he had chronic difficulty rising before eleven and suffered regularly from migraines. The last, and his poverty, may have been contributing motives for his vegetarianism. For less than a shilling, he could dine on macaroni and cheese at the Porridge Bowl in Soho or the Orange Grove in St Martin's Lane. After plays and concerts, he was happy with eggs and cocoa at home.

The tiny, painstaking reckonings at the end of each day grind on one's nerves as they must have on his. You can feel his exhilaration when, with his share of the insurance paid at his father's death in 1885, he walks out to be measured for his first Jaeger suit, "the first new garment I have had for years". It cost him £5.15.0, and (although he blamed its unaccustomed airiness for the cold he caught next day) he loved it so much that he tried, unsuccessfully, to buy a matching Jaeger hat a few weeks later.

Much of his strenuous walking was to free lectures. He attended them omnivorously: in October 1886 he heard lectures on "The Evils of Free Trade", "Can Socialists Be Christians?", "Thought in Holland" and "Primitive Aryan Communities", as well as lecturing himself on "Socialism and Radicalism," "The Division of Society into Classes," "The Unemployed" and "Interest – Its Nature and Justification". Reading the lists brings home the extent to which he made London, the city itself, his university. Its seminars were the dozen literary and debating societies to which he subscribed: the Dialectical, Zetetical, Bedford and Argosy, Annie Gilchrist's Marxist Reading Circle in Hampstead, the Shelley, Browning and New Shakespeare Societies presided over by W.J. Furnivall. The Museum was its library, with its free desks, paper, pens and warmth, and the company of fellow students such as William Archer, Sidney Webb, Graham Wallas and Edith Nesbit, who dragged him out through the portico on June 26, 1886, to declare her passion for him. ("A memorable evening!" he jotted tersely.) The last group, the Fabians, gradually displaced all the others to become the centre of his life: they were his college, club, commune and *Brudersbund*. It was they who brought him to flower, indulging him as their brilliant, outrageous college clown and show-off. It helps to explain the playwright Shaw became, perhaps, if one thinks of him performing for London and its audiences as generations of clever, calculatedly bumptious undergraduates, from Mackworth Praed to Kenneth Tynan, have performed to their alma maters at Oxford and Cambridge.

With the same energy that he gave to his belated education, he flung himself into the other activities that young men discover at university. On his twenty-ninth birthday he was introduced to sex by his mother's friend, the artistic widow Jenny Patterson. "I did not take the initiative in the matter," he wrote, but neither did it come as a total surprise. A week earlier he had purchased a packet of condoms ("French letters 5/-") and taken them home to examine, "which extraordinarily revolted me". By the early '90s, however, when he was dividing his attentions between Mrs Patterson and the actress Florence Farr, he had overcome his revulsion to the extent of buying his supplies in fifty-shilling quantities. Possibly it was his habit of accounting for every penny spent which led him to scribble figures, usually ones or twos, after notations of visits to Mrs Patterson's house in Brompton Square, and sometimes after visits by her to his mother's. One winter night in 1885, he walked her home across frozen Hyde Park and fell on the ice, pulling her down with him. A circled "one" follows in the margin. Whether it refers to an event then and there, or later, is not made clear.

In 1890 Shaw began his concurrent wooing of Florence Farr, plying furtively between new love and old until the night of February 4, 1893, when Mrs Patterson burst into her rival's house in Ravenscourt Park and made the scene which Shaw instantly turned to advantage ("I kept patience and did not behave badly or urgently") as the opening of his play *The Philanderer*. He also paid court, with varying seriousness, to Annie Besant, May Morris, Janet Achurch and Bertha Newcombe, who painted his best portrait at this age, defying hecklers with hands on hips and beard blazing. But the person he saw most regularly in these years, the diaries show, and displayed the most settled affection for, was Graham Wallas. The two bachelors of the inner Fabian junta, they would walk back together from meetings, perhaps share a late pot of tea or cocoa, and if conversation had not flagged, walk a few streets further. In February 1892 he went to hear Wallas lecture on Chartism at South Place Chapel. "Walked home with Wallas after the lecture, which ended in his walking home with me." If Shaw burned a fire in his study to finish a late review, Wallas might come and read beside him companionably: part of the cost of being a nineteenth-century intellectual was having to heat rooms where you worked alone. Youngest of a family of sisters, Wallas was often ill, and Shaw would look in to make sure one of the sisters was nursing him properly. Once, when a snowstorm caught them after dinner at the Webbs, Shaw walked from Grosvenor Street to Westminster to find a cab and send it back for Wallas. Wallas was one of the two witnesses, and the only friend from the Fabian inner circle, invited to Shaw's wedding in 1898.

"A strange, warm-hearted young man," Beatrice Webb wrote of Wallas, "with a bright intelligence, not much beyond commonplace except in its social fervour." It seems to have been that fervour which drew him together with Shaw. Their socialism had an emotional, almost religious basis lacking in that of the Webbs or, later, H. G. Wells. In his Fabian essay on property, Wallas describes the "dreary squalor" of the English industrial working class, then the new and nobler life socialism could bring them. "Socialism hangs above them as the crown hung in Bunyan's story above the man raking the muck heap – ready for them if they will but lift their eyes." It is the same Bunyanesque rhetoric that Shaw brings to his vision of London as hell, miraculously capable of regenerating itself into heaven, in *Widowers' Houses, Mrs Warren's Profession* and *Major Barbara*. His diaries bear witness to that emotion, focused on the image of the great, appalling city, in its flat noting of the miles he and his friends walked across it every Sunday to preach the creed of socialism in remote working-class backwaters, and then to Hammersmith for Sunday dinner with the creed's prophet and patriarch, William Morris, and his family. (Morris, surely, not Stewart Headlam, inspired the hearty socialist vicar in *Candida*, with his cruel madonna of a wife ready to betray him with a poet.) If it was his university, it also became the heart of his religion: his symbol of sin and redemption, the great conspiracy of exploitation, misery and wrong which he and his comrades would build into a new Jerusalem. It would be consoling to believe that there are a few young men like them, dreaming similar dreams, walking the garbage-strewn streets and breathing the limousine-poisoned air of Margaret Thatcher's capital.

SHAW'S
CONTEMPORARIES

ARTISTS IN A LANDSCAPE

Programme note for the Shaw Festival's 1997
production of *The Seagull* by Anton Chekhov

In the third act of *The Seagull*, young Nina Zarechnaya tells the writer Boris Trigorin, with whom she has fallen in love, that she plans to run away to Moscow and go on the stage. "Stay at the Slavyansky Bazaar," he instructs her hurriedly, and gives her an address where she can reach him. The play's first Russian audiences would have seen the point of Trigorin's advice. In spite of its romantically archaic name, the hotel where he urges Nina to stay was one of the newest in Moscow, busy, central and crowded. An unaccompanied young woman of the educated class would encounter no embarrassment there – the Bazaar prided itself on its modernity. Its restaurant was the first in Moscow whose waiters were not just serfs picked off the owner's country estate, but professionals trained in the French manner. Its pancakes were famous; merchants ordered two dozen at a sitting. A century after Nina checked in, it was still serving some of the best food to be had in Moscow, though the hotel proper had gone out of business. Then in 1994 the interior was destroyed by fire, and the restaurant closed.

It is to be hoped that someone will preserve the building so that UNESCO can erect a plaque declaring it a site of cultural importance to the world. Not because Nina stayed there, but to commemorate a meeting that took place in the Bazaar's restaurant a hundred years ago this summer. On 22 June 1897, Constantin Stanislavsky, a wealthy manufacturer with a passion for the theatre, lunched there with Vladimir Nemirovich-Danchenko, a novelist, playwright and critic who taught acting at the Moscow Conservatory. They talked for eighteen hours, most of them in one of the Bazaar's private dining-rooms, through dinner into the small hours

of the morning, when Stanislavsky bore Nemirovich off to breakfast at Liubimovska, his country estate. In that time, they hammered
out most of the details of launching what would become known as
the Moscow Art Theatre. Eighteen months later, their theatre gave
The Seagull its first Moscow production.

Stanislavsky, whose real name was Alexeyev – he took the
name Stanislavsky as a stage pseudonym – had inherited a family
business which made all the gold and silver thread worn by the
imperial Russian court, army and navy. But from childhood he had
wanted more than anything else to be an actor and work in the
theatre. His wealth enabled him to create a private amateur theatre
for himself and his friends, modeled on the private opera run by his
cousin by marriage, the railway magnate Savva Mamontov. But
wanting something more serious and professional, he went on to
launch a Society for Art and Literature, under whose banner he
produced what was generally agreed to be the best theatre in
Moscow, better than the state-run Maly Theatre. In the early 1890s,
he had staged the first production of Tolstoy's *The Fruits of Enlightenment*, as well as Hauptmann's *The Sunken Bell*, Irving's melodrama
The Bells, and *Much Ado About Nothing*, in which his playing of
Benedick was compared to that of the finest actors from France
and Italy.

Although Nemirovich trained actors for the Maly and sat on
the committee that chose its repertoire, he felt increasingly dis-
couraged. The theatre seemed too fearful of censorship to mount
plays about anything other than dead monarchs from picturesque
periods of history or romantic swordsmen in tall Spanish boots. Its
acting drifted equally far from reality. Nemirovich longed for a
Russian equivalent of the lively, engaged new theatres of western
Europe – the Théâtre Libre in Paris, the Freie Bühne in Berlin, the
Independent Theatre in London. There naturalism reigned. Actors
wore modern dress, performed the works of Ibsen, and believed
passionately that the theatre should deal with contemporary problems such as prostitution, venereal disease, the exploitation of workers and the position of women. At the Conservatory, Nemirovich
had a brilliant group of young actors who shared this belief: Vsevolod

Meyerhold, who would play Constantin in *The Seagull*, Ivan Moskvin, who became the Art Theatre's greatest character actor, and Olga Knipper, who would play Arkadina and become Chekhov's wife. Nemirovich wanted to bring them together with Stanislavsky's group and secure for them the highest artistic standards and best direction in Russia.

All that was missing when the deal was done was a house playwright. The new theatres in the west built their fame on Ibsen, Strindberg, Gerhart Hauptmann, various French disciples of Zola, and George Bernard Shaw. The only playwrights in Russia to match them, Nemirovich believed, were his friend Chekhov and himself. He persuaded Stanislavsky that they must secure Chekhov's latest play for their first season. But Chekhov was reluctant to let it be seen in Moscow. *The Seagull* had played five nights the previous October in St Petersburg, where its reception was a humiliating fiasco. Its first night was made a benefit performance for a popular Petersburg comedienne. When the audience learned she was not in the play, they booed and hooted. Chekhov walked the icy quays of the Neva until two in the morning resolving, he told his friend and publisher Alexei Suvorin, "never if he lived seven hundred years to give a play to the theatre again." Some friends believed it was this night walk that brought on later that winter the massive lung haemorrhage which made it clear Chekhov had an advanced case of tuberculosis. Nemirovich had to talk him round, persuading him that he saw the play's quality if no one in Petersburg did, and that he and Stanislavsky could save it for posterity.

In the event, *The Seagull* saved the Moscow Art Theatre. It opened on December 17, 1898, the sixth production of the season. The five previous plays had been praised by the critics, but lost money. By the time *The Seagull* was mounted and costumed, the theatre's capital was exhausted. The actors knew what was at stake. Olga Knipper remembered a strong smell of valerian, the nineteenth century's equivalent of Valium, backstage on the first night. During the first act, the audience was silent. It was customary in those days for curtain calls to follow each act. When the curtain fell, the silence continued. Behind it, pale actors held on to each other, faint with fear. Then, wrote Nemirovich, there was a sound like a dam breaking. Applause and bravos swept the auditorium. There were six curtain calls for that act, more for each that followed. The evening was a triumph: for the first time, most people felt, they had seen real Russian life upon a stage. Out of that success, and the three more great plays by Chekhov that made the Art Theatre famous, Stanislavsky and Nemirovich were able to build a new theatre. On its curtain, to this day, is emblazoned the silhouette of a seagull.

If Chekhov saved the Art Theatre, the Art Theatre also saved Chekhov. No one expected him to live more than a year or two after his lung haemorrhage in March 1897. In fact, he lived on for seven, to write *Uncle Vanya*, *Three Sisters* and *The Cherry Orchard*, and to marry Olga Knipper in 1901. The success of his plays, and the involvement with the theatre represented by his marriage, undoubtedly helped to keep him alive, though his illness forced him to live in the Crimea, far from Moscow. What few people realize is what he really thought of Stanislavsky's productions of his plays. Letters to friends suggest he recognized their quality, finer than anything else in Russia at the time. But he kept protesting that he wrote comedies which Stanislavsky insisted on directing as tragedies. There is evidence to support his complaint. When he sent Stanislavsky *The Cherry Orchard*, unambiguously subtitled "A Comedy," Stanislavsky wrote in ecstasy to tell him that he had read it in floods of tears.

Some of Chekhov's discontent may have been caused by the deliberate pace at which Stanislavsky made his actors explore the subtext between their lines. He was intent on inventing a new kind of acting which captured a reality of which language is only a part. He was right in recognizing that this was the goal of Chekhov's writing. He overlooked the fact that in Chekhov's short stories the work done by his actors was left to the reader. His productions obviously were marvellously clear elucidations of Chekhov's often cryptic texts. They presumably lacked the wiry, economic brevity that in Chekhov's stories has an effect that feels like wit, only finer.

A case in point was his sound effects. His *Seagull* opened with a soundscape of a summer night in the Russian countryside: distant sounds of drunken song, the howling of a dog, the croaking of frogs, the cry of a corncrake. Stanislavsky obviously had read "The Steppe," regarded by most people as Chekhov's finest, most Russian story up to that time, in which the featureless grasslands between the Don and Dnieper are brought to life in a tapestry of natural sounds: the cries of lapwings and petrels, marmots calling in the grass, the chirring music of crickets, locusts and grasshoppers. Chekhov hated Stanislavsky's coarsening of his delicate statement that there is a natural world, almost unnoticed by human beings, which will outlast them.

What Stanislavsky had done was to declare noisily in his overture the still, sad music which Chekhov wanted his audience to recognize when his play was over. *The Seagull* was to him a comedy built on an idea: the unnaturalness of artists appearing in a landscape. It is the nature of most art, he implies subtly, to conquer, appropriate, reshape, declare, make scenes. To let a writer into your life, says the Maupassant novel Arkadina tosses aside in the second act, is to admit a nest of rats to your granary. That there can be a kind of art which is quiet, unassertive, unassuming, as workaday as the world itself, is an idea which has just begun to dawn on Nina and Constantin, with different effects, at the end of the play. To place artists in a landscape, as Manet did in "Le Déjeuner sur l'herbe," is to create an instant joke. To extricate them from nature without their causing harm, the happy ending Nature desires, may be more difficult.

OUT THE NURSERY DOOR

Programme note for the Royal National Theatre's 2000 production of *The Cherry Orchard* by Anton Chekhov

If you asked a representative group of informed theatre-goers, quickly, before the Thought Police could stop you, to name the best play of the twentieth century, it's a safe bet the majority would choose *The Cherry Orchard*. (Being informed means they'd know it wasn't a nineteenth-century product, but had its first performance on January 17, 1904.) Even more interesting, perhaps, would be the number of runners-up which owe their being, directly or indirectly, to Chekhov's play – Maxim Gorky's *Summerfolk*, Bernard Shaw's *Heartbreak House*, Priestley's *Time and the Conways*, Samuel Beckett's *Endgame*, Slawomir Mrozek's *Tango*, Sam Shepard's *Buried Child*, Stoppard's *Arcadia*. Quality is a to-and-fro thing, but sheer quantity suggests that *The Cherry Orchard* is without doubt the most influential play of the last hundred years.

The Thought Police, who hate the idea that any cultural artefact can be more valuable or important than any other, would retort that of course everyone dotes on *The Cherry Orchard* because each generation remakes it to mirror its own moods and concerns. They score a point there. In half a century of playgoing, I must have seen at least fifty *Orchard*s, including the remains of Stanislavsky's, brought to London by the Moscow Art Theatre in 1958. I'm not convinced I've yet seen the play Chekhov wrote.

My first *Cherry Orchard*s, in London in the 1950s, were silvery-grey elegies for the world that ended in 1914, set in the key of Cyril Connolly's "It is closing time in the gardens of the West." My first clues to why Chekhov insisted his play was a comedy came from the Moscow Art Theatre's stately ruin: the woes of its elderly protagonists were doubled by the fact that their domestic help evidently had been recruited from a down-at-heel *commedia dell'arte* travelling troupe. In the '60s, David Magarshack and other scholars told us that, behind the Iron Curtain, Russians revered Chekhov as a great comic artist. British *Orchards* took on the bruised colours of black comedy, in the manner of Joe Orton and Peter Barnes. In those years of Herbert Marcuse and *les évènements*, this was justified by crushing strokes of neo-Marxist satire at the expense of the capitalist sillies who let the orchard slip through their fingers.

But mostly Anglo-Saxon audiences in my time seemed incapable of seeing the loss of the cherry orchard as anything less than tragic. Having grown up on a Caribbean island where half the families I knew kept afloat by selling derelict sugar and cocoa estates, with emotions ranging from regret to relief, nostalgia to elation, I found this view, well, uninflected. Was it the English passion for gardening that could not bear the loss of all that blossom? Or the British passion for Agatha Christie that could not imagine catastrophe without crime? I remember long after-theatre discussions about who dun it. Name the guilty parties! Who killed the cherry orchard?

You come closer to the play Chekhov wrote if you recognize that the orchard's assassin, assassinated himself twenty-two years before the play was written, was Alexander II, the tsar who freed Russia's serfs in 1861. In a world where labour has to be paid for, the cherry orchard is a ludicrous economic absurdity. Have you grasped how enormous it is? Early in the play, the self-made millionaire Lopakhin tells Madame Ranevsky that if she would rent off her estate in one-acre lots at ten roubles an acre, she could have an income of 25,000 roubles a year. Most of those 2500 acres are planted with cherries; at least, we hear of no other crop. No wonder the orchard's yield is irregular. There can't be enough bees in the province to pollinate two thousand acres of blossom. And when the cherries ripen where will you find the army of pickers necessary to strip, pack and ship out 2000 acres worth of cherries? How will you pay them from the proceeds of selling cherries in a market the orchard itself gluts every year?

The orchard is a dying white elephant which cannot be saved. It is pointless, therefore, to accuse the people who fail to save it, as they are invariably accused, of fecklessness. What are they supposed to do? Madame Ranevsky's brother Gayev is certainly a few ko-peks short of a rouble, but he speaks the simple truth when he says that a disease for which so many remedies are prescribed must be incurable. It is stupid of him to promise his nieces on his honour that the orchard will be saved, but behind his idiocy may lie the thought that children should be spared distress if one can. Chekhov never tells us, but it seems possible that one of the children, Ma-dame Ranevsky's adopted daughter Varya, may be his own.

Certainly it is unjust to use the word feckless of Madame Ranevsky. She is careless about money in small ways, leaves things lying about, but she is the one person in the play with a rational, practical plan to save the orchard, and by working tirelessly almost brings it off. If you doubt this, look up Chekhov's 1898 story "A Visit with Friends". You will find there an unmistakable draft for the second act of *The Cherry Orchard*. The one way to save the es-tate is to marry a daughter to the richest man you can find. Ranevskaya applies all her energy, cunning and immense charm to enticing Lopakhin into marrying good, plain, docile Varya, and by the end of the act he says yes. What she cannot see is that, the more she enchants him, the less he finds it possible to love any woman but herself. Chekhov always said it was a comedy.

We're told why Lopakhin loves Ranevskaya in the first minutes of the play. Years ago, when he was a barefoot peasant boy bleeding at the nose from a cuff by his drunken father, the young Lyubov Andreyevna took him into the estate-house nursery, washed his face and told him he would be fine in time for his wedding day. In spite of the transformations his life has brought him, he remains arrested in time on its happiest day. Slowly Chekhov shows us that his is only the first case of an epidemic that infects everyone in Ranevskaya's house-hold. Her brother is arrested at the age when he must have been the stupidest, most beautiful member of the Royal Corps of Pages in Petersburg, probably expelled for winning too often at billiards. She herself has never grown past the age of believing all will be well, the day fine, that love and happiness will come to the pure in heart.

There are moments in Chekhov's play when I smell the influence of his friend Tchaikovsky's ballet *The Sleeping Beauty*. At the opening, the old estate house wakes as if from a century of sleep. At the end, it goes to sleep again forever. At its most wakeful, it seems filled with dancing ghosts: the generals, admirals and barons old Firs the footman remembers at other parties, the dead serfs whose children dance in a house their parents never entered, the circus child who grew into the governess Charlotte cakewalking in clown's trousers, Madame Ranevsky's mother who looked like a flowering cherry tree, the country lawyer Ranevsky who married her money and drowned in champagne, their little boy Grisha who drowned in the river. These moments are presided over by Firs in his century-old livery. He has a rude word for his masters behind their backs which gives trouble to translators. He calls them *nyedotyopy*, and at the end of the play turns the word on himself. It's been rendered as "duffers", "sillybillies", "nincompoops", but really has no English equivalent. In Russian it carries the sense of half-baked, rough-hewn, incomplete, unfinished. Perhaps some day translators will feel free to use the American high-school insult "retards". Then Firs' last word will tell its audience they've seen a play about unachieved lives.

Does that mean Chekhov wrote a Symbolist drama about the strong enchantment of the past, the orchard taking the place of the wall of rose briers cutting off the Sleeping Beauty's palace from the passing of time? I don't think so. To do that, he'd have to show the orchard. In the play he wrote, we never see it, it's an idea in people's minds. That leaves a comedy about people trapped in their own pasts, who need to be liberated from them to live in the present. After *The Seagull*, Chekhov stopped leaving symbols lying about the furniture, giving his plays poetic meanings beyond what their characters do. *The Cherry Orchard* is about what happens in it, the actions that take place in it, especially the last. That is the hardest action most of us have to perform in our lives: walking out of the nursery door.

THE CHERRY ORCHARD'S HEIRS

Programme note for the Royal National Theatre's
1999 production of *Summerfolk* by Maxim Gorky

Early in Anton Chekhov's play *The Cherry Orchard*, the entrepreneur Yermolay Lopakhin tells his bankrupt neighbour Madame Ranevsky that she could pay all her debts and secure a handsome income for life if she would only cut down her cherry orchard, divide her estate into building lots and lease them for summer cottages. "All our towns, even the smallest, are surrounded by summer cottages nowadays. And it looks as if in twenty years or so there are going to be fantastic numbers of these summer people. So far your holiday-maker only has tea on his balcony, but he may very well start growing things on his bit of land, and then this cherry orchard will become a happy, rich, prosperous place."

Chekhov was not the only Russian playwright to have observed this new social phenomenon. During the winter of 1903-4, while the Moscow Art Theatre was rehearsing *The Cherry Orchard*, Maxim Gorky was writing his play *Summerfolk*, about members of Russia's rising industrial middle class renting holiday *dachas* on the kind of development Lopakhin describes. Gorky's wife Ekaterina Peshchova said he got the idea for his play a year or so earlier, when they spent the summer of 1902 in a *dacha* outside Nijni Novgorod. Outraged by the heaps of rusted tins and waste paper the previous year's tenants left behind, he wrote: "The summer visitor is the most useless and perhaps the most harmful individual on earth; he descends on a *dacha*, fouls it up with rubbish and then leaves." What is not clear is how much Gorky was influenced in writing *Summerfolk* by his knowledge of *The Cherry Orchard*.

He was fully aware of Chekhov's play. Ever since the enormous success of *The Lower Depths* in 1902, he had been an honorary member of the Art Theatre family – on its opening night, in fact, he embarked on an affair with the actress Maria Andreyeva, who was to play Varya in *The Cherry Orchard*. As soon as copies of the script were circulated in November 1903, Gorky offered Chekhov 4500 roubles for permission to print the play in his annual *Knowledge*, and it was being set up in type as rehearsals began. *The Cherry Orchard* opened on 17 January 1904, and Gorky finished his first draft of *Summerfolk* in February. He read it to the Art Theatre company – meaning that it was theirs if they wanted it – in April. Had it been accepted, it would have played back to back with *The Cherry Orchard* in the Art Theatre's repertoire, if not in the current season then in the following one.

It was not to be. After Gorky's reading, the Art Theatre's co-founder and dramaturg, Vladimir Nemirovich-Danchenko, criticized the script witheringly. It was structurally weak, he said, and peopled with Aunt Sally characters unworthy of artistic attention. Nemirovich feared the influence of Gorky's left-wing politics on the theatre, and resented the support given them by the company's main backer, the Socialist millionaire Savva Morozov. Nemirovich had a powerful ally in Olga Knipper, Chekhov's wife, who was playing Madame Ranevsky in *The Cherry Orchard*. She detested Maria Andreyeva, whom she saw as a rival, and had persuaded Chekhov she should play Varya, the plain daughter of Madame Ranevsky's household, rather than Anya, the radiant ingénue. During the weeks after Gorky's reading, Knipper managed to goad Andreyeva into quitting the company, after many scenes and much shouting. Gorky took *Summerfolk* to Vera Komisarjevskaya, who had started a new company in St Petersburg. The play had its premiere there in November 1904, but was banned after 25 performances when Gorky denounced the Tsar as a murderer following the massacre of peaceful demonstrators outside the Winter Palace in January 1905.

Did Gorky intend *Summerfolk* as some kind of companion piece, commentary or rejoinder to *The Cherry Orchard*? Because the two plays were separated at birth, so to speak, no one has spent much time considering them as a pair. It's unlikely that Gorky would have written anything pointedly critical of his friend's play – like everyone else, he knew Chekhov was dying. (He did so in July 1904.) If *Summerfolk* was a rejoinder, it's not so much to Chekhov as to his creation Lopakhin, whose vision of the cherry orchard reborn as a hive of happy, virtuous rural industry is accurately described by Madame Ranevsky's birdbrained brother Gayev as nonsense. The tenants of the *dacha* colony in Gorky's play have no taste for husbandry, but see themselves as inheritors of the idle, aristocratic country life they know from the works of Turgenev and his admirers, Chekhov among them. It would be absurd to call *Summerfolk* a parody of *The Cherry Orchard*, but you could call it a play about people whose lives are coarse parodies of the lives of characters in Chekhov's plays.

The real difference between Gorky and Chekhov, which Gorky might well have wanted to put forward as a comment on Chekhov's play – it couldn't have offended Chekhov, they'd often discussed it – is a basic political one. Chekhov perhaps glanced at it in the exchange in *The Cherry Orchard* between Lopakhin and Madame Ranevsky about Russia being a land for giants. "Giants?" says Ranevskaya. "They're all very well in fairy tales, but they'd be a bore in real life." She implies, and one smells Chekhov's agreement with her implicit statement, that all Russia or the world need to better themselves is people who live better, one by one. Whereas Lopakhin's words bring to mind the scene in Gorky's *Lower Depths* where the cardsharp Satin draws drunkenly on the air the giant outline of humanity – Man – in its aggregate, as a symbol of what men and women might achieve collectively.

Gorky has a working man's appreciation of the great things human beings can build together. One of his earliest stories, "Chelkash," opens with a powerful description of the port of Odessa, one of Russia's major nineteenth-century achievements, with huge iron steamers nosing into its vast granite wharves. His play *Barbarians* has an epic sense of how railway builders are transforming the old wooden Russia into a Russia of iron. In his play *Enemies*, about industrial strife, the striking workers agree they must not damage the factory they work in. "We built it," says one of their leaders. "It's ours." The main theme of *Enemies* is how recognition of one's place in a great collective enterprise sharpens the mind and clarifies decisions. *Summerfolk* is its negative companion piece, about the aimless enfeeblement of will that overtakes those with no great idea to command their lives.

Gorky ends his description of the port of Odessa in "Chelkash" with the reflection that the giant works they have made have dwarfed and made prisoners of the workers who built them. "The things they themselves had created had enslaved them and robbed them of their personalities." Gorky himself became a prisoner of the giant revolutionary enterprise to which he gave his life, maintained by Stalin as a kind of public effigy of himself to lie about and apologize for the terror the dictator brought to Russia. However, at the end of a century in which a British prime minister famously declared that there is no such thing as society, it is stirring to be confronted again with one of the great spirits of those hundred years who sold his soul for the opposite belief.

THE AUNT'S PROGRESS

Programme note for the Shaw Festival's 1992
production of *Charley's Aunt* by Brandon Thomas

The Brandon Thomas family cherish a legend that sums up the place in history of their most prized heirloom. During the Second World War, when Cairo swarmed with servicemen, diplomats, refugees, spies and mountebanks of all nations, a cosmopolitan group drinking one night in Shepheard's Hotel discovered that they had two things in common. Before the war all had been actors and all, in their various languages, had played in *Charley's Aunt*. To celebrate the coincidence, they decided to give a performance of the play for wartime charities. Although each played in his or her own language, the gala was a huge success. Everyone in the audience knew the play almost as well as the actors.

Brandon Thomas' comedy started down the road to universal recognition within months of its opening at the Royalty Theatre in London on December 21, 1892. By Christmas 1893, seven companies were touring it round the British Isles. In October 1894, while still only halfway through its 1469 London performances, it opened in New York with a company led by the original Jack, Percy Lyndal. By the end of the century it had been seen in Paris, as *La Marraine de Charley*, Rome (*La Zia di Carlo*), Berlin (*Charleys Tante*) and Tokyo (*The Aunt from Hawaii*). Early in the new century, it was translated into Esperanto. Charley Chaplin's brother Sydney appeared in a silent-film version in 1925, and three sound films starred John Mills, Arthur Askey and Jack Benny. Ray Bolger danced the lead in a Broadway musical adaptation, *Where's Charley?*, in 1948. Its hit tune, "Once in Love with Amy," turns up most Sundays on CBC radio's Royal Canadian Air Farce, ushering in the

Farce's fiery queen of passion and protocol, Amy de la Pompa. Amy is played by a man. Some jokes never die.

The idea for *Charley's Aunt* was hatched on a train travelling down the Thames valley to London. Brandon Thomas, a 42-year-old actor struggling to support a young bride by writing plays, bumped into a colleague, the comedian W.S. Penley, returning from a weekend out of town. Penley, who had made his fortune a few years earlier playing the lead in Charles Hawtrey's farce *The Private Secretary*, was planning to enter management for himself. He asked Thomas to write a play for him – he had seen his short farce *A Highland Legacy* in 1888, and found it uproarious. The only question was what kind of part to write in it for Penley, who had played every imaginable comic type. Perhaps because most Thames valley trains start from Oxford, bearing chattering cargoes of undergraduates, like highly-coloured tropical birds, a thought struck Thomas. Oxford, where women were forbidden to appear in student theatricals, was one of the few places in the world where a man might without scandal appear on stage in female dress. "Have you ever thought," he asked Penley, "of playing a woman?"

Brandon Thomas' upbringing had not been one to instil a fastidious taste in entertainment. His father, a Liverpool bootmaker, married the daughter of a brewing family and wound up selling the family beer behind the counters of various family pubs. His notion of saloon-keeping seems to have been more festive than businesslike, forcing his wife to take in lodgers, some of them theatrical, to support their children. Young Brandon inherited his father's pleasure in setting rooms of beer-drinkers on a roar, and did so by reciting Lancashire dialect poems and singing coon-songs of his own composition in blackface. (Two of these, "I Lub a Lubly Girl" and "Sing Along, Sambo," brought in a small but steady income to the end of his life.) One of Mrs Thomas' theatrical lodgers brought the actor-managers William and Madge Kendal to hear Brandon recite. They invited him to call should he decide to try his luck in London. He dithered for a year or two, then took up their invitation in 1879.

He was 31, but looked older. Because of an astigmatic eye, he wore a monocle. As an actor, he complained later, he found himself playing "shady" parts – officers who return from India to discover in Act II that they have illegitimate daughters fathered twenty years earlier and ripe to make scenes in Act III. But in London he discovered the life of art. He made friends with the debonair George Grossmith, chief clown of the Savoy Operas; with Whistler and his disciple Sickert, Aubrey Beardsley and his sister Mabel. In 1890 he married a young cousin of Oscar Wilde's beloved "Spinx," the novelist Ada Leverson, in whose house they met. Whistler introduced him to Japanese art, and over the years he built up a collection of Hokusai engravings second only to that of the Prince of Wales. It was a taste particularly appropriate for an actor. As Whistler doubtless showed him, Hokusai's drawing of the moving human body was something new in art, both scientific and superbly comic in its notation of geishas fanning, porters running in the rain, fat merchants scratching their rumps.

One can see both where Thomas came from and what he made of himself in *Charley's Aunt*. Its basic joke is a splendidly plebeian raspberry blown at the ruling concern of society drama in the 1890s: the ruin threatening any woman alone in a room with a man for more than a minute and a half. Thomas expels with a blast of fresh air the stink of divorce-court prurience and masculine possession that hangs over the theatre of Pinero and Henry Arthur Jones. But he does so with a nonsensical elegance worthy of Wilde. Lord Fancourt Babberley, dropping by the Oxford rooms of his friend Jack to borrow a few bottles of champagne for luncheon, could be one of Wilde's dandies, and his line "I'm Charley's aunt from Brazil, where the nuts come from," has an echo of Rimbaud or Mallarmé. Great art went into tailoring the role to its star. Penley was a former choirboy who had wound up singing bass-baritone in the Russian Embassy's chapel choir. His best effects came in leaps from choirboy demureness to deep-voiced muscularity in lines like "I'm no ordinary woman," from dainty flirtings of his fan to athletic vaultings over college furniture.

terpart to the French Revolution that Britain never achieved. It is an aristocratic affectation not to hear unwelcome news. Walkley may have been indulging in the very British behaviour burlesqued by music-hall comedians in their lordly dismissal: "I don't wish to know that! Kindly leave the stage!"

Walkley must have known Ibsen's famous declaration of anarchism – that he was not out to dismantle this or that social institution, but to "torpedo the Ark." Presumably he recognized that this budding Ibsenite proposed an even more radical revision of *Genesis*: the redesign of Eden, to give real power to Eve. His snub may have been a message to Barker that so drastic a motion to reverse the whole course of Western civilization needed a weightier mover than a clever young actor of underfed, Italianate good looks.

The British public had met Barker first as a boy actor supporting his mother in seaside recitals of poetry and simulated birdcalls. (His father, an odd-job builder, sporadically converted houses into flats.) Since then he had played small parts with Ben Greet's touring Shakespearians and in Mrs Patrick Campbell's travelling repertoire of plays about tarnished ladies with unrepentant wardrobes. He had distinguished himself fleetingly playing Richard II one afternoon for William Poel and as Marchbanks in the Stage Society's single London matinee of *Candida*, but as a result became identified with his roles as a young man too clever for his own good. The fact that his brilliance as Marchbanks led Shaw to adopt him as a surrogate son and protégé did nothing to help.

To compound his presumption, *Ann Leete* showed a clear debt of admiration to George Meredith. Meredith was the novelist of the intellectual young in the 1890s, as Browning was their poet. ("Meredith is a prose Browning," quipped Oscar Wilde jealously, "and so is Browning.") He was also the saint of the self-made. The son of a tailor, Meredith had perfected a dandified mandarin comedy more elegant and distinguished than the titled world it mocked. Ann Leete's predicament would have reminded Meredith readers of Clara Middleton's in *The Egoist*, struggling to escape her engagement to a vainglorious baronet. The link was clear enough to the American actress Ada Rehan that she asked whether Barker would adapt Meredith's *Diana of the Crossways* for her.

Barker outgrew the Meredith manner, but never abandoned Meredith's main project – to bring down the patriarchal tyranny of the Victorian male. In his essay "On Comedy and the Comic Spirit," urging laughter as humanity's prophylaxis against pomposity and self-importance, Meredith argued that only in societies where male and female are held equal is such sane, health-giving laughter possible. Both male and female visions distort the world with partiality, vanity and sentimentality, he maintained. Only their partnership, in equality, can see life clearly, truly and whole.

All Barker's major plays – *Ann Leete, The Voysey Inheritance, Waste, The Madras House, The Secret Life, His Majesty* – hinge on the sexual equation and its need for balance. All of them end with scenes in which a man and woman, alone together, discuss how to live in the world that is their joint inheritance. Usually their talk ends in recognition that, whatever their individual wishes, they are part of a wider process which demands that they serve it together. Because it contains and drives them, they can know it only as a pair, living it rather than trying to think it.

This sense of a reality larger than either sex can grasp, in which male and female must fit their wills to a current stronger than either, is perhaps what most puzzled Barker's audiences ninety years ago. Plays illustrating such a theme could scarcely be written until the craft of the director, unknown in Britain before 1900, made them possible. Their action consists less of what characters do than of what time does to them. They are plays about process – the groundswell of life which bears human events and motives like driftwood on its surface. To depict this in the theatre required a new art: the orchestration of a performance so that its key moments may be those in which the process makes itself felt – in the cry of a bird before dawn, the first raindrops of a dry summer, the snapping of a cable in a mine miles across a Russian steppe.

Two years before *Ann Leete* was staged, someone else wrote a play in which sisters in a garden discuss how hard it is to find out how life wants us to live it. As Chekhov's Olga, Masha and Irina Prozorov watch the geese fly south, they cry out to know what-

On opening night, the Royalty Theatre's fireman laughed so hard he dropped the fire-curtain, almost causing a panic. The Duke of Cambridge, Queen Victoria's cousin, broke his seat in the stalls falling about, and sat out the act, still laughing helplessly, on the floor. The only person not amused was the Prince of Wales, later Edward VII. He suspected Penley's flying beldam in bombazine, chasing over the stage with the manic energy of a page of Hokusai caricatures, of glancing slyly at the image of his mother. The Brandon Thomas family dismiss his suspicion as foolish. They are almost alone in regarding Edward VII as less than a highly astute man.

GRANVILLE BARKER
AND THE REDESIGN OF EDEN

Programme note for the Shaw Festival's 1993 production
of *The Marrying of Ann Leete* by Harley Granville Barker

Harley Granville Barker's *The Marrying of Ann Leete* was first mounted by the London Stage Society for two matinees on January 26 and 27, 1902. Mostly it provoked bafflement. "It must be difficult to write a play in four acts . . . and throughout them all to keep your audience blankly ignorant of the meaning of it," wrote A.B. Walkley in the *Times*. "Many of the persons who sat through-out *The Marrying of Ann Leete* at the Royalty Theatre yesterday afternoon must have wished it were impossible. Granville Barker calls his piece a comedy. It might more suitably be termed a prac-tical joke."

Seventy-three years later another *Times* critic, Irving Wardle, attended the first revival of Barker's play, with Mia Farrow as Ann, by the Royal Shakespeare Company. He hailed it as a key work of the modern British theatre. "The stage-craft, treatment of charac-ter, attitude towards the audience," Wardle wrote, "all proclaim a man reinventing the art of playwriting and forecasting develop-ments of half a century later." The fact that Barker was only twenty-two when he wrote the play, Wardle added, was only one of the amazing things about it.

What so mystified *Ann Leete*'s first audiences? Doubtless the *Daily Telegraph* spoke for a number who could not fathom its hatred of the English class system. "Why in the name of reason," asked the *Telegraph* plaintively, "did Ann Leete throw over a young, presentable, impassioned and entirely eligible nobleman for a hus-band socially so much her inferior?" Walkley, no fool (though Barker twenty years later still called him irritably "that popinjay"), was hardly so naïve. He must have smelled the Jacobinism of Barker's enterprise: in effect, Ann Leete stages single-handedly the coun-

ever it is that the birds know. "It was when I saw the Moscow people interpreting Chekhov," Granville Barker wrote to William Archer in 1923, "that I fully realized what I had been struggling towards." He did not struggle in vain. No playwright has a better claim to be called the English Chekhov.

"THAT TERRIBLE MASTERPIECE"

Programme note for the Shaw Festival's
2001 production of *Peter Pan* by J.M. Barrie

When Sir James Barrie finally published the text of *Peter Pan*, twenty-four years after its first staging in 1904, he wrote a dedication to it which, while pretending to trace the origins of the play, does its best to obscure them. It is addressed to "The Five" who, it asserts, were co-authors and instigators of the story of the boy who would not grow up. "The play of Peter is streaky with you still, though none may see this but ourselves . . . As for myself, I suppose I always knew that I made Peter by rubbing the five of you violently together, as savages with two sticks produce a flame. That is all he is, the spark I got from you."

One of the curiosities of this very curious piece of writing is that two of its five addressees were dead when it was written. Like a number of characters in his later plays, Barrie was talking to ghosts. The purpose of such conversations is usually exculpation: persuading the dead that the living do not deserve to be haunted. The strenuousness with which Barrie insists on *Peter Pan*'s shared authorship, on its innocent origins in children's games, suggests that perhaps the play had begun to haunt him. A generation of children had grown up – those spared by war – since Peter Pan first asked them to clap if they believed in fairies. People in the '20s had begun to talk of Barrie's work as not just a children's entertainment but as a myth for all ages, about the flight of youth, the loss of innocence, the power of fantasy. For those closest to its history, it had other, darker associations. Barrie's dedication reads almost as if he foresaw and wished to prevent the description of *Peter Pan* by the third of his dedicatees, the publisher Peter Davies, as "that terrible masterpiece".

"The Five" were the sons – George, Jack, Peter, Michael and Nico – of Barrie's Kensington neighbours Arthur and Sylvia Llewelyn Davies. When Barrie and his wife, the actress Mary Ansell, returned from their Swiss honeymoon in 1895 with a St Bernard puppy bought at the foot of the famous pass, they took a house on Gloucester Road, handy to the green, dog-friendly spaces of Kensington Gardens. One day in 1896 two small boys in blue blouses and red tam-o-shanters ran up to ask the dog's name. Barrie told them it was Porthos – Mary had named the puppy after the loyal beast in George du Maurier's novel *Peter Ibbetson* – and spun them some stories about his heroic rescues and other adventures. Enchanted, the boys returned, escaping their nursemaid, the next day and the next, until the stories grew into the untidy bundle of fantasies Barrie published in 1902 as *The Little White Bird*.

In 1897, dining at his lawyer's house, Barrie found himself sitting next to a beautiful young woman with a crooked smile who turned out to be George du Maurier's daughter. It took her not long to work out that the small Scotsman beside her was the owner of Porthos, the man who had told her children those gorgeous stories about fairies in Kensington Gardens, birds who could talk, children who could fly, and pirates shipwrecked on the island in the Serpentine, the artificial lake running down the center of the Gardens. She introduced him to her husband, a handsome young lawyer across the table, and in no time at all – so quickly it was hard to say how it happened – the Barries were the Llewelyn Davies' dearest friends. They took Sylvia with them on holidays to Paris and the Alps; summered together at Black Lake in Sussex, playing pirate games with the children (four of them now); and sat together in a box, provided by Barrie, for Seymour Hicks' children's play *Bluebell in Fairyland*. It seems to have been the last that persuaded Barrie he could make something as good, if not better, out of the stories woven that summer at Black Lake.

It would seem extravagant to say that Barrie fell in love with the whole Davies family if he had not portrayed just such a relationship in the novel that made him famous, *The Little Minister*. Its romantic tale of a Wee Free minister bewitched by a Gypsy girl he finds running barefoot through the forest is complicated by being told by a character with no function in the plot but to breathe great hot sighs down its neck. The retired village schoolmaster once loved the minister's mother; for her sake loves the little minister, the son he never had; and for *his* sake loves the wayward Babbie, who turns out to be the ward of the local laird. The only use he serves in the book is to flood it with unearned sentiment, but he may have done a larger service to its author. He may have shown Barrie how to satisfy emotionally a nature clearly incapable of normal human attachments: a way of loving without the hand-to-hand stress of individual relationships or physical contact. Most of the Barries' friends appear to have recognized that their marriage was largely a formality. Few were startled when Mary ran off in 1909 with the writer Gilbert Cannan. The only surprise was that she let Barrie divorce her for adultery rather than seeking an annulment.

The opening night of *Peter Pan* was a kind of joint Christmas party given by the families involved. Barrie and the Davies boys (except Michael, who was not well, and the baby Nico) watched from a box. On the stage was a du Maurier family jollity: Sylvia's brother Gerald playing Captain Hook and Mr Darling, with Dorothea Baird, the original Trilby in the stage version of George du Maurier's best-seller, as his wife. To cover the elaborate scene-change from the Frozen River to the House Underground, Gerald du Maurier gave impersonations, on the pretext of having Hook summon the famous pirates of history for advice on dealing with Pan, of his West End peers Henry Irving, Beerbohm Tree and John Martin Harvey. (When the critics frowned on this self-indulgence, Barrie wrote in the Mermaids' Lagoon scene.) The last act took place in Kensington Gardens, with Hook and his sidekick Starkey turned into schoolmasters rounding up the Lost Boys to drag them off to the Davies boys' Notting Hill preparatory school.

This was probably why the script was not published. Christmas plays and pantomimes were occasional entertainments, changing from year to year depending who starred in them and what personal "material" they brought with them. *Peter Pan*'s script evolved like any other. Kensington Gardens disappeared and was replaced by the final glimpse of Wendy's house in the Never Land. An epilogue in which Wendy grows up and lets her daughter Jane visit Peter to do his spring cleaning was added in 1908, then relegated to the children's book *Peter and Wendy*. In 1909 a new front cloth, purporting to be Wendy's sampler, paid tribute to "dear Robert Louis Stevenson and R.M. Ballantyne" of *The Coral Island*. Barrie was beginning to see that his family joke must be taken seriously, assert its lineage among the children's classics. No one had expected it to succeed. Beerbohm Tree, who turned down the chance to produce it, told Charles Frohman, who seized it, that Barrie clearly had gone out of his mind. But the play made Barrie a rich man, earning nearly a quarter of a million dollars – its biggest profits came from Maude Adams' American tours – in its first year alone.

Then tragedy struck. In 1907 Arthur Davies died painfully of cancer of the jaw. Barrie, who sat by him when his wife could not look at his ruined face, promised to take care of his sons. Neither the Davies family nor the du Mauriers had the money to do for them what Barrie could, and he had persuaded Arthur and Sylvia that *Peter Pan* was as much their children's as it was his. He bought Sylvia and the boys a house on Campden Hill, finagled George and Peter into Eton, and got Captain Scott of the Antarctic to put forward Jack for a place at Dartmouth Naval College. George was fourteen, Jack thirteen, Peter ten, Michael seven and Nico four. Then, almost as suddenly as her husband, Sylvia was taken by what sounds like a breast cancer. Keeping on the little boys' nurse as a housekeeper, Barrie maintained the house for them, while living in an apartment off the Strand, but to all intents and purposes he became their adoptive father. The fiction that they were co-authors of *Peter Pan* was his justification for what amounted to a kidnapping.

It was an arrangement both splendid and tragic. Barrie could afford to give the Five the best of everything – Eton, Oxford, fishing holidays in Scotland, excursions to Paris – but he could not become a father or give the children back what they had lost. Jack particularly, whom he told after Sylvia's death that she had agreed to become his wife, never forgave him, and seems to have turned

Peter partly against him. George, the eldest and most grateful of the boys, deeply attached to him, was killed on the Western Front in 1915. Michael, the most beautiful and brilliant, who gradually made himself the centre of Barrie's life, drowned in the Thames near Oxford in 1921, swimming with a friend who drowned with him, in circumstances which led the remaining brothers to suspect suicide. Peter Davies at the age of sixty, after reading and sorting all their family history, threw himself under a London Underground train. At twenty Michael confided to a friend how oppressive he found their position, what a burden Barrie's love and expectations laid on them. Loving and understanding Barrie best of the five, he found himself paralyzed by fear that he could never live up to what Barrie wanted of him.

Late in the 1920s, after Michael's death, Barrie made a last important change to the script of *Peter Pan* before publishing it. In Act I, when Wendy tries to give Peter a "thimble" or kiss, he starts back, saying "Don't touch me. No one must ever touch me," and Barrie adds in a stage direction "No one touches him in the course of the play." Biographers have attributed the change to the other-worldly performance of Jean Forbes-Robertson as Peter in this period, but in fact it crystallized the play's deep logic. From an adult point of view, it can be seen as a version of the incubus legend – the idea of a being who comes to us by night, in our dreams, seducing us to live with him in his own fantastic realm, growing in strength and power from the vital fluids he draws from us. But if you allow yourself to join him in his dark kingdom, you discover that it is a cold, forbidding place of no return, where in the pursuit of fantasy you lose touch with your real life and soul. It is the most brilliant part of Barrie's invention that he shows Peter, the almost innocent baby incubus, to have a full-grown incubus of his own: the diabolic Captain Hook, with his ringlets like melting black candles, who slithers down a hollow tree to the cavern where Peter sleeps and squeezes a drop of poison into the glass of milky cordial by his bed.

That Barrie knew what he was hinting at in *Peter Pan*, and came to see what he had done to the Davies boys, appears in his last play *The Boy David*, produced in 1936, the year before he died. David and Saul, the first king of Israel, haunt each other's dreams. David is what Saul has been and would return to, Saul is what David dreams of becoming. They love each other, but Saul knows he can only bring David harm, and drives him from his court. The relationship of David and Saul is that of Peter and Hook, understood by a mature mind. The play failed, and its failure could be said to have killed Barrie. The actress Elisabeth Bergner, who played the boy David, said years later that the intensity of Barrie's need for it to succeed, of his expectation and love for her, unstrung her, made her ill, and forced her to fail. Trapped in Neverland, his hunger for real life was a torment to him and to all those he loved. But terrible though it is, he made a masterpiece. Year after year, children clap to save the life of Tinker Bell and weep to stay after the play with Peter and Wendy.

THE PRISONER OF NEVERLAND

On a London remount of *Peter Pan* by J.M.Barrie.
Originally published in the *Observer*, December 1966

In the freezing Byzantine cavern of the Scala Theatre in Charlotte Street, a white-haired rehearsal pianist in great-coat and muffler peered forward under a reading lamp and rippled off a shimmering sequence of minor chords. Like a bat swooping out of its stalactites, a small girl in black tights and a pony-tail ran down the empty aisle, a leather harness clasping her armpits and groin like those of some junior astronaut. On stage, before a frozen, painted river, a small stout man in a fisherman's sweater listened to a thin one with a nose like a nutcracker, who wore a hooked cylinder over one sleeve of his pinstriped suit.

"They will find the cake and gobble it up," he was announcing, "because, having no mother, they don't know how dangerous it is to eat rich . . . damp . . . cake! They will die!" He laughed, a descending scale of such Victorian villainy that the shorter actor recoiled, knocking over a plaster toadstool. Both broke up, grinning.

It was a rehearsal for the sixty-first season of *Peter Pan*. The BBC had just declared Jonathan Miller's version of *Alice in Wonderland* unsuitable for younger viewers, and turned down a modernized version of *Cinderella* which translated the ball into a Chelsea drug-orgy. But J.M. Barrie's tale of the three Bloomsbury children who flew out of their nursery window to a fairyland of pirates, Indians and ticking crocodiles, was back on the boards inviolate, rock-like and aloof above the tides of modernism. Psychiatry might come, types of ambiguity go, generations of cynical fathers echo Anthony Hope's sigh, on the first night in 1904, for an hour of

Herod. But the Edwardian children's classic remained, last strong-hold of the vanishing British custom of family Christmas theatrego-ing, preparing for the same squealing infant hordes it had drawn every year, with the exception of 1940, since it was written.

If you asked the Daniel Mayer Company, which has held sole production rights to the play in this country since 1929, what they'd say to a new *Peter Pan*, re-thought and re-staged for adults, you'd probably get much the same ghastly smile as that with which the first Hook, Gerald du Maurier, sent children home shuddering. They may add the occasional new crocodile, with red Magicoal eyes, or a repainted Mermaids' Lagoon, but largely their production is the same post-war replica which faithfully recreated in 1946 the rigid traditions of Barrie's lifetime. They can point to the fact that all prof-its from the play go to the Hospital for Sick Children in Great Ormond Street; to the barrage of letters in the *Times* and *Stage* which denounce with outrage the smallest innovation.

Yet every year or so comes a suggestion that the play be remounted in an adult version – there was gossip recently of a National Theatre production, and Tyrone Guthrie has long been known to be interested in directing a version for which he was given a free hand. On the whole, the suggestions are serious, not mischievously aimed at the sort of send-up success achieved by *Young England*, before the war. They argue that, like most fairy tales, the play has an adult content – isn't "Beauty and the Beast" one of the archetypal Freudian myths, "The Sleeping Beauty" an echo of the Proserpine fertility-story? – which needs bringing out to re-veal the play as the masterpiece in its kind that it surely is.

Actors have always known this – producers have never found difficulty in contracting leading stars to play Hook and Pan. "Peter's much the deepest part I could hope for at my age," said Julia Lockwood, tackling the part for the second time. "Each time I play it, I find new things in it. Most of the time, I'm offered 20-year-old juveniles." Ron Moody, playing Hook for the first time, revelled in the role. "He's the greatest villain in theatrical history, except pos-sibly Richard III. You've got to play him entirely seriously, in the melodrama convention, without worrying about frightening the children. Children like to be scared."

Toby Robertson, the director responsible for the play's seasons in 1963, 1964 and 1965, considered that the first thing to be done was restoring the play to a small theatre where the acting could be subtler. "You know it was originally produced at the Duke of York's, don't you? And think of what modern scenery could do. The nursery scene could be much more solid, entirely realistic, while the Never-Never Land could be pure dream, all light and hallucination. Of course, it ought to end in the nursery, as it began. Barrie floundered around inventing innumerable alternative endings, of which the house in the treetops was only the last, but the real ending is the children's home-coming, and Peter being barred out."

The best argument for a new *Peter Pan* is that it could eliminate this uncertainty whether the play should be aimed at adults or children; the discomfort of wondering how to take such lines as Peter's cry to Wendy, "You *musn't* touch me! No one must ever touch me!", or the doubling of the same actor as Mr Darling and Hook. Barrie wrote before the notion of a separate market, a separate world for children, when critics had not yet coined the modern cliché that children's stories should be for children only, with no knowing glances over the tiny heads from author to parent. For all his period obeisances to the purity of the infant mind, he knew that most children's stories are read, and most theatre-tickets bought, by parents for their offspring. His civilization had not yet split into separate realities for young and old: in his first draft (which called it the Never-Never-Never Land), Peter was guardian not only of the Lost Boys but of all children dead in childhood – Edwardian nurseries knew all about death, and infant mortality.

All the best literature for children, surely, offers meanings and pleasures on different levels to adults and young: a double vision of the single world which both inhabit. It may be too much to start children on *Anna Karenina* or *Tess of the D'Urbervilles* – they'd be bored and baffled – but it's possible, as Kipling showed in his Puck stories, to wrap an adult story within one for children, with a meaning which grows and deepens, like that of real events, as they grow older. Barrie surely did the same, and deliberately, in *Peter Pan*.

To begin with, as Toby Robertson's comment suggests, the form of the play is a junior version of the traditional Edwardian adventure-novel: a solid, buttoned-leather London interior from which the characters take off on fantastic travels, to Ruritania, the island of Dr Moreau or around the world in eighty days. This sandwich-formula – two slices of realism enclosing one of dream – is the customary one of a majority of Barrie's mature plays, in whose context one should seek the meaning of *Peter Pan*. He used it earlier in *The Admirable Crichton*; he was to use it again in *A Kiss for Cinderella*, *Dear Brutus* and *Mary Rose*.

It is the natural form for expressing the theme he used over and over: the transformation of character by fantasy or masquerade. In *The Little Minister*, Lady Babbie romps through the woods disguised as a gypsy, with rowanberries in her hair, to involve Gavin Dishart in a love their social positions would otherwise make impossible. In *Quality Street*, shy Miss Phoebe escapes spinsterhood by going to a ball disguised as her own niece. In *Crichton*, the perfect butler blossoms on a desert island into one of nature's chieftains, robed in feathers and skins.

The masquerades fulfil the characters' real natures, but in each case they carry a curious charge of guilty excitement and shame, disproportionate (the disproportion is used for comedy, but seems exaggerated even so) to the peril of discovery. The liberating disguises seem to take on a culpable identity of their own, are hidden or smuggled away as if they might stand up and incriminate their users like blood-stained linen.

That is only part of the hangover. With every play, the central fantasy dissolves into a more acrid mouthful of dust and ashes the morning after. Crichton, returned from his island kingdom, subsides into a wan figure who goes perpetually through the motion of washing his hands. He seems stooped, almost emasculated: there is no question now of marrying his Lady Mary, and almost as little, it appears, of his return to the faithful Tweeny. The heroine of *A Kiss for Cinderella* wakes from her dream-ball lying in snow, apparently to die of exposure and tuberculosis. The characters of *Dear Brutus*, stumbling back from the magic wood of second chances, discover that they would most of them squander a second life as they have their first.

The most curious escape into fantasy is that of the eponymous heroine of *Mary Rose*. On an island in the Hebrides, she disappears mysteriously for twenty-five years. When she returns, the parents and young husband she left behind have grown old, but she seems if anything younger, more fragile, with a slighter hold on life. She slips from the stage, and re-appears as a ghost to the grown-up, runaway son who has dreamed her story. Her long absence in whatever elfland held her seems to have arrested her short of maturity, lessened her grip on reality, and also somehow to have made her a guilty spirit, haunting her family home as if in expiation of some forgotten wrong which she must right before going to her rest.

Mary Rose is fascinating because, if you think about it, it tells the same story as *Peter Pan* back-to-front. We are never told to what Never Land she vanishes, nor what kind of magic takes her, only that as a result of going there she can never grow up. There is, however, a stage direction describing the music with which the island's magic carries her away as infinitely sweet, seductive but evil. Clearly it is a rape of some kind, like Proserpine's by her dark lord of the underworld, but one from which she returns somehow sinning as well as sinned against. She is both virginal and soiled, intact yet broken by her experience. A mother who has never known her son, she rages through the house in search of him; yet the action she requires from him for her release is to be taken on his knee, like a forgiven child.

Is this what would have happened to Wendy had she stayed in the Never Land? Then what kind of dark fairy is Peter Pan, the boy whose shadow announced him before his own appearance, who tries to hold her and the other children there? He too seems, like Mary Rose, a victim as well as a sinner, unable to return to the real world of human relationships. He also is a ghost: a face at the window and shadow on the floor, a dream haunting the sleep of other children. His flight from window to window is also a search for release from his condition;

for the relationship – mother-son, wife-husband – which would free him from unreality.

Barrie's secretary, Cynthia Asquith, tells in her memoir of him how she found him one morning wan and hollow-eyed on the great settle in the Adelphi flat where he lived alone, dismissing his servants each evening, after his wife's elopement with Gilbert Cannan. He had had a dream, he told her, in which he struggled with another body for the leather sofa: a body which tried to push him off, but which was also recognizably his own.

There is a recurrence in Barrie's writing of half-dreamed figures who try to share, if not take possession of, the lives of living people. In *Quality Street*, Miss Phoebe is almost displaced by the imaginary "niece" who was in fact her own self-projection. In *Dear Brutus*, there is the painter Dearth's might-have-been daughter: innocent enough in her possession, but completely altering his life by bringing him fatherhood. But the most overt occurs in his last story, "Farewell, Miss Julie Logan". In this, the young dominie of a snowbound Scottish village is haunted by a flirtatious young woman who dogs his steps and drags him into a passionate, invisible kiss at the heart of a blizzard. Eventually she disappears, after helping a crofter's wife through labour by climbing naked into the woman's bed and warming her body with her own.

Julie Logan is fairly readily recognizable as the true version of Babbie in *The Little Minister*: fantasy, not fact. She is equally evidently a de-sexualized form of the mediaeval succubus: the legendary dream-body supposed to attach itself to men in their masturbation fantasies, drawing increasing strength and reality from the semen they lose. Her masculine equivalent was the incubus, a shadowy-faced demon-lover who performed the same function for women, sucking its strength from their imaginations.

Mary Rose, the sad little ghost held to earth and immaturity by the incompleteness of her marriage and motherhood, is a kind of innocent, maternal succubus, hovering enviously on the fringes of life trying to steal a little of its reality. But the experience which blighted her has all the marks of commerce with an incubus: a sinister, life-draining dream from which she returns inviolate but lessened, frozen in withered girlishness.

What of Peter Pan, the boy who never grows up? He covets Wendy's real life, but cannot bring himself to accept the responsibilities which would make such a life possible. So that they meet only in fantasy, unable to touch however Wendy longs to "squdge" him. "It has something to do," reads Barrie's last stage-direction in the published text, "with the riddle of his being. If he could get the hang of the thing his cry might become 'To live would be an awfully big adventure!' but he can never quite get the hang of it, and so no one is as gay as he."

Instead he remains in the Never Land with Hook, the shadow who haunts his sleep as he haunts Wendy's. Hook's relationship with Peter is an odd seesaw of envies: in a way, both would like to become the other, play with each other's identities. What is one to make of him, that tall, peremptory presence, pale between his black curls, so proud yet so quickly wilting with fear of further mutilation in the crocodile's jaws? Who forces himself as far as he can down the tree-tunnel that leads to the children's snug, blind home, to squeeze into Peter's medicine the poisoned drops which would end forever the sleep of innocence?

He is surely, as the doubling of the part with Mr Darling suggests, the other, frightening face of fatherhood and male maturity. It's not necessary here to suppose that Barrie intended all of this fully from the first. Although Gerald du Maurier played both parts in the original production, he relinquished Mr Darling to another actor toward the end of the long, tiring run, with Barrie's consent. The line in which Peter warns Wendy not to touch him was added in the '20s for Jean Forbes-Robertson, apparently the most unearthly and fey creator of Peter's part. But both touches were incorporated in the text which Barrie finally published in 1928, evidently representing clarifications of purpose which had come to him, however accidentally, in the twenty years since the play was written.

It seems as if he went on clarifying it until the end of his life. For his last play, *The Boy David*, is to a startling extent a re-exploration of Hook and Peter's relationship in that between David and

Saul, the mad, brooding king whose throne David will inherit. Like Peter, David is uncertain of the line between fact and fantasy. Like him, he is played by an actress. Like their earlier counterparts, he and the saturnine king haunt each other's dreams with desperate, loving enmity, Saul yearning to become again the innocent young shepherd, David aware that he must kill and supplant Saul.

Even after David has slain Goliath, replacing Saul as Israel's hero, they remain more friends than enemies – Saul teases David fondly about his inability to raise Goliath's spear. At the end of the play, their rivalry now plain and inescapable, David takes leave of Jonathan with a warning for his father – he can lift the spear now. Previously, he had performed all his feats in states of dreamy ecstasy which made it difficult afterwards to tell whether they were real or fancied. Not this time. "I did it for myself," he boasts, "none did help me."

A certain amount of creative innocence may be granted writers about their intentions. I decline to believe that when Barrie wrote *The Boy David* in 1935 he incorporated that bit of symbolism unconsciously. Was he so much more innocent in 1904 when he wrote *Peter Pan*?

The play was originally written for the sons of his friends and neighbours in Bayswater, the Llewelyn Davieses. Barrie seems to have been more than half in love with Mrs Llewelyn Davies, and after the parents' deaths adopted the children as his own. It was not a wholly happy arrangement: as they grew up, the boys found their foster-father demandingly possessive and moody, and drifted into degrees of alienation from him.

The message of *Peter Pan* for children has always been plain enough: linger too long in the Never Land, and you will never grow up to find a wife and children of your own. Did Barrie, with some part of his mind, mean to warn the Llewelyn Davies boys that their beloved story-teller could become, as he later did in fact, a kind of incubus, frustrating real, mature relationships with one which was a sort of fantasy-surrogate for adult loves he could not achieve?

For an adult who knows the rest of his work, the message seems starkly, despairingly overt. It has always been there in the play for those who cared to look at it; which is why serious actors are still drawn to the parts, and why *Peter Pan* survives while other contemporary children's plays on which it was partly modelled, such as Seymour Hicks' *Bluebell in Fairyland*, are forgotten. It requires no distortion of text or playing to bring it out, only an adult attention and expectation which takes Barrie more seriously than we have been willing to.

The meaning is the same for children and grown-ups. Only a deeper experience should distinguish the shudders of parents at the Scala from those of their children at the moment when the sixty-first Peter climbs from waist-deep scrim to the top of the Mermaids' Rock to declare to the gathering darkness that, to fantasy's victim, life itself is indifferent. "To die would be an awfully big adventure."

A Shaw Festival Album
PHOTOS BY DAVID COOPER

MRS WARREN'S PROFESSION, 1997

JAN ALEXANDRA SMITH AS VIVIE AND NORA MCLELLAN AS
MRS WARREN. DIRECTED BY TADEUSZ BRADECKI, DESIGNED
BY LESLIE FRANKISH, LIGHTING DESIGNED BY KEVIN LAMOTTE.

ARMS AND THE MAN, 1994

TOP: LUNCHEON AT THE
MARINE HOTEL. BOTTOM:
RICHARD BINSLEY AS
VALENTINE AND MICHAEL
BALL AS MR CRAMPTON.
DIRECTED BY CHRISTOPHER
NEWTON, DESIGNED BY
WILLIAM SCHMUCK,
LIGHTING DESIGNED
BY KEVIN LAMOTTE.

LEFT: SARAH ORENSTEIN
AS LOUKA AND ANDREW
GILLIES AS SERGIUS.
DIRECTED BY JIM MEZON,
DESIGNED BY EDUARD
KOCHERGIN, LIGHTING
DESIGNED BY ROBERT
THOMSON.

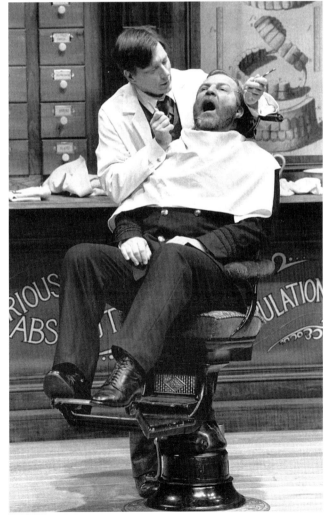

GORDON RAND AS RICHARD DUDGEON WITH TOWNSPEOPLE. DIRECTED BY GLYNIS LEYSHON,
DESIGNED BY PETER HARTWELL, LIGHTING DESIGNED BY ROBERT THOMSON.

CAESAR AND CLEOPATRA, 2002

TOP: JIM MEZON AS CAESAR AND CAROLINE CAVE AS CLEOPATRA. BOTTOM: SARAH ORENSTEIN
AS FTATATEETA AND KARIM MORGAN AS A NUBIAN SLAVE. DIRECTED BY CHRISTOPHER NEWTON,
DESIGNED BY WILLIAM SCHMUCK, LIGHTING DESIGNED BY KEVIN LAMOTTE.

MAJOR BARBARA, 1998

TOP: KELLI FOX AS BARBARA AND JIM MEZON AS UNDERSHAFT. BOTTOM: SHARRY FLETT AS LADY BRITOMART. DIRECTED BY HELENA KAUT-HOWSON, DESIGNED BY WILLIAM SCHMUCK, LIGHTING DESIGNED BY ERECA HASSELL.

OPPOSITE: SARAH ORENSTEIN AS HESIONE, DAVID SCHURMANN AS MAZZINI DUNN AND JIM MEZON AS BOSS MANGAN. DIRECTED BY TADEUSZ BRADECKI, SETS DESIGNED BY PETER HARTWELL, COSTUMES DESIGNED BY CHRISTINA PODDUBIUK, LIGHTING DESIGNED BY KEVIN LAMOTTE.

THE APPLE CART, 2000

THE MILLIONAIRESS, 2001

SARAH ORENSTEIN AS EPIFANIA, DONNA BELLEVILLE AS
THE OLD LADY AND WILLIAM VICKERS AS THE OLD MAN.
DIRECTED BY ALLEN MACINNIS, DESIGNED BY WILLIAM
SCHMUCK, LIGHTING DESIGNED BY MICHAEL KRUSE.

OPPOSITE, TOP: DAVID SCHURMANN AS KING MAGNUS
AND PAMELA RABE AS ORINTHIA. BOTTOM: THE CABINET
MEETING. DIRECTED BY RICHARD GREENBLATT, DESIGNED
BY KELLY WOLF, LIGHTING DESIGNED BY BONNIE BEECHER.

FIONA REID AS ARKADINA AND BEN CARLSON AS CONSTANTINE. DIRECTED BY NEIL
MUNRO, DESIGNED BY PETER HARTWELL, LIGHTING DESIGNED BY KEVIN LAMOTTE.

*THE MARRYING OF
ANN LEETE, 1993*

TOP: CHRISTOPHER NEWTON AS CARNABY LEETE AND SEANA MCKENNA
AS LADY COTTESHAM.BOTTOM: ANN BAGGLEY AS ANN LEETE. DIRECTED
BY NEIL MUNRO, DESIGNED BY YVONNE SAURIOL, LIGHTING DESIGNED
BY ROBERT THOMSON.

PETER PAN, 2001

CLOCKWISE FROM TOP: FIONA BYRNE
AS WENDY WITH THE LOST BOYS; JENNY
L. WRIGHT AS TINKER BELL; DYLAN
TROWBRIDGE AS PETER PAN. DIRECTED
BY CHRISTOPHER NEWTON, DESIGNED
BY SUE LEPAGE, LIGHTING DESIGNED
BY KEVIN LAMOTTE.

GOLDIE SEMPLE AS LARITA AND FIONA BYRNE AS HILDA. DIRECTED BY CHRISTOPHER NEWTON, DESIGNED BY WILLIAM SCHMUCK, LIGHTING DESIGNED BY ALAN BRODIE.

FIONA REID AS LINDA AND SIMON BRADBURY AS MARTIN.
DIRECTED BY CHRISTOPHER NEWTON, DESIGNED BY YVONNE
SAURIOL, LIGHTING DESIGNED BY ROBERT THOMSON.

TOP: DAVID SCHURMANN AS CHARLES
WITH DIANE D'AQUILA AS RUTH AND
SARAH ORENSTEIN AS ELVIRA. BOTTOM:
JENNIFER PHIPPS AS MADAME ARCATI.
DIRECTED BY SUSAN COX, DESIGNED BY
LESLIE FRANKISH, LIGHTING DESIGNED
BY ROBERT THOMSON.

TOP: FIREWORKS AT THE END OF ACT II. BOTTOM: MARY HANEY AS PENELOPE,
NORMAN BROWNING AS MR KIRBY, JENNY L. WRIGHT AS ESSIE, JILLIAN COOK
AS MRS KIRBY AND DOUGLAS E. HUGHES AS ED. DIRECTED BY NEIL MUNRO,
DESIGNED BY SUE LEPAGE, LIGHTING DESIGNED BY KEVIN LAMOTTE.

PLAYER VERSUS GENTRY

Programme note for the Shaw Festival's 1999-2000
production of *Easy Virtue* by Noel Coward

Noel Coward came to look back on the year 1924 as a watershed
in his life. When the year began, two weeks after his twenty-fourth
birthday, he was a young actor usually described as promising, who
had also written a few popular songs and two amicably received
but short-lived light comedies. His name had just appeared in lights
for the first time outside the revue *London Calling*, to which he had
contributed songs and sketches as well as his own appearance in
person. Also for the first time, he found himself earning forty pounds
a week. Twelve months later, he was a celebrity: hobnobbing with
royalty, photographed in glossy magazines wearing oriental dressing gowns and wielding long cigarette holders, the author of the
most talked-about play since Pinero's *The Second Mrs Tanqueray*.

That play was *The Vortex*, which no one today would claim as
major Coward. But during the summer of 1924, he had also written his first great comedy, *Hay Fever*, and a neglected but important
companion piece to it, *Easy Virtue*. It was important because it
expressed, with *Hay Fever*, one of the crucial decisions of his life:
that gentlefolk – the class that British people called "the gentry" –
cannot mix with people of artistic temperament, and should not
try to. That the Mrs Worthingtons of the world should not put their
daughters on the stage. Whereas the stage, he decided, was his world
and where he belonged. To rise in his profession, he decided in
1924, was more important to him than rising in society. If John
Osborne was right in describing Coward as his own invention and
contribution to the twentieth century, 1924 was the year he invented himself.

To choose between the stage and social advancement was
unusual in Britain in the 1920s. Ever since Henry Irving had been

made the theatre's first knight in 1895, British actors had behaved increasingly as if ennoblement were the main purpose of their endeavours. Beerbohm Tree, Forbes Robertson, George Alexander and Gerald du Maurier, the next four knights of the stage, conducted themselves as if their highest ambition were to be buried in Westminister Abbey. They joined West End clubs, played golf with stockbrokers at Sunningdale, and wore silk hats and morning coats to open charity bazaars. Actresses too dreamed of grandeur. Gaiety girls married into the peerage. Gladys Cooper, reigning beauty of the stage, married the founder of Buck's Club, and had the Buck's Fizz – champagne and orange juice – created in her honour. Kenneth Barnes, younger brother of the Vanbrugh sisters Violet and Irene, the first girls of "good family" (their father was Dean of Exeter) to go on the stage, was hired to run the new Academy of Dramatic Art on Gower Street, as a token that its female products would be as ladylike as his sisters.

Society in its turn opened its arms to people from the stage. During the run of *London Calling*, Coward discovered that to star in a popular revue was to become an honorary member of the horde of Bright Young Things. It helped that his co-star was Gertrude Lawrence. Every night after the show her dressing-room was crowded with fascinated young Guards officers, one or two of whom Coward was able to fascinate himself. One night during the show's interval, he looked into Gertie's dressing-room and found a handsome youth trying on one of her huge, curly wigs. He turned out to be the youngest of the royal family, Prince George, later Duke of Kent, and he and Coward became close friends, perhaps more if the rumours of the time are to be believed. If true, the rumours would perhaps explain why Coward and the prince's eldest brother, later Edward VIII, later still Duke of Windsor, detested each other all their lives.

Coward's new intimacy with the aristocracy would have delighted his mother. The Cowards – his father's family – were a large tribe of middle-class music-lovers, forever singing chummily in choirs and amateur productions of Gilbert and Sullivan. But his mother came from the kind of family Jane Austen wrote about –

her father was a captain in the Navy – and she suffered a good deal when her husband found himself selling pianos for a failing manufacturer. She put their savings into a house in Ebury Street big enough to take lodgers; and when her husband's company went bankrupt, she took on most of the cleaning and cooking herself, while Arthur Coward sailed model boats on the Round Pond in Kensington Gardens.

Coward's forty pounds a week enabled him to rescue his mother from all this. In January 1924, he rented a cottage for her at Dockenfield in Surrey, and hired a village girl to do the housekeeping for her. Having grown up in the country, Mrs Coward preferred genteel poverty there to the genteel poverty of Ebury Street, and in theory it would provide a hideaway for Coward to write. He also acquired a small open car – like a fast red tin bath, he described it – in which they could view the countryside and call on desirable neighbours. Among these were a rather pompous family, as he writes in *Present Indicative*, his first volume of autobiography: "Their name escapes me at the moment, but they were overgrand, and their house was large and ugly. It was filled with silver teapots, family paintings, tennis racquets, young people in flannels, sporting and hunting prints, mackintoshes, golf clubs, tweed coats, pipe-racks, and huge truculent cakes. I still retain a certain bitterness towards them, knowing that they were the type that would fawn upon me now, and remembering how distantly, insufferably polite they were to me then."

Seen in their natural habitat, Coward decided, the English upper classes were considerably less bearable than when they were making much of Gertrude Lawrence and himself in the dressing rooms of the Garrick Theatre. Gertie had left *London Calling* in the New Year to star in a new André Charlot revue in New York, with Beatrice Lillie and Jack Buchanan. Tired of cottage life and a failing show, Coward threw up his part and followed. New York as always stimulated him. He spent time with his friends the Lunts, resumed his acquaintance with the actress Laurette Taylor and her husband Hartley Manners, and in their eccentric Gothic mansion on Riverside Drive, always pullulating with temperament and extraordinary parlour games known only to the family, he met the Holly-wood equivalent of royalty, Douglas Fairbanks and Mary Pickford. That, he decided, was the life for him. When he got back to Dockenfield he sat down to write *Hay Fever*, a comedy about an artistic family so bohemian and individual they are incapable of nego-tiating a country weekend with a houseful of ordinary guests.

With *Hay Fever* written, he escaped again. A society hostess named Ruby Melville invited him to come and sing for his supper at her house in Deauville, and in July Coward sped across the Chan-nel to the French resort. This was a branch of society more rackety than he had met before. Its star personality that summer was James Dunn, the Canadian mining millionaire who had broken the bank at Monte Carlo, with a yachtload of guests including Duff Cooper, his wife Lady Diana, and Dunn's future wife, the Marchioness of Queensberry. To Coward's surprise, Dunn decided to invest in him, guaranteeing him a hundred pounds a month for five years in return for twenty percent of all his earnings in that period. It took Coward some time to work out that if his prospects were that prom-ising, he would do better to keep his earnings for himself.

His other principal memory of Deauville, he told his friend and biographer Cole Lesley, was the number of expensive and stylish kept women in its cosmopolitan summer population. The most imposing was a woman named Elsie Scott, who drove about in a white Rolls Royce with a liveried chauffeur. Like her companions in luxuri-ous sin, she was immensely elegant, well bred, and had impeccable manners. Coward burned, he told Lesley, to know where she and her like had been schooled in their exacting profession, how they had learned never to put a foot wrong, never to go too far.

Out of this memory of Deauville, when Coward returned home to Dockenfield, came *Easy Virtue*. What would happen to a woman like Elsie Scott if she found herself set down in that ugly house of silver teapots, tennis racquets and truculent cakes? In effect, it would be the story of Pinero's Mrs Tanqueray all over again, but with a difference. No Mrs Tanqueray in 1924 would commit suicide – or need to. She would find a way of triumphing over the Philistines. She would have a world elsewhere to which she could return, where people did not suppose Proust a writer of dirty books or consider you a scarlet woman if you carried a scarlet ostrich-feather fan.

First staged in New York in 1925, with the actress Jane Cowl playing Larita, *Easy Virtue* moved to London the next summer after a couple of try-out weeks in Manchester. The Manchester watch committee refused to license the play's title, so it opened with the cryptic legend "A New Play in Three Acts" displayed on the theatre's marquee. It never achieved the kind of success *The Second Mrs Tanqueray* enjoyed in the 1890s, but it is important in the canon of Noel Coward's plays as being the first in which he declared one of his central themes.

Whenever Coward needed to work up a plot at short notice in the future, he would come up with a variant on the question posed in *Easy Virtue*: can a person with artistic values live with people whose values are silver teapots and tennis? In *Cavalcade*, *Conversation Piece*, *Operette*, *Pacific 1860* and *Relative Values*, the question becomes: can an actor marry into the aristocracy? A performer into the audience? The answer is usually no. In 1924, Coward realized that the theatre has its own aristocracy, that of professionalism, and there is no higher society for an artist to aspire to.

THE HOUSE PARTY FROM HELL

Programme note for the Shaw Festival's 2002
production of *Hay Fever* by Noel Coward

Noel Coward wrote *Hay Fever* in 1924, the same summer he completed *Easy Virtue*. But the seed of his first great comedy had been planted three years earlier, during his first visit to New York.

In the spring of 1921, a few months after coming of age, Coward decided it was time he conquered the New World. He had not yet conquered London completely, but felt he had made a large enough breach in her indifference to climb through whenever he felt ready. He had played the juvenile lead in his first comedy, *I'll Leave It to You*, for five weeks in a major West End theatre, and been praised with an enthusiasm not too damningly coloured with surprise at finding talent in one so young. He had sold an option on a thriller, *The Last Trick*, to the New York producer Al Woods, and written a second comedy, *The Young Idea*, only slightly plagiarized from Bernard Shaw's *You Never Can Tell*. He had spent a profitable winter playing sizeable roles in a revival of an Elizabethan curiosity, *The Knight of the Burning Pestle*, and a successful comedy from Broadway, *Polly with a Past*, and spent the proceeds on a dashing new wardrobe of smart suits, pastel shirts, silk socks and his first suit of tails.

With these, he felt ready for a sparkling social life with the circle of theatrical friends he had acquired – Gertrude Lawrence, Beatrice Lillie, Fay Compton, Ronald Colman, Ivor Novello, and "a scraggy, friendly girl with intelligent brown eyes and a raucous laugh" named Lynn Fontanne. She had become a protégée of the American star Laurette Taylor, spent most of the war in New York playing in her company, and was back in London for the run of her latest vehicle. It may have been she who brought along to one of Ivor Novello's parties the latest Broadway sensation, a dark, smouldering beauty named Jeanne Eagels, who told Coward he really ought to go to New York. Impressed by the idea of a city filled with personalities like hers, he bought a one-way ticket on the *Aquitania* and sailed the last week in May. After paying for his ticket and a suitcase to hold his new wardrobe and a sheaf of playscripts to sell to New York producers, he had exactly $85 left in American money.

He arrived early in June to find New York shimmering in the grip of an early summer heat wave. No one had warned him that summer temperatures in the delta of the Hudson rivaled those of the Niger and Congo. Air conditioning had not yet been invented. Nearly all the New York theatres were closed or closing, and all the producers he hoped to sell plays to – Al Woods, Charles Dillingham, David Belasco – had left or were about to leave for the Adirondacks, Colorado or Europe. After one night in a small, airless room at the Algonquin Hotel, choice of visiting theatricals, he moved to an even smaller one under the eaves of the Brevoort, at the bottom of Broadway, which cost only $2.50 a night.

While his money lasted, he dutifully toured the sights of the city – the Woolworth Building, Pennsylvania Station, Grand Central, Coney Island and Harlem – with his friend Jeffery Holmesdale, over to represent his father, the Earl Amherst, at the centenary of Amherst College in Massachusetts. They managed to see two or three shows before the theatres closed down entirely: Tallulah Bankhead and Katharine Cornell in Rachel Crothers' *Nice People*; Marilyn Miller in *Sally* at the New Amsterdam; Fanny Brice singing "Second-Hand Rose" in the Ziegfeld Follies. Then Jeffery returned to England and the last of Coward's dollars ran out.

He had brought with him a small book of burlesque memoirs he had written with a friend, *A Withered Nosegay*, bits of which he managed to sell to *Vanity Fair*. Then providentially two expatriate friends of Jeffery's, Gabrielle Enthoven and Cecile Sartoris, took pity on him and lent him a room in the studio-apartment they shared in Washington Square. Gabrielle wrote plays and collected theatrical memorabilia – her collection eventually became the kernel of the British Theatre Museum. Cecile, part of the vast Kemble connection, recited Symbolist poems to music in fashionable drawing-rooms. Neither had much money, but they were not prepared to see a fellow member of the profession starve. They told him he could stay as their guest, until he could afford to pay them. They were pleasantly bohemian. While the heat wave lasted, they all dined in pyjamas and drank cheap red wine from an Italian grocery on the corner.

In July, the heat growing worse, Coward's hostesses decided to leave town too. He was left in charge of the studio. He lived on wine and bacon, bought on their credit from the Italian at the corner, and spent his days sitting among the down-and-outs in Washington Square or sometimes in Battery Park, watching liners bound for England steam past the Statue of Liberty. His only visitor was a policeman who knocked one day to reprove him for frying bacon in the nude by the window of his stifling kitchen. He stayed, according to Coward, to drink three glasses of wine and warn about the roughness of the neighbourhood. Lonely, friendless, hungry much of the time, Coward felt he had reached the lowest ebb in his life so far.

Then the tide turned. Lynn Fontanne arrived from Chicago, where she had been trying out the comedy *Dulcy*, which made her a star. She asked him up to the boarding-house on West 71st Street where she was cohabiting discreetly with Alfred Lunt. (They maintained separate apartments, but slept in one and ate in the other.) Together the three of them ate delicatessen pickles and cold potato salad and fantasized about their futures. Coward promised when they were international stars to write a play for them which all took place in an enormous bed. Ten years later they co-starred in *Design for Living*, hopping in and out of each other's beds. But the original idea survives in *Ways and Means*, one of the best of the one-act plays Coward wrote for himself and Gertrude Lawrence, in which a couple as penniless as he was that summer in New York never leave the bed they share in a guest-room on the Riviera, and for much of the play share it with a burglar whom they help to steal their hostess's jewels.

Desperate, Coward borrowed twenty dollars from Lynn. The very next day, the editor of the Metropolitan magazine offered him

$500 to turn *I'll Leave It to You* into a short story. Coward persuaded him to do the same for *The Young Idea*, and with $1000 in his pockets finally was able to book a return fare to London. But before he sailed he determined to enjoy with his new wealth a city now cooling down and filling with theatrical folk returning for the new theatre season. Among those returning were Lynn's great friend and protector Laurette Taylor and her husband the playwright Hartley Manners. Their Sunday evenings at home were famous, and Lynn took Coward off to one or more.

In his memoir *Present Indicative*, Coward runs together his memory of meeting the Manners in 1921 with that of his next visit in 1924, when he saw much more of them. In the interim, they had been to Hollywood and filmed their greatest hit *Peg o' My Heart*, written for Laurette by Hartley in 1912. It had made millions for them on the stage, and made even more on the screen. They spent part of the film's profits on a huge, ugly red-brick mansion on Riverside Drive in upper Manhattan, with a sunken reception room two stories high for their Sunday entertainments. In Hollywood, still in those days without restaurants or nightclubs, Laurette had acquired the local habit of home entertaining with parlour games. Guests were conscripted to take part in word-games and charades whose main purpose, increasingly, was to allow the actress to display at home the talents for which her husband's plays no longer provided sufficient scope. Hartley had not written a real hit since *Peg*, and was utterly at odds with the Broadway theatre of the '20s.

Hartley was Laurette's second husband. At the age of sixteen she had escaped the back streets of Harlem by marrying Charles Taylor, the Dumas of the fifty-cent melodrama circuit. Tough, handsome and slightly deaf, he wrote heroines for her to play in vehicles with such titles as *Rags to Riches, Daughter of the Diamond King* and *White Tigress of Japan*. Touring up the west coast through Oregon and Alaska, she discovered she really could act and loved it. She mentioned Shakespeare. Charlie hit her and told her to shut up. She took their children, Dwight and Marguerite, back east with her and signed with the Shubert Brothers. They found her a string of sentimental comedies by a former British actor of decorous but warm-hearted clubmen, who was a perfect gentleman. Used, presumably, to husbands who wrote plays for her, she married him.

Hartley Manners was as bogus as his absurd stage name. At his death she discovered he had an Irish-Cockney family in London named Dunne. But for want of a character of his own, he became the perfect gentleman he had played on stage and wrote his secret fantasy into *Peg o' My Heart*, the story of an Irish waif adopted by a noble family. The end of the Edwardian world of Pinero and Henry Arthur Jones threatened his invented identity. Repelled by the '20s informality, candour and pursuit of pleasure, he withdrew from them into baronial seclusion, taking Laurette and the children with him – it would never do for *Peg o' My Heart* to be seen in a speakeasy. Quietly, he slipped into alcoholism. Laurette followed, less quietly.

Their Sunday nights became horrific Broadway legends. Almost everyone in the profession had been told off by Laurette for acting "the manner of the word" quite wrong, and shown by her how to do it properly. If you refused to play, you were bawled out as a spoil-sport. One night during the run of *Dulcy*, Lynn Fontanne pleaded tiredness and begged to be excused. "Getting too grand to play with us now you're a star?" Laurette asked dangerously, jeering at her former protégée in front of the other guests. Lynn left in tears, and was persuaded by Alfred never to go back. It was the beginning of twenty years in the wilderness for Laurette, which ended with her triumphant return to the stage in 1945 as Amanda in Tennessee Williams' *The Glass Menagerie*.

Coward recognized the material for a great comedy and seized it. Yes, the profession had sheltered and succoured him in his summer of need, but had also shown him its ingrown, egotistical, fiercely competitive side. He sailed home to try life among the gentry in the English Home counties, and was driven by what he found there to balance *Hay Fever* with a corrective companion piece, *Easy Virtue*. A weekend with the Blisses might be hell, but not nearly so hellish as a weekend with the Whittaker family in the second play. There was a kind of generosity of scale, if not of behaviour, to the

Blisses. They put more into the world than they took out. And if you were dying of toothache, they would certainly share with you their last spoonful of oil of cloves, if anyone could remember where to find the bottle. In the showbiz way, they are irresistibly shameless. "They're not a bit like us," declared Laurette when *Hay Fever* opened in New York. "We would never insult a guest unintentionally."

THE HOTEL BY THE
DRAGON'S MOUTH

Programme note for the Shaw Festival's 1992
production of *Point Valaine* by Noel Coward

On October 31, 1931, two weeks after opening *Cavalcade*, Noel
Coward sailed by freighter for South America. He meant to stay
out of England most of a year. He was exhausted and confused.
So, he felt, were his critics. In just over two years, he had staged the
three greatest hits of his life so far – *Bitter Sweet* in 1929, *Private
Lives* in 1930, and now his panorama of Britain since the death of
Queen Victoria. Because they were all so different – operetta, ultra-
modern comedy, family chronicle (*Cavalcade*, in effect, was the pi-
lot for *Upstairs, Downstairs*) – the critics had carped suspiciously.
Talents so diverse, they hinted, could not all be authentic. Would
the real Noel Coward please stand up? *Cavalcade's* reception had
ranged from demands that he be knighted for calling his country
to greatness in a dark hour (Britain had abandoned the gold standard) to cries that he was exploiting tinpot jingoism to make theatrical hay in a national crisis. The air of London, Coward decided,
was overheated and bad for his sense of himself. It was time to get
as far from the theatre as possible and work out who he really was
offstage.

He did so successfully, travelling from Brazil through Argen-
tina to Patagonia with his friend Jeffery Amherst, for nearly three
months. Then in Santiago, Chile, a cable forwarded from Buenos
Aires caught up with him. OUR CONTRACT WITH THEATRE GUILD UP
IN JUNE, it read. WHAT ABOUT IT? Its senders were Alfred Lunt and
Lynn Fontanne, reminding him that he owed them a play. Ten years
earlier, when all three were penniless beginners starving on delicatessen sandwiches through a New York summer, he had promised
when they were famous to write a play they could all star in. The

same summer the promises became a debt when Fontanne introduced him into the eccentric household of Laurette Taylor, who had brought her to New York to act in her company. The mad Gothic mansion on Riverside Drive was Coward's inspiration for *Hay Fever*.

The play he wrote, crawling from Panama to Los Angeles on the Norwegian freighter *Toronto*, was *Design for Living*, set firmly in Paris, London and New York. But the habit of travelling with an imaginary proscenium arch to frame what he saw would not go away. He and the Lunts made more money from *Design for Living* than they had ever earned before. As a result, they formed a company, Transatlantic Productions, to invest their gains in further money-making ventures. On a Caribbean cruise to recover his strength after five months as the toast of Broadway, Coward stumbled on a backdrop for their next collaboration: the ramshackle tropical hotel that became the setting for *Point Valaine*.

It was a real place: a rambling, two-floored bungalow on the island of Gasparee, in the gulf that separates Trinidad from Venezuela. I can vouch for its reality. The summer after Coward's visit in 1933, my family rented a house on the island for the month of August. We rowed round to the hotel frequently to visit friends there, and swam in its sheltered bathing place while our parents drank rum punches on the long verandah. It was all as Coward depicts it. I remember my mother warning us to beware of splinters on the water-chute, whose wood split in the dry season, and not to swim out too far for fear of jellyfish and sharks.

Its real name was Point Baleine. A century before, when Trinidadians mostly spoke French, it had been a whaling station. Two iron vats for melting down blubber rusted above the bathing place. The islands linking Trinidad to Venezuela form a kind of filter through which silt and vegetation from the mighty Orinoco pour into the Caribbean. As a result, the channels between them are rich feeding grounds for deep-sea fish. No one had seen whales in my time, but kingfish, manta rays, tarpon and sharks abounded. Particularly sharks, or so everyone believed. One of the islands, Carrera, housed Trinidad's long-term prison. It scarcely needed bars. No prisoner had ever swum the mile to shore. From the sea, the islands' volcanic peaks look like the drowned spine of a gigantic lizard. Perhaps for that reason, Columbus's sailors named the largest channel *La Boca del Dragon* and the next widest *La Boca del Sierpe* – the Dragon's Mouth and the Serpent's Mouth.

Coward records it in photographic detail: the rock in the narrowest Boca which he calls "Mother Amos," beyond which tides raced dangerously; the little government steam-launch that delivered mail and groceries to island houses; the afternoon downpours of rain in June and July. There's only one odd omission. The young journalist in the play takes "the path to the caves," with no further explanation. The most dramatic feature of Point Baleine is a labyrinth of caves a hundred yards or so from the hotel. An underwater channel links them to the sea; on still days the sound of the ocean sighs in the stalactites like the roar in a conch shell. In a sense, the most interesting thing about *Point Valaine* is Coward's decision to leave the caves out.

They must have been part of his original conception. *Point Valaine* was his boldest attempt to reach past comedy and romance to the reality he had barely glanced at before, what people feel and do "deep in their private lives." The one sour note in the raves for *Design for Living* had been the familiar complaint that Coward dealt in veneers, skating on the surface of life. This time he obviously determined to explore the underworld of personality, the depths from which the people of Shakespeare, Strindberg and Dostoyevsky come. But to dramatize his purpose by using the caves would have been clumsy, over-symbolic. Setting Linda and her Russian tormentor over a labyrinth deep as the sea would have romanticized them. Coward was no longer interested in that. He had decided what the centre of his life and art should be: not romance, but passion. From Somerset Maugham, to whom he dedicated *Point Valaine*, he had learned that passion is not rare or exotic but universal – as matter-of-fact as headaches, insomnia or murder in the home.

To write his first play about the ordinariness of passion, he made its setting as real and mundane as possible. Unfortunately, in

1935 hotels in the Caribbean still struck audiences as exotic and romantic. Coward might have done better to set his play in Brighton, where Terence Rattigan was to rework it shamelessly twenty years later in *Separate Tables*. *Point Valaine*'s realism disappointed everyone, including the Lunts. They told the press how difficult Alfred had found it to learn the accordion, Lynn to imagine herself as a promiscuous woman. On tour the set gave trouble. The rain-machine flooded the stage. Audiences didn't like it when Alfred spat in Lynn's face, twice. Three weeks after opening at the Ethel Barrymore in January 1935, the play closed with heavy losses.

Coward was philosophical. None of the characters, he wrote later, was sufficiently sympathetic. He presumably meant that Broadway in 1935 was not ready for plays about sado-masochistic bondage, let alone the play he obviously really wanted to write, about passion between a white woman and a black man. But he could afford to move on. He had learned the lesson he wanted. He headed home to write a one-act play about an English housewife who encounters the passion of her life when a cinder flies into her eye on the platform of a suburban railway station.

HOW NOEL COWARD
LAID HIS GHOSTS

Programme note for the Shaw Festival's 1993
production of *Blithe Spirit* by Noel Coward

Noel Coward wrote *Blithe Spirit* in six days, beginning after breakfast on Sunday and finishing in time for dinner on Friday May 9, 1941. He did so, he admitted freely, because he needed money – in April his accountants had broken it to him that he had nothing in the bank. For these and other reasons, *Blithe Spirit* has been regarded as his lightest, most frivolous comedy, written with no motive but to make audiences laugh and pay up. Coward described it so himself. He lied.

John Lahr in his book on Coward shows how subtly *Blithe Spirit* reflects the circumstances in which Coward wrote it. In comic terms, the murderous violence of its ghosts mirrors the turbulence of Britain, and of Coward's emotions, in 1941. In its farcical geometry you can see Coward resolving something like a midlife crisis in his career. This makes it no less funny, but twice as interesting.

Coward was broke in May 1941 because he had written and earned nothing since the outbreak of World War II in 1939. He had spent the intervening time chasing vainly round the globe trying to find a job in which he might serve his country worthily in wartime. In his pre-war plays he had argued, lightly but firmly, that individuals owe no more to society than the disciplined, professional discharge of their professional duties – everything else belongs to their private lives, and is nobody's business but their own. Suddenly in 1940 the code he had lived by throughout his career seemed inadequate. He burned to do something personal, passionate, larger than professional, for England.

Going to the top, as always, he asked Winston Churchill's advice. To his chagrin, the great man bade him serve his countrymen by amusing them: "Sing 'Mad Dogs and Englishmen' while the guns are firing." While France fell and London burned, Coward gritted his teeth and obeyed. With a vague mandate from Duff Cooper, Minister of Information, he travelled the USA, Australia and New Zealand giving concerts and banging the drum for Britain in her hour of need. He wrote back to Cooper about American and Antipodean opinion, hoping to edge into intelligence work, and was actually recruited in New York for his spy circus by William Stephenson, the man called Intrepid. But Whitehall said no. Coward's junketings to Hollywood and the South Pacific while bombs fell on London had been reported, widely and nastily, by the British press. Hopeless to involve him in any work requiring secrecy. Besides, the Treasury was preparing to prosecute him for spending $50,000 of his American royalties on his travels. Unknown to Coward, all British dollar accounts overseas had been frozen when war broke out.

Such was his state, jobless and publicly friendless, when he flew back to London in March 1941. Early in April, to crown it all, he became homeless as well. Bombs falling next to his studio flat off Eaton Square blasted in all its doors, windows and skylights, burying the premises in glass and debris. His bedroom was untouched, bed turned down, pyjamas neatly folded, but covered entirely by a black velvet mantle of soot, like a room in Pompeii. Repairs obviously would take months, and thousands of pounds. "There was a hopeless, beastly smell in the air," he wrote in his war memoir *Future Indefinite*. "I suddenly felt miserable and most profoundly angry."

Walking out of the house where he had written so many hits, given so many marvellous parties, he checked into the Savoy. He had never stayed in a hotel in his own city before. He felt disembodied, like a visitor from another world, but exhilarated. He bought a bicycle from Fortnum and Mason's and pedalled through the rubble of the West End, falling off only once. What cheered him most was the proximity of his friend Winifred Ashton, who wrote plays and novels under the name Clemence Dane. Her small house in Covent Garden, a stone's throw from the Savoy, was open nightly to writers, musicians and theatre folk. This was her way of keeping the home fires burning, and she fed them with the same patriotic gusto she poured into her radio plays about Drake, Nelson, Shakespeare and Elizabeth I – invocations to the great ghosts of England to stand by their land in her dark hour.

Cole Lesley, Coward's companion and biographer, confirms that Clemence Dane was the model for Madame Arcati, the boisterous, bicycling medium in *Blithe Spirit*. There was even talk of her playing the role. Certainly Coward stole from her Madame Arcati's schoolgirl propensity for innocent double entendres. He had to enlist the actress Joyce Carey to explain why a sentence in the latest Dane novel could bear rephrasing: "He stretched out and grasped the other's gnarled, stumpy tool."

Joyce Carey was his companion when he set off for North Wales in May to write the comedy taking shape in his mind. They stayed at Portmeirion, a remarkable luxury hotel six miles down the coast from the house where Shelley saw a ghost in 1813, a less "blithe spirit" than the skylark of his famous ode. Modelled by its architect, Clough Williams Ellis, on an Italian fishing village, it suggests a set for a 1930s Hollywood musical – its rococo piazzas cry out for Fred and Ginger to lead a Busby Berkeley chorus in the Piccolino. Deserted in wartime, it must have seemed a haunted place: a ghostly memory of foolish pre-war elegance, Riviera honeymoons, nights playing *Private Lives* with Gertrude Lawrence. It evidently played a part in defining the character of Elvira, the dead wife called back to life in the play. Her strongest character note is her claim that her marriage was soured by honeymooning at Budleigh Salterton, a blameless Devon resort as unlike Portmeirion as possible.

Coward dramatized in *Blithe Spirit* the plight of a writer torn between a chafingly mundane present, all demands and duties, and a glamorous past unrecapturable this side of the grave. At the end of the play, freed by Madame Arcati, he walks out of the door into the future, leaving his ghosts reducing his house to much the state in which Coward had left his studio. Back in London, clearly indebted to Clemence Dane, he wrote the best patriotic song to come out of the war: "London Pride," an ode to the flowering pink weed that had turned the ruins of Covent Garden into a garden again. He then embarked on something he had never done before: writing and directing a film, *In Which We Serve*, about the Royal Navy. Personal, passionate, and larger than its extreme professionalism, it may well have been the best film about the war, too. Meanwhile, *Blithe Spirit* opened at the Piccadilly Theatre on July 2, 1941, and outran the war that evoked it. It's never really stopped.

KNIGHT OF THE
GASLIGHT JUNGLE

Programme note for the Shaw Festival's 1994
production of *Sherlock Holmes* by William Gillette

If it had not been for William Gillette, the bones of Sherlock Holmes probably still would be whitening at the foot of the Reichenbach Falls, where Arthur Conan Doyle dumped them unceremoniously in 1893.

Doyle took a Swiss holiday with his wife early that year and walked up from the village of Meiringen, in the Bernese Oberland, to the famous gorge. "A terrible place," he wrote in his memoirs, "and one that I thought would make a worthy tomb for poor Sherlock, even if I buried my bank account with him." By the first week in April he was halfway through "The Final Problem" and happily planning Holmes' Miltonic plunge, locked in struggle with the diabolic Professor Moriarty, into the Alpine abyss. The story appeared in *The Strand* magazine for December 1893 and raised a nationwide howl of grief and outrage. "You brute!" began one woman's letter of remonstrance to Doyle. Young City men paraded to their offices with mourning bands of crape round their hats.

Doyle killed off Holmes, he said, because he was sick of inventing the intricate puzzles his detective unravelled monthly for *Strand* readers. One Holmes story took more plotting than any of his novels. Besides, he felt that the fame of his popular creation cheapened his reputation as a serious writer. He wished to be remembered not as a contriver of mysteries, but as a historical novelist comparable to Walter Scott or Robert Louis Stevenson.

He no longer needed Holmes. He had invented the detective when he was a newly married young doctor in Portsmouth, earning barely £300 a year from his practice. *A Study in Scarlet* took a year to get published and netted him only £25. But it encouraged him to embark on a sequel, *The Sign of the Four,* and two historical novels, *Micah Clarke* and *The White Company*. These were successful enough to enable him to move his practice to London. When he failed there – he lacked the fashionable connections to attract patients to fashionable Devonshire Place – he resorted to Holmes again. The new *Strand* wanted series that would addict new readers without requiring them to know the story so far. The adventures of Holmes and his loyal Dr Watson filled the bill sensationally. The fame of Holmes and his creator went round the world, making Doyle rich enough to abandon medicine and, he decided, detective fiction.

He might have chosen differently had he known that, even as "The Final Problem" was going to press, his wife would be diagnosed to have a rapidly advancing case of tuberculosis. She would die in months, doctors told him, unless moved to a climate dry and clear enough to arrest the disease. From 1893 to 1895 the Doyles shuttled miserably between summers in Davos and winters on the Nile. Then the novelist Grant Allen told them how his tuberculosis had been checked in the high, clean air of Hindhead in Surrey. Homesick for England, they commissioned an architect they had known in Portsmouth to build them their dream house facing south toward the Sussex Downs and the Channel. It was to have a billiard room, a tennis court, four acres of landscaped gardens, and its own electric generator to power every modern convenience. They gave their friend *carte blanche* and went abroad again. He took them at their word. For the next two years, money poured into the cleft of the Surrey hills which Doyle christened Undershaw.

Which explains why, late in 1897, Doyle reluctantly resolved to call Holmes back from the dead, not in print but on the stage. His one-act play *Waterloo*, written for Henry Irving, had been praised by all the critics save an upstart named Shaw. Why not a play about Holmes, set prior to his vanishing? Doyle's agent A.P. Watt tried it on Beerbohm Tree, who expressed interest if he could rewrite Holmes' part to fit his own idiosyncrasies. Doyle shuddered and put the play shamefacedly in a drawer. But a copy had also gone to the New York impresario Charles Frohman, who showed it to America's most intelligent actor, William Gillette. Gillette saw in it the chance of a lifetime. He made Frohman buy the play and persuaded Doyle to let him reshape it. Doyle no longer cared, except for Frohman's dollars. When Gillette cabled MAY I MARRY HOLMES?, Doyle answered "You may marry him, murder him, or do anything you like with him."

In May 1899 Gillette brought the rewritten play to England. Having invited him to Undershaw, Doyle met Gillette at Hindhead station. Out of the train stepped a tall, thin man with deep-set eyes and a Roman profile, wearing a long grey cape and a deerstalker cap. It was all Doyle needed to know. Holmes lived.

Doyle biographers puzzle over the ease with which he accepted Gillette and his version of Holmes, a being different in subtle but profound ways from the eccentric genius first described by Watson in the chemical laboratory at Bart's Hospital. John Dickson Carr suggests Doyle was overcome by the discovery that the player was also a gentleman: son of a Connecticut senator, educated at Yale and Harvard, descended from one of New England's oldest families. But Doyle also discovered that Gillette was a finer playwright than he was, author of several successful farces and two superb Civil War melodramas, *Held by the Enemy* and *Secret Service*. "Gillette has turned it into a fine play," he told his mother. He seems to have destroyed his own original – it has never been found.

Gillette sensibly gave himself a human being to play. Doyle's original Holmes had been a Darwinian freak, a warning example of the narrowness produced by evolutionary differentiation. He lost interest in Holmes, he said, because the character was simply a calculating machine, capable only of ideas. Doyle wanted to get back to the broader humanity of his knight errant Sir Nigel and his swaggering Napoleonic Brigadier Gerard. But he did not notice how much his wishes had seeped into the Holmes stories, changing their protagonist. In *A Study in Scarlet* in 1887, Holmes was impervious to literature; by 1891 he was quoting Flaubert and comparing the poetry of Hafiz and Horace. The subsequent invention of Holmes' sedentary brother Mycroft, a brain in a chair, gives away the extent to which Sherlock had abandoned fireside ratiocination for adventure, plunging disguised into the flickering labyrinth of gaslit London like Livingstone into darkest Africa. Earlier fictional detectives knew the underworld because they rose out of it. Holmes is the first gentleman detective, entering it as an explorer, alone as Doyle believed the best explorers should travel – unless trailed, like a mediaeval knight, by his trusty squire Watson.

Doyle's first thought, clearly, was to imagine a man who, noting everything that comes under his eye, has in effect no subconscious – no buried memories, blurred imaginings or bad dreams. But in what he wrote, London gradually takes the place of all these. Its underworld was Victorian England's subconscious – suppressed and unadmitted, *terra incognita* to the classes who made up its articulate public mind. Venturing into its depths, digging up crimes committed by its respectable citizens in remote corners of the Empire, Holmes becomes both psychiatrist and martyr to the nation, taking its guilts and traumas on himself as he lies pale and exhausted on his couch in Baker Street. As Gillette realized, Doyle had transformed Holmes from a scientific freak into a mythic hero.

As such, he needs a mythic antagonist. Gillette's main addition to the myth is the flowering of Moriarty. Hastily run up by Doyle in "The Final Problem" purely to dispose of Holmes, Moriarty is vivid but unreal. Gillette's villain, by contrast, is as gigantic a figure as Holmes himself. It was the play, not the story, that popularized Holmes' deerstalker cap, and it was the play that made Professor Moriarty a household name.

The play ran a year in New York, a year in London, years and years on the road in Britain and America, and made millionaires of both Doyle and Gillette. As a result of its popularity, American publishers offered Doyle $5000 for every new Holmes story he would write. He wrote 34 more, as well as the novels *The Hound of the Baskervilles* and *The Valley of Fear*. But he is said to have agreed with the critic who complained that his detective was never the same man after his return from the Reichenbach Falls. Holmes plunged into the abyss a superman. What returned to the stage was only a hero, so human he might even be marriageable.

THE GOLD-DIGGER'S TALE

Programme note for the Shaw Festival's 1993 production
of *Gentlemen Prefer Blondes* by Anita Loos et al

Anita Loos published several accounts of how she came to write *Gentlemen Prefer Blondes*. They agree on three points. Early in the 1920s, she was riding the Santa Fe Chief from Chicago to Hollywood. The men in her Pullman ignored her struggles with luggage (she was four feet, ten inches tall) but fell over each other picking up books and pillows for a strapping blonde bound for the Coast to make her film debut. To pass the stifling hours crossing the desert, Loos wrote up this Darwinian glimpse of natural selection at work for her friend H.L. Mencken, editor of the *American Mercury*. Between the lines she hoped to convey her pique at his preferring the company of fair-haired showgirls to her own. To underline his poor taste, she couched her essay in the form of a diary kept by a blonde gold-digger, with a passion for diamonds on the side, of the type he favoured. As a further dig, she made her siren hail from Arkansas, pronounced by Mencken "the Sahara of the Bozarts".

Mencken guffawed and insisted she publish it; not in the serious *Mercury*, but perhaps in glossy *Harper's Bazaar*. *Bazaar's* editor Henry Sell liked the story so much he commissioned a series and illustrations from America's wittiest cartoonist, Ralph Barton. As the series ran through the summer of 1925, the *Bazaar's* circulation rose. Even men bought the women's fashion magazine to read the adventures of Lorelei Lee.

When the publisher Horace Liveright printed a Christmas gift edition, it sold out before lunchtime. A second printing of 65,000 disappeared by the new year. There were forty-five more editions in Anita Loos' lifetime.

Loos was not the first writer to seize on the image of the predatory, empty-headed Broadway chorus girl. Avery Hopwood, author of *Getting Gertie's Garter*, had produced a successful farce called *The Gold-Diggers* in 1919. But Loos was the first person to write of women like Lorelei and her friend Dorothy from personal, shared experience. Like Lorelei, she had slaved for D. W. Griffith on the Babylonian set of *Intolerance*; having provided the story of his early hit *The New York Hat*, she became Griffith's most trusted source of plots and titles. Later, tailoring silent comedies to the talents of Douglas Fairbanks and Constance Talmadge, she had moved in the Talmadge sisters' circle of friends from Ziegfeld's Follies – Marion Davies, Marilyn Miller, Justine Johnstone, Lillian Lorraine. The most beautiful and highly paid women in America, she discovered, all clung to rich "protectors" who hung them with jewels when pleased with them and beat them up when displeased. Lorelei derived her pleasure in finding new places to wear diamonds from Lillian Lorraine, the first woman in New York to wear a diamond anklet.

Loos made gentle fun in the voice of Lorelei of the Ziegfeld beauties' desire for gentility. The blonde man-eater performs in prose the decorous equivalent of their stately progress over the New Amsterdam stage – heads high to sustain headdresses for pagan empresses, majestically oblivious to the scandalous, scantily feathered and spangled nakedness supporting them. But Loos also understood and pitied them. Contrary to myth, she wrote in her memoir *A Girl Like I*, they were touchingly kind to and about each other. She saw this as a result of a bond of shared persecution. The Ziegfeld girls all knew "the revulsion that comes from being mauled by practically every man they meet ... forced to listen while males who happen to be in their liquor make absolutely appalling declarations in words of four letters. They learn too early that married men are cheaters and that those who don't cheat aren't real men... Pretty girls have an unusually deep sympathy for each other, a feeling that they stand together with the world of men lined up against them."

Behind her baby talk, Lorelei is the vengeful Tamburlaine of this undeclared war between the sexes. In her rage to be at once rich, independent, invulnerable and respectably married, she lies, pillages, blackmails and murders, defoliating her victims of their assets like a corporate raider. But in the end she seems a pathetic monster. She is going to get everything she wants. She obviously is going to discover she doesn't want it.

Her portrait is defined but also softened by her friendship with Dorothy, Loos' voice and representative in the story. Dorothy prefers a good laugh to a diamond any day, and would rather support the men she loves than depend on them. Vainly, she tries to show Lorelei that her old-fashioned code of decorum, proper to the clinging women of Victorian fiction, is what traps her in her endless guerrilla warfare with men. Stop pretending to cling, depend on yourself, urges Dorothy, and you actually can make a man a pal.

A few people in 1925 recognized that Loos had made a profoundly wise, sophisticated contribution to the discussion of women's place in the modern world. Santayana, asked what was the finest American work of philosophy, smilingly named *Gentlemen Prefer Blondes*. But more people, including Loos' sad, dreadful husband John Emerson, rushed to cash in on the gold-digger's gold mine. The producer Edgar Selwyn commissioned Loos to turn her book into a play which ran for six months in 1926-27. A film version, directed by Malcolm St Clair, followed in 1928.

Too late, Loos said, she recognized that her story could only work on stage in the idiom of musical comedy, and heard that Ziegfeld had wanted to make one of it for Marilyn Miller, with music by Jerome Kern. She had to wait twenty-two years for her second chance. The musical *Gentlemen Prefer Blondes* opened at the Ziegfeld Theatre on December 8, 1949, ran for most of two years and another on the road, and made a star of Carol Channing. Herman Levin, its producer, had feared she would be too big for the little girl from Little Rock. Loos disagreed, in a revealing image. "She can play Lorelei as a Great Dane under the delusion it's a Pekingese," she said. Trapped lifelong herself in a Pekingese body, she dreamed of a world where all women might be Great Danes.

WHAT THE STATUE PROMISED

Programme note for Theater Plus' 1977
production of *Awake and Sing* by Clifford Odets

In his history of the American Group Theatre, *The Fervent Years*, Harold Clurman tells disarmingly how he resisted for nearly two years staging the play which finally put the Group on the map. During the winter of 1932-33, at the Group's lowest ebb, he shared with several of its actors a musty ten-room apartment in an old West Side brownstone where they lived communally, pooling expenses, alternating the chores and dividing the cooking among four or five of the men. The smallest and coldest room housed a young actor from the Bronx named Clifford Odets whose principal talent appeared to be potato pancakes. During the winter, however, Clurman learned that he was typing away at night, huddled on his camp-bed (there was no room for a desk), at a play which he then called *I've Got the Blues*.

In the following year, Clurman and Odets became close friends, but Clurman resisted all Odets' hints that his play might be the salvation of the Group. He found the first act "cluttered with some rather gross Jewish humour and a kind of messy kitchen realism," the last act "almost masochistically pessimistic". The most he would agree to was a try-out of the second act as a studio exercise when the Group went into summer bivouac at a holiday camp in the Adirondacks. Audiences there were enthusiastic, but Clurman still doubted the piece's "playability" as a whole. It took an actors' revolt in January 1935 to persuade the Group's directors, Clurman, Lee Strasberg and Cheryl Crawford, that instead of going out of business they should try their luck one more time with Odets' play, now re-titled *Awake and Sing*. It opened at the Belasco Theatre, New York, on February 19, 1935, and made American theatre history.

The kind of history made that night justifies, as Clurman clearly knew, his story against himself. Anyone can spot a good play. What is hard to recognize is the kind of play – it may not be conventionally "good" at all – which has that special relationship with its time, that power to seed the future, which lay claim to greatness. One of the problems of reviving *Awake and Sing* now is that it so drastically changed the American theatre, the very nature of American acting and playwriting, that it no longer seems the original it was. Odets' style in his first play has been so frequently imitated that it runs the risk today of appearing an imitation of its imitations.

For example, consider that charged, hyper-electric style of American staging which, at its worst, seems the unshaven face of sentimentality. Sentimentality, says the dictionary, is emotion in excess of its occasion. This type of staging has a violence, a coiled aggressiveness, in excess of its material. It can liven flaccid writing as vodka peps up carrot juice, but it ends by seeming specious, disproportionate, a cry of "Wolf!" when there's nothing in the pen but sheepishness. It blurs the individuality of the plays to which it is applied indiscriminately by overlaying their flavour with a bor-rowed one – the flavour of Odets.

Odets hooked the American stage on high-tension electri-city and surging adrenalin. But in *Awake and Sing* they belong to the subject-matter: urban America in the Depression years when twelve million people in a nation of less than 120 million were unemployed. Clurman tells in his book how, the winter Odets fin-ished his play, they roamed together the midnight streets of a Man-hattan where derelicts haunted soup-kitchens, businessmen lay idle all day on the grass of Central Park, and talented young actresses were reduced, in order to eat, to stripping in dismal burlesque flesh-shows. Thirties audiences could recognize in Ralph Berger's anger at his inability to get his teeth fixed an anger bred of larger impo-tence: inability to change a world gone bankrupt. They could read, behind the "nervy" irritability with which Bessie Berger slams down the phone on her son's orphaned girlfriend, a fear of dispos-session which extends to the dispossessed. What Blanche represents for Bessie is the loss of sixteen dollars a week if Ralph moves out: a vision of herself as one more nice-looking, grey-haired woman standing with her furniture on the sidewalk outside the house from which she has been evicted.

The other stimulant to which Odets introduced the American theatre, of which it has become an addict, was the poetry of inarticulacy. It's hard to recall a Broadway drama of the past thirty years in which some baffled stage son hasn't shouted at his father: "Why can't we talk to each other? Every time we try to talk, we end up fighting!" The characters of *Awake and Sing* come by their inarticulacy honestly. Odets wrote of the generation whose parents had stepped off boats from Europe, their first experience of America having their names altered by immigration officials on Ellis Island. The generation gap in his play is a real one, between parents who cling to the safe obscurity of a transplanted ghetto life and children who demand belligerently that America live up to the promises made in Emma Lazarus' poem on the Statue of Liberty's pedestal. Their inability to communicate is historical fact: a genuine gulf of language and assumptions. Ralph Berger is no James Dean hero, a rebel without a cause. He has a cause as big as the Atlantic, the distance between Old World docility and North American expectations. When Moe Axelrod, refused by the girl he loves, growls "What the hell kind of house is this it ain't got an orange?" he is singing a threnody of pain in the only language the New World has taught him.

The tragedy is that Odets became one of his own plagiarists. He never again wrote as well as in *Awake and Sing*. He continued to supply the demand for the electricity and baffled, violent eloquence which had brought him success, but success became the only subject to which he could apply it. He railed in *Golden Boy* against the glittering snares of the fight-game, in *Rocket to the Moon* against ambitious wives, in *The Big Knife* against the gilded treadmills of Hollywood, where he wasted himself as a scriptwriter and married the actress Luise Rainer. In the lotus air of California he became enervated, apathetic. He would start things and lay them aside to write yet another B-picture – the last work he completed, two years before his death in 1963, was the script for Elvis Presley's *Wild in the Country*. The energy he had poured into his first play evaporated with the anger which had fuelled it. All that was left was anger with himself. Probably the best of his later plays is *The Country Girl* (1950), the portrait of an alcoholic middle-aged actor struggling to make a comeback. It has the pathos of a portrait in a mirror. But nothing can take away from his achievement in *Awake and Sing*. The history of the American theatre since 1935 is sufficient testimony to it.

A GOLDEN AGE
IN THE DEPRESSION

Programme note for the Shaw Festival's 1998-9
production of *You Can't Take It With You*
by George S. Kaufman and Moss Hart

In February 1921 the playwright Booth Tarkington wrote a concerned letter to his New York producer and friend George C. Tyler. Tyler had bought a new comedy called *Dulcy* from two young journalists, George Kaufman and Marc Connelly, and sent a script to Tarkington for his opinion. Tarkington was worried on his friend's behalf. The play's main character, Dulcinea, was a theatrical fleshing-out of a running joke in Franklin P. Adams' *New York Post* column "The Conning Tower". Dulcy is a fashionable Westchester wife with complete sets of everything, including the latest clichés. "New York is a wonderful place to visit," she announces with conviction, "but I wouldn't want to live there. There's nothing like the country!" She adds "My books are my best friends." Dulcy also believes that there is a time and place for everything, that sleeping dogs should be let lie, that a burnt child dreads the fire and that people unlucky at cards will be lucky in love. The things Dulcy says, Tarkington wrote from his home in Indianapolis to warn Tyler, are things that ordinary people say every day. How is the play to make clear without excessive exaggeration that they're meant to be laughable? "Dulcy is a character for wise guys," wrote Tarkington. "The audience, being commonplace, won't be amused by commonplaces unless they are rather heavily *shown*."

In the event, *Dulcy* ran for 250 performances, delighting its audiences and making the reputations of Kaufman, Connelly and its unknown star, Lynn Fontanne. Those audiences consisted entirely of New Yorkers. Tyler had not the heart to tell Tarkington of the decision he and most other New York producers had come to since the end of the First World War. Before 1914, most of the money made in the American theatre came from touring. A run of a hundred nights on Broadway was a "success," but barely covered the costs of a production. Profits were made "on the road," shipping shows stamped successful by New York critics to the entertainment-starved towns of the Middle West, South, mountain states and California. The first question asked of a show was "How will it play in Peoria?" Producers looked for scripts to appeal to the broad farmlands of Middle America. They usually found them in Indiana. The most popular American plays of the century's first decade were *The Man from Home* by Tarkington, born in Indianapolis; *The County Chairman* and *The College Widow* by George Ade, born in Kentland, south of Chicago; and *The Great Divide* by William Vaughn Moody, born in Spencer, near Bloomington. All in different ways declared that the residents of America west of the Ohio were the salt of the earth. But during the war years, the economics of touring changed for the worse. Costs went up, and competition from the vaudeville chains and silent movies cut into profits. By 1920 most Broadway producers had resolved to get out of touring and find plays to appeal to New York audiences. Plays, as Tarkington put it, for wise guys.

In fact, *Dulcy* was the first crocus of a great flowering of American comedy. We're often asked why the Shaw Festival includes revivals of the commercial Broadway comedies written between the wars in its predominantly "classical" seasons. One reason is that we want to show Shaw's work in its historical context, the commercial theatre of his lifetime – there were no subsidized stages in the English-speaking world he lived in. But the second reason is that Broadway between 1920 and 1945 housed one of the world's golden ages of comic playwriting: the coming together, like hand and glove, of a generation of marvellous urban wits with an audience of sharp, high-spirited intelligences, celebrating a city they saw coming into its own as the capital of the world. Nothing quite like it had happened since Aristophanes mocked and harangued Athens in the fifth century BC, or Ben Jonson, John Marston, Thomas Middleton and Thomas Dekker revelled in their city comedies in the sleaze and energy of Elizabethan London.

You can see the characteristics of the new comedy assembling themselves – speed, smartness, scorn for out-of-towners and sentimentalists – in Kaufman's other early collaborations with Connelly, *Merton of the Movies* (1922) and *Beggar on Horseback* (1924). They found their full voice in *Broadway*, the 1926 melodrama by Philip Dunning and George Abbott, about Prohibition gangsters and speakeasy chorus girls. That was followed in 1928 by Ben Hecht's and Charles MacArthur's *The Front Page*; Preston Sturges' *Strictly Dishonorable* in 1929; Kaufman's and Ring Lardner's *June Moon*, scarifying Tin Pan Alley, the same year; Hecht and MacArthur's *Twentieth Century* in 1932; John Holm's and George Abbott's *Three Men on a Horse* in 1935; Clare Boothe's *The Women* in 1936; Philip Barry's *The Philadelphia Story* in 1939; and throughout the 1930s the brilliant collaborations of Kaufman with Moss Hart – *Once in a Lifetime* (1930), *You Can't Take It With You* (1936), and *The Man Who Came to Dinner* (1939). The last of their kind was probably Garson Kanin's *Born Yesterday*, written in 1945.

They sang the splendours of New York for audiences of New Yorkers, but mostly it was a New York of the mind. Few of the circle of wits who frequented the Algonquin Hotel's Round Table were born in New York. Kaufman came from Pittsburgh; Connelly from McKeesport, Pennsylvania; George Abbott from Hamburg in upstate New York; MacArthur from Scranton, Pennsylvania; Hecht from a Wisconsin upbringing. Of their friends, Robert Benchley came from Worcester, Massachusetts; Dorothy Parker from West End, New Jersey; Alexander Woollcott from Phalanx, New Jersey; James Thurber from Columbus, Ohio; Philip Barry from Rochester, New York. The New York they sang about was the city they had conquered and made their oyster. Its splendour was a function of theirs: hymning it as the toughest city in the world, where only the toughest could survive, they flattered not only their audiences but themselves. Their plays' only messages would have been familiar to Ben Jonson – it's a great life if you don't weaken, never give a sucker an even break, and don't take any wooden nickels. Sometimes their comedies revolve around innocents too guileless to realize that they are drowning in guile – *June Moon* and *Three Men on a Horse* fall into this category. But the innocents are sent home at the end of the play to South Bend, Dubuque or wherever they came from, to demonstrate that they can never be New Yorkers. They have served their purpose – to display the speed, cunning and ruthlessness, with occasional fits of kindness, of the witty hatchet-folk who sit on top of New York's Darwinian ladder.

As a result, the Broadway comedies of those years have the polish of high comedy. High comedy was a product of the European class system. At its best, in Congreve, Marivaux and Wilde, it has an assured edge and precision which come from dealing with characters who know exactly who they are and how they relate socially to everyone else on stage. In the nineteenth century, heyday of the bourgeoisie, high comedy gave way to farce, which builds on the desperate uncertainty of people skating the thin ice of precarious respectability. But the New York comedies between the wars revel in the total assurance of characters who know, like Wilde's, that they are lords of the earth. Their high-comedy finish is one part sophistication, one part rapier wit and one part sheer arrogance.

Kaufman's and Hart's *You Can't Take It With You* is an exception to some of these rules, which may be why it has outlived many of its contemporaries. It does not praise toughness. Rather, it reflects the question Moss Hart expressed in his memoir *Act One*, whether the "toughness and competitiveness which have become an ingrained part of our character as a people, and a symbol of our way of life as a nation, are not a sign of weakness as well as of strength." At the time it was written, near the bottom of the Depression, *You Can't Take It With You* offered a recipe for beating the Depression blues: get out of the rat race, retire from the national pursuit of getting and spending, and build a West Side chapter of Rabelais' Abbey of Thelema, whose motto above the door says "Do What You Will". For all its coziness and innocence – its living-room is a Norman Rockwell *Saturday Evening Post* cover gone haywire with snakes, ballet-dancers, plaster skulls and mottoes from the works of Trotsky – the Sycamore household is deeply subversive of American values. At the start of the play, Grandpa Vanderhof returns choking with laughter from listening to Commencement speeches at Columbia University, around the corner. He laughs at talk of progress, idealism, the great American future. With this, the family maintains a New York confidence in its superiority. No Sycamore ever questions that he or she knows better than anyone else. They are heirs of all the ages, and it seems fully appropriate that as the play ends a Russian grand duchess should be serving them mountains of blintzes.

Kaufman and Hart wound up pure New Yorkers too, equally devoted to seizing the day. One of the most charming glimpses of their collaboration is the story of how, with the profits from *You Can't Take It With You*, Hart bought a farm in Bucks County, Pennsylvania, and spent the pre-war equivalent of several hundred thousand dollars foresting it with some four thousand mature trees. Kaufman, who lived nearby, came to inspect the results. Hart showed him about nervously, clearly afraid his partner might find his extravagance vulgar or excessive. "Mossie," said Kaufman affectionately, "it's just what God would have done if he'd had the money."

The beginning of the end came on March 31, 1943. The musical *Oklahoma* opened at the St James Theatre, and for the next five years every man, woman and child in the United States fought for tickets to see Rodgers' and Hammerstein's dancing cowboys and singing daughters of the soil. Servicemen, before embarking for overseas, paid scalpers insane prices to remind themselves of the wholesomeness America was fighting for. The Broadway economy changed again. Producers sought out family musicals about family values in order to bring out-of-towners into their theatres for endless runs. The New York theatre gradually turned itself into a theatre for tourists, and remains one today. Kaufman never forgave Oscar Hammerstein II for destroying, as he saw it, the Broadway of Kaufman and Hart. He refused to admit that Hammerstein had any theatrical gift beyond his ability to draw attention to the birds in the trees. "For my money," he said morosely, "he's definitely and exclusively a birds in the trees man. I'm just as definitely a son-of-a-bitch in the trees fellow."

A STRANGER AT THE FEAST

Programme note for the Shaw Festival's 2000
production of *The Matchmaker* by Thornton Wilder

We owe the plays of Thornton Wilder – *Our Town*, *The Skin of Our
Teeth*, *The Matchmaker*, and the remarkable string of one-acters running from *The Long Christmas Dinner* in 1931 to *The Rivers Under
the Earth* thirty years latter – to the strong Scottish mind of his
mother, Isabella Niven. It was Isabella who rescued her second,
most sensitive child from the imperial schemes of his father, Amos
Wilder, to raise his sons as knights of muscular Christianity. Appointed U.S. consul to Hong Kong in 1906, Amos dragged his
family after him, evidently confident that, if no suitable schools
could be found, he could rear them himself by the light of his own
patriarchal wisdom, like Noah in the Ark. Discovering that there
were indeed no suitable schools they could afford, Isabella snatched
her children from her husband's grasp, fled back with them across
the Pacific, and entered them in ordinary American schools in Berkeley, California.

It was at Berkeley that Thornton discovered the theatre. The
university there had just built a Greek amphitheatre on a hillside
shaded with eucalyptus trees, and Isabella volunteered for work in
its costume department, sewing small togas – blue for Thornton,
green for his brother Amos Jr – to wear in the choruses of plays by
Aeschylus, Sophocles and Euripides. Wilder told Alexander
Woollcott that he played Miss Prism in a school production of *The
Importance of Being Earnest* – "Oh, the evils of typecasting!" said
Woollcott. It was at Berkeley, too, that Wilder first read the name of
Max Reinhardt, emperor of the European stage, and made an idol
of him. Thirty years later, he wrote *The Matchmaker* for Reinhardt,
under its original title *The Merchant of Yonkers*, parodying in it, he
explained in a 1957 preface to his three most successful plays, the

stock company farces and melodramas he used to see as a boy at Ye Liberty Theatre in nearby Oakland.

Two of Wilder's mature works, *The Skin of Our Teeth* and his novel *The Eighth Day*, contain sons who try to kill their fathers, one successfully. It is hard to resist the conclusion that Wilder would have led a fuller, happier life had he managed to kill his own father. Amos Wilder was a rock-ribbed Congregationalist from Maine who clearly had been born to be a leader of men. In another time, he might have been a bishop, Pope or president – his handsome, obstinate head would have looked at home on Mount Rushmore. Instead, he chose the nineteenth-century equivalent of a pulpit and edited a regional newspaper, preaching the gospel of Republicanism to the passionate Democrats of Madison, Wisconsin. It was from this failure that Yale friends in Washington rescued him with a consulship in Hong Kong. Cheated of the following he felt it his right to lead, Amos conscripted his family to be his legion.

He succeeded with his eldest son. Amos Jr distinguished himself at the physically and spiritually demanding Thacher School in Ojai, California, a forerunner of Kurt Hahn's Outward Bound forcing-grounds for boys, and became an eminent Harvard theologian. Thornton was a perennial disappointment, possibly because no one had noticed that he was acutely shortsighted. Promoted to a senior consulship in Shanghai in 1910, Amos enrolled his problem son in the China Inland Mission School at Chefu, up the Yellow Sea coast, where English teachers taught Greek and Latin to the children of English and a few American missionaries, to prepare them for Oxford and Cambridge. A year there taught Thornton mostly how to feel like a foreigner. One of his contemporaries at Chefu was Henry Luce, future editor and proprietor of *Time* and *Life*. Never close, they maintained an edgy lifelong relationship, based perhaps on their shared need to erect and glorify an imaginary American norm from which both felt forever excluded.

In a final stroke to save his son for the armies of God, Amos sent Thornton to join his brother at Ojai. Once more his son failed him. Asked what he was doing wandering in a meadow while the other boys were disciplining their flesh in athletic contest, Thornton replied that he was looking for an asphodel. Isabella was allowed to rescue her son a second time and return him to school in Berkeley, the only place where he had been happy and achieved satisfactory grades. Thornton plunged back into the school's theatrical life, writing sketches for his class revue and poetic playlets for the school magazine. When Amos returned finally from China in 1915, his son showed these shyly to him. "Carving olive pits! Carving olive pits!" the father snorted. Neither then nor in the future was Amos able to persuade himself that his son had any capacity as a writer. He was convinced that only some freak of fashion had allowed Thornton to win a Pulitzer prize for *The Bridge of San Luis Rey*, which was translated into several languages, and take over the support of his family when another of Amos's journalistic ventures failed.

Another writer would have revenged himself on the old monster by putting him in a book – Balzac might have done him justice. There may be glimpses of Amos in the character of Mr Antrobus in *The Skin of Our Teeth*, inventing the wheel and leading the human race out of the ice age, but it's an amiable caricature. Instead, Wilder wrote his best and funniest novel, *Heaven's My Destination*, to portray the son he might have become had he been all his father wanted. George Brush is a Bible-college graduate selling school textbooks across the southwestern plains at the bottom of the Depression: a Dust-Bowl Don Quixote forever falling afoul of the law for proclaiming the truth, combating lies and rescuing damsels from equivocal situations, whether they wish to be rescued or not. George is a muscular all-American saint who can find no place in America to lay his head. Baffled, sweet-natured, invincibly sure he is doing right, it is he who has somehow become a monster to his American kind. It's a devastating accusation, but it seems unlikely Amos ever read it. He suffered a series of strokes the year it appeared, and died in 1936.

Read *Heaven's My Destination*, and you start to see that almost everything Wilder wrote is about outsiders. The six who fall to their deaths with the bridge of San Luis Rey are already rejects from life – stretcher cases from the wars of love, they are all consumed by passions requitable only in a better world than this one.

Emily Webb in *Our Town* becomes an outsider by dying in childbirth. From her grave on the hill overlooking Grover's Corners, she can see the beauty and fleetingness of everyday life, invisible to the living. George Antrobus in *The Skin of Our Teeth* is a Moses who can never enter the promised land he labours to bring into existence. Leading the human race toward its humanity, he is always too many steps ahead to be part of it himself. For similar reasons, Julius Caesar in *The Ides of March* is the only person of consequence in Rome not to know that is the date fixed for his assassination.

The exception is *The Matchmaker*. Wilder wrote it to welcome the exiled Max Reinhardt as an insider to America. He had discovered Johann Nestroy's comedy *Einen Jux will es sich Machen* in Vienna in 1935 (a rough translation might be *He's Going to Have Himself a Time*, or as Tom Stoppard called his 1981 version, *On the Razzle*). He showed it to Reinhardt in Salzburg that summer, suggesting it as something he might direct on Broadway. When Hitler occupied Austria in 1938, driving Reinhardt from his Salzburg Schloss Leopoldskron, Wilder followed him to Hollywood to put his adaptation in Reinhardt's hand. He had turned Nestroy's slangy Viennese farce into a New York comedy of the 1880s, borrowing from those stock company plays he had enjoyed in Oakland as a boy. There are echoes in it of Charles Hoyt's *A Trip to Chinatown*, of Dion Boucicault's *Forbidden Fruit*, and of the German-immigrant vaudeville of Weber and Fields, whose monument is "Dat vas no lady, dat vas my wife." But most of all it recalls Reinhardt's greatest success, *A Midsummer Night's Dream*, which he had filmed for Warner Brothers in 1935: young lovers fleeing elderly tyrants through the forest of Manhattan.

In its original form, *The Merchant of Yonkers* was an affectionate reminder to German-Americans that they had been Americans since the Revolution, and still were in 1938 no matter what happened in Europe. The Harmonia Gardens, with its oom-pah-pah band and emotional German waiters, is a recognizable likeness of the much-loved restaurant Luchow's, which went on serving spiced beef, wurst and cabbage to New Yorkers until the 1970s. Herman Shumlin's production at the Guild Theatre in December

1938 had every ingredient for success: a script by the winner of the last Pulitzer prize for drama, the greatest director in Europe, a star adored by New Yorkers since her triumphs in *Lilac Time* and *Smilin' Through*. In the event, *The Merchant* opened on December 28 and closed three weeks later.

What went wrong? Gottfried Reinhardt, the director's son and biographer, blames the star, Jane Cowl, for attempting to play Dolly Levi in the grand manner she had acquired playing Juliet and Cleopatra. His father, he implies, never grasped the great gulf laid by the Broadway class system between star acting and character work. Asking her to play Dolly as a character, he mortally offended Miss Cowl, and without her cooperation the comedy dragged and sagged.

Wilder regretted bitterly not offering the part to his friend, the actress Ruth Gordon. But she was living with Jed Harris, who had directed *Our Town*, and could have felt obliged to demand his direction. Fourteen years later, however, looking for a play to star in, Ruth Gordon remembered *The Merchant* and suggested a revival of it to Tyrone Guthrie. They agreed on a new title to blot out the memory of earlier failure, and publicized *The Matchmaker* as a wholly rewritten play. In fact, the two scripts are virtually identical. Wilder lengthened Dolly's monologue, tightened up the high jinks at the restaurant, and substituted for a Germanic drinking song in praise of "Old Father Hudson" the melting pot's anthem "The Sidewalks of New York."

Obviously there was nothing wrong with the play itself. It ran almost a year in London, longer in New York, and was turned into the musical *Hello Dolly* which ran for nearly 3000 performances. Perhaps the old and exiled Reinhardt was not the man to express the message Wilder had found in Nestroy's comedy: Life is a feast to which we are all bidden, and if you don't turn up for it, it's your own fool fault.

THE ASPIRING DOLPHIN

Review of *The Letters of Oscar Wilde*, edited by Rupert
Hart-Davis. Originally published in the *Nation*, November 1962

Why should the Wilde case still seem important? It has grown into
one of those myths, like the *Titanic*, which resurrects itself, year
after year, in shoddy "studies" and Sunday supplement features. Even
now, if you go to Père Lachaise to visit the great French dead in
their small stone city, its Lilliputian streets and palaces climbing
above Paris like a miniature citadel where glory has been stored
against siege, the old men sweeping leaves refuse to credit that an
Englishman could come to honour Delacroix, Balzac, Colette. *"Le
tombeau d'Oscar Wilde, monsieur? Tout droit, par là"* − and they point
firmly through the wet trees where Epstein's monster looms with
spread wings, lion haunches and long, epicene, Egyptian-Irish face.
Only last year, Paris papers reported that someone had mutilated
it, obscenely. In literature, Wilde may be the minor master of a
secondary period, the author of one classic farce, two well-written
essays, some clever epigrams and dubious verse. In life, in his death,
he still has power, apparently, to arouse passions, fascination and fear.

Rupert Hart-Davis' edition of his letters seems as much, as
disproportionate, a monument as Epstein's. It runs to 950 pages,
contains 1098 items, less than 200 of which have been published
before, and at least twice that number, I'd estimate, of notes. Every
name, every reference, has been tracked with superb patience.
Transient Oxford nicknames have been pinned onto forgotten
Edwardian bankers, judges of Indian high courts. Shadowy youths
who flit across the last letters from Paris are identified. Two of the
major sources for Wilde's last years, Frank Harris and Lord Alfred
Douglas himself, were congenital liars, and other of his friends had
cause to cover their tracks. Mr Hart-Davis uncovers them calmly
but ruthlessly, correcting dates, straightening out chronology, re-

storing suppressed passages, generally demonstrating who lied, who paltered, who stood by Wilde or betrayed him. Worth it or not, the result is a magnificent piece of scholarship. For the first time, we have the materials for a true biography, can jettison at last the mounds of inaccurate anecdote and prurient rubbish which have accumulated round Wilde's name.

What new image emerges from their wreckage? The first thing to be said is that no trace remains, if Auden left any, of the effigy of St Oscar, Martyr of the Homintern. The notion of Wilde as a pioneer of the dark, free self, a rebel against a Philistine society which crushed him, rests on the truncated versions of *De Profundis*, with its vague, Romantic gestures toward artistic "self-realization" regardless of convention. Mr Hart-Davis prints the whole letter for the first time. It becomes in this form, thank heaven, much more readable. The purple lagoons of self-pity remain, but take their place in a lucid, weary, on the whole restrained explanation to Alfred Douglas precisely how he had destroyed Wilde's life, and what he had destroyed. He had taken from Wilde his "distinguished name, high social position . . . the brilliant successes of my first nights and the brilliant banquets that followed them . . . that beautiful unreal world of Art where once I was King." This was the life Wilde thought destiny had intended him for, the true life for which his nature suited him. "Two things were absolutely necessary for him," wrote Robert Ross, the faithful friend, "contact with comely things, as Peter says, and social position." Wilde did not choose exile, he had it thrust upon him. "I simply loathe my life at present," he wrote Ross pathetically, toward the end, from Italy.

Wilde never rebelled against the society which rejected him. He sought to glitter in it, by the dandy's technique he epigrammatized: nothing succeeds like excess. Dandiacally, he mocked its taste; but the velvet suits Gilbert satirized in *Patience* were the confident joke of a young man who knows that within his milieu – the square mile or so of Mayfair and St James's – he will meet almost no one who is not an acquaintance. After his American tour he discarded costume, married and settled down like any fashionable young husband in a fashionable Chelsea street, a few doors away from

Whistler, Sargent and a well-known judge, Mr Justice Wills, who was to sentence him in 1895. Wilde loved society, swam in it as his element, rose to the top of it like an aspiring dolphin.

What is difficult to understand now is that he rose to the top of an almost wholly masculine society. In Victorian London no decent woman dined in public – the brilliant after-theatre suppers at the Café Royal were exclusively masculine affairs. Serious conversation took place only in smoking rooms, which no woman ever penetrated – as no "well-bred" women had been to a university, there was little place for one in serious conversation. It was a society of all-male offices, all-male professions, governed by an all-male parliament, and its masculine institutions represented an economic fact. The wealth of Victorian England rested on enforcement of protracted male celibacy. The Empire was ruled by subalterns and civil servants who could scarcely hope to marry before forty; only India had developed a small community of white wives, and they belonged chiefly to the senior grades. The riches sent flowing back to London were counted by thousands of unmarried clerks, whose salaries would not support a family until well after thirty. At the universities which moulded the pro-consuls, celibacy had been compulsory for all dons until the 1870s. It was an age of bachelors, when a man could drift into single old age without suspicion of being more than a crusty "woman-hater" – they filled the clubs and smoking rooms and chophouses in which a celibate society consoled itself by evolving a whole separate masculine culture.

This was the culture to whose beaded brim Wilde rose. It had its own tone, its slang, its sentimentalities, all of them exemplified in Wilde's early correspondence with his artistic Oxford and London friends. "My dear Boy"; "My dearest Jimmy"; "Harry, why did you let me catch my train? I would have liked to have gone to the National Gallery with you, and looked at Velasquez's pale evil King. . . ." The last opens a letter to one of the many undergraduates who came to him with their poetry, their artistic ambitions, beglamoured by the poet who had made himself monarch of that adult masculine world with its wit, its urbane style, its sublimated friendships. They thronged round Wilde, admiring, flattering him; and he, gregarious, uneasy, found in their admiration the emotional confidence he needed. In 1891 his help was sought for a handsome, titled Oxford youth who was being blackmailed. It was not a long step from the harmlessly effusive notes to various Harrys to the fatal letter which was read out at his trial: "My Own Boy, your slim gilt soul walks between passion and poetry. . ."

The case shook Victorian society to its foundations because it exposed the latent homosexuality upon which so much of its fabric rested. It stripped away the innocence which was its safeguard. Not every exiled subaltern on the Indian frontier, as a result of it, turned to his batman with new eyes; not every schoolmaster fell upon his charges; but that was how it felt to the English at the turn of the century. The Wilde affair gave them a self-consciousness which no amount of co-education, women's suffrage, their admission to smoking-rooms, clubs and universities, has been able to remove. Like the *Titanic*, it became one of the great images of collapse, of a whole society cracking down its façade to reveal hidden, ignoble motives within. "I was a man who stood in symbolic relations to the art and culture of my age," wrote Wilde in *De Profundis*. In an unintended sense, he spoke the truth. The next decade was to knock wider, more fundamental cracks – the Dreyfus affair, the Russo-Japanese War, the revolution of 1905 – in the world he belonged to before it came crumbling down in 1914. But his was the earliest, uncomprehended omen. It keeps the horror and fascination of prophecy.

FANTEE SHAKESPEARE

Review of *O'Neill* by Arthur and Barbara Gelb.
Originally published in the *Spectator*, November 1962

"A Fantee Shakespeare." It was Shaw who coined the phrase for O'Neill, obviously with *The Emperor Jones* in mind, ignorant – they had not yet been written – of *The Iceman Cometh* and *Long Day's Journey into Night*. He meant, he explained to the mutual friend who asked his opinion, that O'Neill was a great natural talent without the literary equipment to control it. The judgment was premature, we know, but it raises – O'Neill is bound to raise – the most fascinating of literature's illicit questions. Can a writer be born in the wrong time and place? Is it possible to imagine a genius who fails to flower because he has grown in a language and culture inadequate to the kind of statements he wants to make?

Of course the question is improper. A writer is what he has written. The greatest service Oxford has done literature has been to scotch the fallacy that ideas can exist independently, prior to the language and syntax in which they are expressed. Yet again and again with O'Neill, one seems to feel some mountainous conception labouring to free itself from insufficient words and images. The experimental frameworks he erected in play after play shake like the gorilla's bars in *The Hairy Ape*, with an effort and intensity you can't but think of as straining toward some unachieved articulation. Certainly O'Neill believed himself so caged. "Oh, for a language to write drama in!" he wrote to Joseph Wood Krutch while planning *Mourning Becomes Electra*. "For a speech that is dramatic and isn't just conversation! I'm so strait-jacketed by writing in terms of talk! I'm so fed up with the dodge-question of dialect! But where to find that language?"

If it were possible to believe in favourable and unfavourable periods for art, one could argue that O'Neill was a great playwright spoiled by being born in an America unready for him by twenty or thirty years. Time and again, his plays seem about to soar when they stub their toes on some crudity of feeling or phrase, a bathos or over-simplification which has the air of being less the fault of O'Neill than of his generation. They strike one as anachronisms, those dated feeblenesses of slang, woodennesses of character, leaving an exasperating sense that, had he only grown in a more sophisticated society, finished his education, faced a more demanding audience – had he only written in America now – it might have been a different story.

Yet how can you imagine a writer out of his time? How could there be an O'Neill not part and parcel of that younger, marvellous America of the early twentieth century, of immigrants, ragtime and saloon-politics, prairie radicals, puritanism and infinite possibility? He preserved it in *The Iceman Cometh* and *Ah, Wilderness*, and his achievement, its ambition reaching past its means, is inseparable from that huge, buoyant evolution.

It becomes even more inseparable after reading Arthur and Barbara Gelb's biography. This is not just a life, but a Life and Times. Mr Gelb, a reporter on the *New York Times*, has excavated with his wife everything about O'Neill that is fit to print. Every surviving acquaintance has been interviewed, every life which crossed the dramatist's has been accorded a pocket biography in its own right (we learn that his landlord during his eight months at Harvard was a Mennonite minister from Hillsboro, Kansas, taking a postgraduate course in Greek while his brother studied painting in Boston). The result is a thick, thumbily-written, 950-page canvas of American intellectual and theatrical life from 1870 to the present. It takes in Edwin Booth and David Belasco, Lillian Russell, Emma Goldman, Mabel Dodge Luhan, John Reed, Edna St Vincent Millay, Jack London, Oscar Wilde, Marx, Freud, Jung, Yeats, Strindberg, syndicalism, expressionism, the Dempsey-Firpo fight, Charlie Chaplin, and a youthful beau of O'Neill's daughter Oona named J.D. Salinger. It is useful to be reminded that O'Neill's life embraced them all.

The wonder is that he became what he did, given his family and his upbringing. His father was a matinee idol of the 1870s, a curly-haired famine-Irish immigrant with a large, flexible voice he liked to call "my organ". He employed it touring the States for forty years as Edmond Dantès, starting the day with a whisky to settle his breakfast, climbing nightly from painted waves to shout exultantly, "Mine the treasure of Monte Cristo! The world is mine!" His mother, the convent-bred daughter of an Ohio stationer, retreated from the vulgarities of backstage life into her Catholicism and morphine addiction. His elder brother Jamie introduced him in his teens to alcohol and whores; at twenty-one Eugene had left Princeton after nine drunken months, fathered a child, and deserted its mother to dig for gold in Honduras. His education, a scrappy reading of Nietzsche and the Romantics, took place in the fo'c's'les of tramp steamers and between bouts of drinking at Jimmy-the-Priest's flop-house on the New York waterfront. His first literary masters were Kipling, London, Francis Thompson – he never outgrew the arch Kipling habit of capitalized slang (the tinhorn gambler in his last one-acter, *Hughie*, clings to "the One True Grapevine, the Real Know") or a Thompsonesque strain of histrionic, self-pitying daemonism.

Even when he had taken his life in hand (after tuberculosis and an attempt at suicide), spent a year in George Pierce Baker's playwriting course at Harvard and been accepted by the Provincetown intellectuals, he wrestled ideas with the clumsy earnestness of an autodidact. Every concept that boiled up with the twentieth century found its way into his work, wrapping each play in a stiff scaffolding of theory. Each, he supposed, demanded a new definition of drama, and he experimented ruthlessly. If he read Marx, he must devise a Marxist theatre-epic; while Brecht and Piscator argued the notion he wrote *Marco Millions*. If he read Bergson, he must dramatize the Life Force in *Lazarus Laughed*; in *Strange Interlude*, he made the subconscious articulate, in interminable asides which tried to accomplish theatrically what Joyce and Virginia Woolf had done in the novel. In *Mourning Becomes Electra*, he mixed Freud and Frazer, bringing mythology up to date like Giraudoux and Cocteau.

There was something in the charge, leveled by his successors in the '30s, that O'Neill's '20s fame had a tinge of intellectual modishness. You couldn't accuse so massively dour a writer of pursuing fashions; but hadn't many people set him with Sophocles simply for putting the Oedipus complex and machines on the stage? There was an element in common between the culture-hero of the Theatre Guild and the loyal ladies who turned up at tea-time for his five-hour marathons. O'Neill belonged to the period of America's self-education, of little theatres, touring lecturers, women's groups, the Book-of-the-Month Club. To the college-bred generation of the '30s, he was a solemn old popularizer, and a bore. They laughed at Groucho Marx muttering behind his hand, "pardon me while I have a strange interlude!" and stayed away in droves from the play in which O'Neill made his most ceremonious profession of faith, *Days Without End*.

Surely one can blame partly the time he wrote for? A writer must try to deal with the changes of his world, and the first half of the twentieth century brought as many as literature had to cope with in the previous millennium. If O'Neill floundered more than his contemporaries, surely it was by tackling more ambitiously than they a history intolerably accelerated. After *Days Without End*, he gave up. He retreated into himself, brooding painfully on his past and his family's. He had become trapped by the public mask of the tragic prophet, the bardic image his third wife fiercely protected; but when she was absent he relaxed more and more into his father's Irish gregariousness, following the fights and races, lunching young actresses, escaping on galvanic drunks with the old friends who shared the songs and slang of his flop-house days.

Out of this turning backward came the great, late plays. Baffled, ill, middle-aged, he began to look back with forgiveness at the youth he had tried so violently to flee. The gentle comedy of *Ah, Wilderness* led on to the marvellous pity of *The Iceman Cometh*, the tremendous pardon of his family ghosts in *Long Day's Journey* and *A Moon for the Misbegotten*. There were no more experiments: in *A Touch of the Poet*, he cast back across his own lifetime, as if the modern theatre had never been, to write about a stage-Irishman like his father in precisely the Boucicault genre James O'Neill had played. One of the wonders of *Long Day's Journey* is to see all the techniques and Freudian themes he had wrestled with tranquilly absorbed into sure and perfect naturalism. Mary Tyrone watches her husband and sons disappear into fog, pitying herself, blaming them for abandoning her, then plunging below all self-deceptions to whisper her guilt, her relief, the joy of being alone, unwatched and drugged, single and secure as a child. All the asides of *Strange Interlude*, the masks of *The Great God Brown*, the wooden symbolisms of *Electra*, are superbly bypassed, rolled together into the reality they were meant to stand for.

O'Neill made the same error as most of his contemporaries. He supposed that machines and science, Frazer and Freud, had altered everything, the very definitions of man and art. He could not see until he stopped thinking about it that neither definition had changed: they had only been extended. The fundamental difference the twentieth century has made for artists is the discovery that humanity goes back further and deeper than our grandparents knew, starting not with history and consciousness but including in itself all the primitive darkness, cruelty and innocence of Africa, Lascaux and Greece before Aeschylus. Looking back on the art of our time, the great figures are those who grasped these lengthened perspectives to their world, without supposing that they reversed history or made humanity less human. Forster, Lawrence, Stravinsky, Picasso – narrowly but ultimately, O'Neill belongs with them.

There are flashes of historical impressiveness in his earlier plays, as the conception dawns crudely on him: the confrontation of Brutus Jones with his crocodile god, of Yank in *The Hairy Ape* with his gorilla, of parents and children in *Mourning Becomes Electra*, formalized round the huge family bed like a brood of Minoan figurines. But the plays which make him a kind of primitive Shakespeare are the last, nostalgic ones, in which the dark violence surviving in the psyche finds the language of his own America – the songs, the slang, the imagery of his youth in that tormented family of black Irish exiles, among the whores, sports and derelicts of the old New York which, for better and worse, was his place and time.

LONG DAY'S JOURNEY
INTO SELF

Review of *Eugene O'Neill: Beyond Mourning
and Tragedy* by Stephen A. Black. Originally published
in the *National Post*, February 2000

On the face of it, Broadway's hottest playwright today is a man dead forty-six years. On the heels of last season's prizewinning revival of *The Iceman Cometh* with Kevin Spacey, there's news of a similarly starry production of *A Moon for the Misbegotten* with Gabriel Byrne due this spring. It's as if the ghost of Eugene O'Neill were stalking the ruins of the American theatre he helped to build, determined to show that if any American playwright has legs to carry him into the new century, he's the one.

Posthumous booms in reputation like this usually follow some critical revaluation, an influential book or essay. Not this one. O'Neill's plays always surprise by turning out better than the literature about him leads you to expect. He may have been helped by the chill on O'Neill studies since his centenary in 1988, when news leaked out that Arthur and Barbara Gelb, authors of his first full-dress biography in 1962, were planning a vast revision of it in three volumes.

In the shadow of that impending juggernaut, there's little O'Neill scholars can do but shuffle the old facts into new patterns, trying to answer the question critics always ask. How did a life so agonized and disordered, ravaged by alcohol, depression, nervous disease and a spectacularly dysfunctional family background, yield such amazingly ordered, satisfying plays?

Stephen A. Black may have found the answer – part of it, anyway. A member of the English faculty at Simon Fraser University, Professor Black is also a trained psychoanalytic therapist. He mines a rich vein of Freudian material in his study of O'Neill's life and career. O'Neill was one of the earliest modern writers to be influenced by Freud's theories – his first major expenditure out of his royalties from *The Emperor Jones* and *Anna Christie* was on a course of sessions with the psychoanalyst frequented by his friends Robert Edmond Jones, his designer, and Arthur Hopkins, his producer.

Thereafter his plays were deeply coloured by Freudian ideas and archetypal Freudian situations, many of them obviously based on his own life. But the virtue of Professor Black's book, which is both good and serious, is not its Freudian reading of O'Neill's biography. We've been there before and seen that, as Oscar Wilde said of the poet Wordsworth, if he found sermons in stones and books in the running brooks, it was usually because he had put them there himself. The novelty of Professor Black's study is its suggestion that O'Neill used his plays as exercises in psychoanalyzing himself, and that his whole writing career was one long, astonishingly successful psychoanalysis.

Anyone who has seen his autobiographical masterpiece *Long Day's Journey into Night* will recognize the truth of this. The play spends four hours dredging up the distressing, painful circumstances of O'Neill's home life, such as it was, and the reasons why every member of his family blamed the others for ruining their chances of happiness. James O'Neill, his father, blamed his wife Ella for demanding a style of life which led him to abandon his career as a rising Shakespearian ("That boy's Othello is better than mine," said Edwin Booth) to make a fortune touring the romantic warhorse *The Count of Monte Cristo*. Ella blamed James for a life spent in hotels, one of which supplied the doctor who delivered Eugene so clumsily he had to dose her with excessive quantities of morphine. As a result, she became a morphine addict.

James Junior, O'Neill's elder brother, took her side in blaming their father, but also secretly blamed Eugene for turning their mother into a dope-fiend. Meanwhile, Eugene himself blamed all of them for making him curse the day he was born and feel like the agent of a curse on his whole family. Cursed families became the staple of his drama, most notably his own, renamed the Tyrones, in *Long Day's Journey*. The play is an orgy of recrimination, each member of the family accusing the others unforgivingly. Yet at the end of it, you come away curiously peaceful and satisfied, as if someone had tidied the bottom drawers of your subconscious while you dreamed the Tyrones' nightmare. The dramatized psychoanalysis has worked.

One way in which O'Neill felt cursed, Professor Black points out, was that he felt the death of anyone he cared for as a personal offence. Like Hamlet, he could not accept that dying is common. The loss within five years of each other of his father, mother and brother, left him almost crippled by depression and alcohol. In his major plays of the 1920s, Black argues, you see him working out how to deal with loss by mourning, especially in the play which won him a Nobel prize, *Mourning Becomes Electra*. This becomes the main burden of the great plays that followed, culminating in *Long Day's Journey*.

It's an interesting new way of reading O'Neill, and convincing as far as it goes. The book's shortcoming is that of any attempt to uncover the secrets of Bluebeard's castle using only one key. Professor Black isn't interested in any non-psychoanalytic approaches to O'Neill's work, and therefore pays little attention to one of the great late plays, *A Touch of the Poet*, except to point to it as a comedy remarkably free of angst and personal anguish thanks to O'Neill's self-analysis in his other works.

Yet his widow, Carlotta Monterey, told someone that if he wanted to know what O'Neill's voice sounded like, he should look at the scenes in *Touch of the Poet* where its protagonist, Con Melody, talks to himself in a mirror. Con, the son of Irish peasants, fought in Wellington's army in Spain against Napoleon, and now passes himself off in the New World as an officer and hero, to the shame of his daughter. It's hard not to read the play as the plaint of James O'Neill's younger son about the difficulty of finding an authentic identity for himself. Was he the child of an uneducated emigrant from the slums of Kilkenny, or the heir to the king of the romantic stage, the Count of Monte Cristo?

All O'Neill biographies, I'd say, show him trying to have it both ways. He sees through and is shamed by his father's pretensions to be a prince of the theatre, and atones for them by leading the guttersnipe life in the dives of Greenwich Village that James

O'Neill would have led but for Shakespeare. But at the same time, he hugs to himself the secret knowledge that he is of blood royal, a child of destiny, cheated of his inheritance by the curse on his family.

Several of his early plays deal with figures he called "tramps royal," blown by fate about the world but always in search of the fountain of youth, the white whale and its oil, the treasure of far Cathay. Like Peer Gynt, great liar and son of a bankrupt, they are capable of dreaming a kingdom for themselves; but like Hamlet and Orestes, they are kept from the throne by a tragic destiny. It was not until he had clearly surpassed his father's fame in the American theatre that O'Neill began to find a voice for himself.

He was helped to do so by Carlotta Monterey. Professor Black does not attempt to explain this extraordinary and evidently maddening woman, who obfuscated O'Neill's last years by keeping a diary which she then falsified after his death and gave to Yale. But he gives her credit for weaning O'Neill from the bottle and isolating him from his drinking friends so that he could concentrate on his writing. They fought violently and savagely, like a Strindberg husband and wife, but Carlotta was with O'Neill when he died, and *Long Day's Journey* is dedicated to her.

It seems to me possible that Carlotta cured O'Neill in more ways than one. She brought order into his life, rationing his drink and providing meals at regular hours. But she may also have cured his identity problems by being a hundred times more zanily inauthentic than he could ever be. The daughter of a Danish sailor and a woman who became rich running boarding-houses in San Francisco, she changed her name, Hazel Tharsing, to go on the stage, where she cultivated the Spanish appearance "Carlotta Monterey" suggested. Making her way to New York, she was kept by various wealthy protectors, both female and male, before playing the part of an heiress in O'Neill's *Hairy Ape*. Groomed and educated by her various lovers, she made herself the almost uncannily perfect hostess the winner of a Nobel prize would need, with lapses into Viking rage when crossed or thwarted.

O'Neill seems to have seen through her yet remained attached gratefully to her. One of the things which distinguishes his great late plays from his early ones is that they use the bar room and college slang of his youth with an accuracy he was proud of. In *The Iceman Cometh*, *Long Day's Journey* and *Moon for the Misbegotten*, you can say he found his own American voice. Perhaps it was the phoniness of his faux-Spanish enchantress and dominatrix that set him free. No matter how stagey and accursed his family may have been, compared with Carlotta they were folksy as apple pie.

CRITIC AT LARGE

let the memories he was forswearing rush in and stop him, gasping with pain, until he caught breath. Then, at "By yond marble heaven," he tore the crucifix from his neck (Iago, you recall, says casually Othello'd renounce his baptism for Desdemona) and, crouching forehead to ground, made his "sacred vow" in the religion which caked Benin's altars with blood.

Possibly it was too early a climax, built to make a curtain of Iago's "I am your own for ever." In Act Four he could only repeat himself with increased volume, adding a humming animal moan as he fell into his fit, a strangler's look to the dangling hands, a sharper danger to the turns of his head as he questioned Emilia. But it gave him time to wind down to a superb returned dignity and tenderness for the murder. This became an act of love – at "I would not have thee linger in thy pain" he threw aside the pillow and, stopping her lips with a kiss, strangled her. The last speech was spoken kneeling on the bed, her body clutched upright to him as a shield for the dagger he turns on himself.

As he slumped beside her in the sheets, the current stopped. A couple of wigged actors stood awkwardly about. You could only pity them: we had seen history, and it was over. Perhaps it's as well to have seen the performance while still unripe, constructed in fragments, still knitting itself. Now you can see how it's done; later, it will be a torrent. But before it exhausts him, a film should be made. It couldn't tell the whole truth, but it might save something the unborn should know.

CLOSING TIME

Review of the Windmill Theatre, a London burlesque house.
Originally published in the *New Statesman*, November 1962

At the bottom of the narrow street off Shaftesbury Avenue I could
see only the old black and yellow sign saying "We Never Close,"
and for a moment wondered if there'd been some reprieve. But at
the door a board announced bookings for closing day, October 31.
It faced with the dignity of baldness the glowing marquees opposite of the Nosh Bar and the cinema showing *Violent Ecstasy* and an
item of *ciné-nudité*; the stripclub photograph of a girl squeezing her
breasts at you like vintage motor-horns. Before the war, the year
they sang "The Umbrella Man," my father had taken my older
brothers in a school holiday for their first grown glimpse of what
he called "a bit of honest tit". I'd been too young, and the nearest
I'd ever come was a Rita Hayworth film, with Gene Kelly, gas-masks
and bombs in the dressing-room, called *Tonight and Every Night*. I
couldn't let the Windmill close without knowing what two generations had found there.

Inside three boys in collegiate blue mohair were stamping
and whapping out the "Mexican Marriage Dance" on guitars. According to the illuminated numbers on either side of the stage they
were Act 11 – the Harbour Lites, from New Zealand. They paused
panting, mourned through a Loewe and Lerner show-tune calling
the wind Maria, and then invited us to clap along while they jumped
down, turned around, picked a bale of cotton, jumped down, turned
around, picked a bale of hay. The audience, mainly men smoking in
twos and threes, didn't seem to feel like clapping.

Twelve was the finale. A little band, squashed against the left
corner of the proscenium, launched into flamenco sounds. The audience stirred agreeably. The girls were coming back, in skin-tight
gold matador pants and sequined bodices open between the breasts.

OLIVIER'S MOOR

Review of the National Theatre's production of *Othello*.
Originally published in the *New Statesman*, May 1964

All posterity will want to know is how he played. John Dexter's National Theatre *Othello is* efficient and clear, if slow, and contains some intelligent minor novelties. But in the long run all that matters is that it left the stage as bare as possible for its athlete. What requires record is how he, tackling Burbage's role for the first time at fifty-seven, created the Moor.

He came on smelling a rose, laughing softly with a private delight; barefooted, ankleted, black. He had chosen to play a sub-Saharan African. The story fits a true Moor better: one of those striding hawks, fierce in a narrow range of medieval passions, whose women still veil themselves like Henry Moore sleepers against the blowing sand of Nouakchott's surrealistically modern streets. But Shakespeare muddled, giving him the excuse to turn himself into a coastal African from below the Senegal: dark, thick-lipped, open, laughing.

He sauntered downstage, with a loose, bare-heeled roll of the buttocks; came to rest feet splayed apart, hip lounging outward. For him, the great Richard III of his day, the part was too simple. He had made it difficult and interesting for himself by studying, as scrupulously as he studied the flat vowels, dead grin and hunched time-steps of Archie Rice, how an African looks, moves, sounds. The make-up, exact in pigment, covered his body almost wholly: an hour's job at least. The hands hung big and graceful. The whole voice was characterized, the o's and a's deepened, the consonants thickened with faint, gutteral deliberation. "Put up your bright swords, or de dew will rus' dem": not quite so crude, but in that direction.

It could have been caricature, an embarrassment. Instead, after the second performance, a well-known black actor rose in the stalls bravoing. For obviously it was done with love; with the main purpose of substituting for the dead grandeur of the Moorish empire one modern audiences could respond to: the grandeur of Africa. He was the continent, like a figure of Rubens allegory. In Cyprus, he strode ashore in a cloak and spiked helmet which brought to mind the medieval emirates of Ethiopia and Niger. Facing Doge and senators, he hooded his eyes in a pouting ebony mask: an old chief listening watchfully in tribal conclave. When he named them "my masters" it was proudly edged: he had been a slave, their inquisition recalled his slavery, he reminded them in turn of his service and generalship.

He described Desdemona's encouragement smiling down at them, easy with sexual confidence. This was the other key to the choice of a Negro: Frank Finlay's Iago, bony, crop-haired, staring with the fanatic mule-grin of a Mississippi redneck, was to be goaded by a small white man's sexual jealousy of the black, a jealousy sliding into ambiguous fascination. Like Yeats's crowd staring, sweating, at Don Juan's mighty thigh, this Iago gazed, licking dry lips, on a black one. All he had to do was teach his own disease.

Mannerisms established, they were lifted into the older, broader imagery of the part. Leading Desdemona to bed, he pretended to snap at her with playful teeth. At Iago's first hints, he made a chuckling mock of twisting truth out of him by the ear. Then, during the temptation, he began to pace, turning his head sharply like a lion listening. The climax was his farewell to his occupation: bellowing the words as pure, wounded outcry, he hurled back his head until the ululating tongue showed pink against the roof of his mouth like a trumpeting elephant's. As he grew into a great beast, Finlay shrank beside him, clinging to his shoulder like an ape, hugging his heels like a jackal.

He used every clue in the part, its most strenuous difficulties. Reassured by Desdemona's innocence, he bent to kiss her – and paused looking, sickened, at her lips. Long before his raging return, you knew he had found Cassio's kisses there. Faced with the lung-torturing hurdle of "Like to the Pontic sea," he found a brilliant device for breaking the period: at "Shall ne'er look back," he

Somebody sang "Granada" while the boys, in broad hats and sashes, handed them round the stage. Two taller girls came on, in Spanish veils, G-strings and brassières with panels of chiffon through which you could mistily see nipples. The tune changed, and the front lights went out. A girl entered silhouetted against the cyclorama, wearing high heels, a sort of loose chiffon poncho and, as far as one could see, nothing else. She paced and turned among others in a parody of a bull-fight. Whenever she came near exposing her front to the lights one of them would be there to screen it with a flourish of a muleta.

The lights went up. There was time before the show started again to read the programme. It gave photographs of the girls, with numbers which appeared later on beside their names – Shendah, Deirdre, Serena, Doris, Hala, Dawn – so that you could identify them in each act. Captions told you where they came from and what their hobbies were. "Shendah's greatest ambition is to own a race-horse." There were pictures of Jimmy Edwards, Bruce Forsyth and Harry Secombe as they'd looked when they were Windmill comics; some of the girls helping to clean Sheila Van Damm's car, but none of Vivian Van Damm, who had persuaded the Lord Chamberlain in 1932 "that a really pretty girl, artistically posed with tactful lighting, could have every bit as much 'art' as a classical painting." At the back in small print it said: "Any additional artificial aid to vision is NOT permitted."

The seats were filling up. There were two young Indians in smart blazers, one openly carrying binoculars, some Rockerish boys with shaggy, oiled hair, but mostly it seemed to be men in their forties who filled the front rows, down from the North in tweed jackets and pullovers. A few middle-aged couples sat nearer the back; in my row, a woman with spectacles and a frizzy perm sat with an elderly man with blue miner's scars on his forehead. A man in white socks and a white mackintosh came and sat a seat away from me and leaned over looking at the nudes in my programme. I concentrated on the Pearl and Dean advertisements projected on the safety curtain.

The lights went down again and the girls came on in blue and gold, with gold pineapple head-dresses and flesh-coloured chiffon in front through which they pointed politely to their navels with long, gloved fingers. A singer with a waxy black quiff welcomed us to the 341st edition. They danced off, and were followed by a small blond comedian named Roy Douglas. He made jokes about Liverpool and Bradford ("that's the capital of Pakistan"), mothers-in-law, and some of the advertisements we'd seen.

There was a sketch called "Rancho Divorcee," an excuse for the singer with the quiff to do some songs from *Seven Brides for Seven Brothers*. Doris was a much-divorced heiress who stripped off her coat to reveal a G-string hung with mink tails, the other girls wore gingham with the same odd little chiffon insertions to show their breasts. The American parody was coarse and slightly quaint. Jackie Joy, a short, wiry girl in pink, sang three or four songs in the manner of a younger Sophie Tucker. During one, "I Wish You Love," the lights turned blue; she stared fiercely into them, looking like a two-colour photograph in some back-number of *Screen Romances*. There was a Polynesian turn, all orange, greens and magentas: the girls mamboed with the boys, twisting shaved, feathered bodies while Dawn, it looked like, sat naked and artistic on a rock, breathing carefully.

The big number came: Serena's fan-dance. Obviously it was the model for the bull-fight bit: she carried two huge white wafers of plumes, one front, one back; nothing on between. The other girls, dressed, carried black and red fans the same size. As Serena swung a fan aloft a red or black one would take its place; the girls passed her round the stage as if with huge feathered tongs. Most of the time she was swathed in plumage from shoulder to instep, looking like Ginger Rogers in an old musical; but from time to time the tremulous foam of coloured feathers would dip to show her small, pretty breasts. At the end the lights turned rose-red behind her, the great white fans parted and she posed for a moment silhouetted in the nude. It was lovely.

One could see why a Cardiff patron, quoted in the programme, had written: "I had heard it was *not very nice*, but I was pleasantly surprised!" One could also see why it was closing. It was a good Northern pier show with a thin veneer of London gloss: nothing to come from Blackpool for, certainly nothing to bring in the Mod young at whom Messrs Pearl and Dean's Players and hair-cream adverts were aimed. They could see all the skin they wanted at the club across the street with no wisps of chiffon and no need of artificial aids to vision. They didn't want their sex and fantasies of luxury packaged for them in this coy, remote old format. They'd had enough of images being dangled in front of them, of being handed packages for which they were expected to be grateful. They could get all they wanted for themselves, the real thing.

But the seats were filling up, and the Harbour Lites, once more jumping down, turning round and cotton-picking, were collecting an affectionate clap from an audience with more frizzy perms, more grey hair and spectacles. Presumably most of it came as I had, because the place was closing; they no longer needed it, but could remember it gratefully. It had offered them fantasies of luxury and sex, but it had never lied about them, never pretended that the idea of wealth could be anything but comically remote as Reno or that you could take the girls home afterwards. It had talked their language, sung them the old songs, mocked the advertisements and let them meet that family of nice young bodies. It's an old show now, it might as well close; but, in the Depression days which bore it and the never-had-it-so-good days which finally outbid it, it was a bit of honest tit.

REMEMBERING OLD TIMES

Programme note for the American Conservatory
Theatre's 1997 production of *Old Times* by Harold Pinter

In more ways than one, *Old Times* was a turning point in Harold
Pinter's career. Up to 1971, when Peter Hall first produced the
play at the Aldwych Theatre in London, Pinter had been the Dark
Stranger of postwar British drama. Reviews of the '60s treat him as
a difficult, deliberately obscure puzzle maker, from whose mazes of
bleak metaphysical chic audiences have to find their own way out,
unaided. People went to see *The Birthday Party*, *The Caretaker* and
The Homecoming less as entertainment than as strenuous games of
intellectual squash, designed to tone the synapses. The object of
this testing mental exercise was to keep up your end of the conversation at Chelsea cocktail parties or small Hampstead dinners, about
whether Pinter should be classified as an Absurdist, in the line of
Beckett and Ionesco, or as belonging to a new genre called "Comedy of Menace," along with Joe Orton's *Entertaining Mr Sloane*,
Max Frisch's *Fire Raisers*, and the early James Bond films. The phrase
"black comedy" was also tossed about (Peter Shaffer caught and
fastened it on a funny short play in 1965) which linked itself vaguely
in the public mind with the young fashionables who already dressed
all in black, with optional biker boots.

All this fretting with names suggests, accurately, that people
felt threatened by the Pinter phenomenon and wanted to fix some
controlling device on it. Even clamorous admirers seemed defensive in their efforts to explain the plays away with the help of Freud,
Jung, and Robert Ardrey's *Territorial Imperative*. The critic Kenneth
Tynan suggested that the three men in *The Caretaker* represented
the superego, ego and id, while Terence Rattigan put it to Pinter
that, consciously or not, they evoked the Holy Trinity of Father,
Son and Holy Ghost. I was one of a number of theatre folk asked

by a publisher to comment on a bulky typescript by a lady who claimed to have seen *The Homecoming* more than twenty times and to have plucked out the heart of its mystery. The cause of the publisher's interest was a brief note by Pinter, either to the writer or some friend who'd shown him her work, congratulating her on recognizing that his play was about the freedom of women, but demurring gently from her conclusion that his character Ruth, faculty wife and former call-girl, was intended as an analogue of the Virgin Mary.

The best early Pinter story was the one about the woman who wrote him the following letter:

> Dear Sir,
>
> I would be obliged if you would kindly explain to me the meaning of your play The Birthday Party. These are the points I do not understand: 1. Who are the two men? 2. Where did Stanley come from? 3. Were they all supposed to be normal? You will appreciate that without the answers to my questions I cannot fully understand your play.

Pinter replied:

> Dear Madam,
>
> I would be obliged if you would kindly explain to me the meaning of your letter. These are the points which I do not understand: 1. Who are you? 2. Where do you come from? 3. Are you supposed to be normal? You will appreciate that without the answers to these questions I cannot fully understand your letter.

The publication of this story in Martin Esslin's book *The Peopled Wound* in 1970 did much to make Pinter seem less dark and strange. So did the fact that, throughout the '60s, British television broadcast an increasing number of television plays written in obedience to those first laws of televised drama laid down in New York in the '50s: audiences will switch off if you halt the action to explain who your characters are and where they've been. Anyone who watched

TV even occasionally in the '60s could scarcely avoid the conclusion that Henrik Ibsen must be dead.

So the reception given to *Old Times* in 1971 was partly the result of audiences growing familiar with the elements of Pinter's dramaturgy. Nothing that happens before the curtain goes up, or offstage, can be known for certain. Nothing the characters say can be taken as truth. Dialogue is action; characters use words not to convey meaning, but to do things to each other. But neither audience familiarity with the rules of Pinter's game, nor the gleaming assurance with which it was played by Peter Hall's original cast – Dorothy Tutin, Colin Blakely, and Pinter's first wife, Vivien Merchant – fully explains the glowing notices the play received, the best of Pinter's career up to that point.

For the first time in a Pinter play, the world evoked offstage did not sound like the ominous landscape of an alien planet. There was no more certainty than ever that what lay beyond the play was as its characters described it, but what they described aroused memories the audience could share. Anna's description of the time when she shared a London flat with Kate aroused nostalgia, as it was intended to do, for a time most Londoners of Pinter's age remembered well.

> Queuing all night, the rain, do you remember? My goodness, the Albert Hall, Covent Garden, what did we eat? To look back, half the night, to do things we loved, we were young then, of course, but what stamina, and to work in the morning, and to a concert, or the opera, or the ballet, that night, you haven't forgotten?

The references to queuing all night or half the night gave Anna's vagueness a specific time frame. They called up the postwar years when, food and clothes rationed, consumer goods in short supply, there was little for the British to spend money on but culture. One had to queue all night to see Laurence Olivier, Ralph Richardson, and the Old Vic Company at the New Theatre, or to secure gallery seats for performances when Margot Fonteyn and Robert Helpmann danced with the Sadler's Wells Ballet at Covent

Garden Opera House. Concerts still happened at the Albert Hall because the Festival Hall south of the Thames had not yet been built. It was a time when the young could feel that the old, grey, partly destroyed city belonged particularly to them. The Labour Government that swept into power at the end of the war had promised to build a new Britain whose opportunities would be open to all. As the Empire began to slip away, its capital started to seem a more domestic, familial home to its inheritors.

According to Michael Billington, Pinter's biographer, the playwright sent a script of the play when it was finished to the actress Dilys Hamlett with a note saying: "This will ring bells." Miss Hamlett confirmed that it did indeed. She and Pinter had a short but intense affair in the spring and summer of 1950, when he was still a mostly out-of-work actor, some of whose circumstances the play echoes. But what she found most authentic in it was its evocation of that postwar London of the young, still singing Eric Maschwitz's ballad "These Foolish Things," excited by the new wave of postwar British films such as Carol Reed's 1947 *Odd Man Out*, Powell and Pressburger's 1948 *Red Shoes*, and David Lean's screen versions of Dickens' *Great Expectations* and *Oliver Twist*. It was a time when, if you were young and hopeful, the future looked as if it might fulfil all your hopes: bring to success in Britain's old, highly civilized democracy the socialist experiment that was evidently going so wrong in Eastern Europe.

In 1971, Anna's attempt to bring back the bliss of that dawn when to be young was very heaven struck deep, painful chords within British audiences of Pinter's generation. The promised Utopia had not arrived. Instead the island seemed to be sinking deeper and deeper into economic crisis and class warfare. The smell of what eventually would identify itself as Thatcherism was in the air. With this shipwreck of postwar hopes came the realization that youth had vanished, too. The title of Pinter's play summed up poignantly the emotion at its heart, which also gripped the hearts of its audiences – the dull shock of recognition that their youth, still so present to them in imagination, had become with the passage of twenty years old times. From this point in his career, his main theme would be time lost.

As usual, Pinter added his additional turn of the screw: How sure could anyone be, anyway, that the past had been as one imagined? Twenty-seven years later still, what seems remarkable about *Old Times* is the way it can be seen to make its contribution to what now seems the common endeavour of the quarter-century of British drama after World War II – to explain to the British that most of what they had been told about their past was a lie. As the twentieth century nears its end, it becomes clear that its most important events have been mass refusals to believe – America's loss of belief in the '60s in the national dream according to Eisenhower, the Soviet empire's loss of belief in the gospel of Stalin, Chinese youth's loss of belief in Mao and his little red book. With these can be placed the postwar British struggle to wake up from the Churchillian dream of the Empire and its finest hour. Like all really great plays, *Old Times* seems to float above and beyond politics, but nevertheless to articulate in its bones the central idea of its time.

DRAGON KILLER

Programme note for Toronto Arts Productions'
1977 production of *The Sea* by Edward Bond

Edward Bond is the last of a distinguished theatrical line in Great Britain. In March 1968, six months before the Lord Chamberlain's 200-year-old power over the stage was abolished, he chose as his final act of censorship to refuse a performance licence to Bond's play *Early Morning*. It was rumoured that the current Chamberlain, a literate and intelligent man as eager as any to see his office discontinued, was concerned chiefly lest the piece provoke a scandal and outcry for retaining censorship. But it would be pleasant to think that he was prompted also by admiration for Bond's work. He must have known that at a stroke he was creating the playwright one of a brilliant company, junior member of the theatre's most select and illustrious club – Henrik Ibsen (for *Ghosts*), Bernard Shaw (for *Mrs Warren's Profession*), Oscar Wilde (for *Salome*), Harley Granville Barker (for *Waste*), Percy Bysshe Shelley (for *The Cenci*), Henry Fielding (for suspected authorship of *The Golden Rump*) and Sophocles (for *Oedipus Rex*).

If to be banned at the start of one's career is the sign of greatness, it seems Bond should indeed be the great dramatist John Fraser proclaimed him earlier this year in the *Globe and Mail*, when *The Sea* was first performed in Toronto. *Early Morning* was not his first work to be refused the censor's licence. In 1965 his play *Saved* had also been banned from public performance. When played under club conditions at the Royal Court Theatre, it was howled down by a majority of London critics. A piece of sadistic pornography, the *Times'* reviewer called it, while another declared its subject matter – the lives of some violent, inarticulate slum youths who stone a baby to death in its perambulator – the proper concern of police and magistrates, not theatre audiences.

Saved was defended by a number of theatrical figures (including Laurence Olivier, who pointed out that baffled passion and violence was also a feature of Shakespeare's *Othello*) and went on to be hailed as a superb and compassionate social study in dozens of European theatres. But when *Early Morning* came to be banned two years later, few voices spoke up for it. How could one claim seriousness for a dramatist, critics implied, who travestied Britain's nineteenth-century history as a succession of futile, comic-strip civil wars behind whose lines Queen Victoria pursued a lesbian liaison with Florence Nightingale? "Call me Victor," she was imagined growling tenderly to the Lady with the Lamp while her subjects plucked limbs from each other and gnawed them hungrily.

Bond's vindication did not come until 1969, the year after the Lord Chamberlain's powers were abolished. Then, in an unprecedented gesture, the Royal Court Theatre devoted an entire season to the three plays he had written so far: *Saved, Early Morning* and *Narrow Road to the Deep North*. Words were eaten handsomely all round. The seriousness and poetic quality of *Saved* was generally admitted. *Early Morning* was recognized as a savagely brilliant satirical fantasia in the Expressionist style of *Ubu Roi*, with the frock-coated pantheon of Britain's nineteenth-century public heroes taking the place of Alfred Jarry's monstrous, egotistical monarch of bourgeois greed. *Narrow Road*, Bond's fable of art and tyranny in antique Japan, was greeted, simply, as the work of the finest, most original playwright to emerge in Britain for over a decade. "You ought to be satisfied now," said one of the critics who had championed *Saved* four years earlier, bumping into Bond on the way out of the theatre after a performance. Bond's eyes narrowed, "I suppose so," he said slowly, "but they don't enjoy me, do they? Audiences actually *enjoy* my plays in Germany and Poland and Czechoslovakia. Why don't they here?"

Even now, Bond is still something of a prophet without honour in his own country. Since the productions of his *Lear* in 1971, *The Sea* in 1973 and *Bingo* in 1974, most British critics concede that he is probably the best serious playwright working in the country. His most recent work, *The Fool*, was voted the best play of 1975 by a majority of London reviewers. But the concession is grudging, rather in the spirit of André Gide's answer to the question, who was France's greatest poet: "*Victor Hugo, hélas!*" In Europe, Bond is probably the most successful and admired of living playwrights. In Britain, he has still to win a large popular audience. *Lear*, perhaps his masterpiece, played to 30 percent audiences for four weeks at the little Royal Court, and has yet to be revived. *Bingo*, in spite of the presence of John Gielgud playing the aging Shakespeare, could not muster sufficient business to justify transfer to the West End, where audiences normally would queue to hear Gielgud read extracts from the telephone book. Although his European royalties have made him rich, most of Bond's British income has come from writing film scripts – Antonioni's *Blow-Up*, Nicholas Ray's *Walkabout* – and the libretto of an opera for Hans Werner Henze, *We Come to the River*, staged at Covent Garden Opera House last year. Bond's relationship with his countrymen remains uneasy: that of villagers with a neighbour whom they feel to be watching them with a pale, preternaturally clear eye and documenting their behaviour for some higher, even clearer-eyed tribunal – posterity, perhaps, or God.

Bond clearly suffers over this. As *The Sea* demonstrates, he knows how it feels to be treated as an alien observer from another planet. He is no Ibsen, proudly aloof from his patriots and contemporaries, addressing his plays to a wiser future. Bond writes, he told an interviewer in 1966, to persuade audiences to change the world – if for no other reason, he cares about reaching a wide audience. But he also cares for his countrymen in a simpler way. His plays are full, if you look deep enough, of love for the ordinary English, Chesterton's "people of England, who have not spoken yet" and who, because of their silence, have figured little on English stages since Shakespeare. No one since Shakespeare has captured so movingly the poetry of the inarticulate – of the farm-folk of East Anglia, where Bond lives in a Cambridgeshire village, or the layabout boys of a working-class London suburb such as Willesden, where Bond was born forty-one years ago. His ear can catch the emotion compressed in a few burred country syllables ("O dear my boy," says a farm-girl in *The Fool* to her brother, awaiting hanging in Ely jail) or a laconic Cockney offer like the one in *Saved*: "If y'buy me the wool, I might knit y'a sweater." Bond once told a journalist that he had been drawn into the theatre by seeing a school matinee when he was eleven of *King Lear* with Donald Wolfit. "My family didn't talk, nor did any of the people I knew. I'd never known people could talk like that, live like that." He speaks in the theatre for the unspeaking English. He wishes his plays could also speak to them.

Unfortunately they are not the British theatre public. Instead Bond finds himself addressing the well-to-do middle-class, fashionably "radical" audiences of central London. They feel accused by his plays. They identify themselves with Judith Shakespeare in *Bingo*, who cannot understand why her father holds out against her husband's scheme to enclose common land near Stratford, nor why, when a vagrant girl is hanged for stealing fruit from his orchard, the creator of Lear takes to his bed, muttering tormentedly: "But was anything done?" They feel got at, affronted, by the horrific, Goyescan caricature in *Early Morning* of Queen Victoria and her family picnicking on human flesh. They feel exposed with the luckless vicar in *The Fool*, Bond's play about the East Anglian poet John Clare, stripped naked in a moonlit wood by rioting farm labourers. The scene is a prose translation of the brutal poetry of *Early Morning*'s metaphor of cannibalism. "Where you stole that flesh, boy?" cries one of the labourers, pinching the churchman's white plumpness. "Your flesh is stolen goods. You're covered in stolen goods when you strip! How you climb your altar steps like that? What God say when you raise Chriss flesh in service — more flesh they stolen, doo he say? You call us thief when we took silver. You took 'us flesh!"

Bond's plays are accusing. They agonize over the cruelty of men to men. The shock of that first experience of *King Lear* is still sending waves through his work. His own fantasia on the theme of the maddened old king piles modern torments on Shakespeare's mediaeval ones, until the wars of Lear's dragon daughters reverberate with echoes of Guernica, Dresden, Vietnam. Prince Arthur in *Early Morning* tells of a dream in which the world is a mill, in which men, women, children and cattle grind each other endlessly to bone dust. Even the critics who grudgingly admit Bond's supremacy among living British playwrights complain of the bleakness of his vision of life. It is hard, they argue, to love a dramatist who is so unrelenting a pessimist.

This is the fundamental misunderstanding, Bond would reply, with which his critics have kept him from the audience he seeks. He regards himself as an optimist. Man, he maintains, is an innocent, born for happiness. It is the timid, the fearers of life, who have taught us dread of our animal natures and with it the guilt we transfer onto each other. It is our fear of ourselves which becomes our fear of other men; the walls of repression we build around our own natures which turn the rest of the world into enemy territory, hateful and tantalizing in its freedom. At the beginning of Bond's *Lear*, the king is building such a wall around his kingdom, making his realm a forced-labour camp to construct a defense against the barbarian, the unregulated, the other. By the end of the play, victim of the tyranny he himself created, Lear is trying to tear it down — to heal the breach in nature we make by dividing it into personal kingdoms.

The effect of Bond's *Lear* is tragic, the hope it holds out — Lear dies spread-eagled on his wall, but will become legend — desperate rather than cheering. Bond's only completely hopeful play, his one comedy so far, is *The Sea*. Matching the East Anglian coast where it is set, it is bare, windswept, dark-toned comedy only marginally lined with silver, like the cloud masses which pile over the North Sea beyond East Anglia's long beaches. Its Edwardian background makes no effort to hide that it, too, is an accusing play, pointing a finger at perennial ills of English society — its class-consciousness, its repression, its insular fear of the alien. But there is no escaping, either, its warmth and compassion. Unlike *Lear*, its local tyrant, Mrs Rafi, recognizes that she is her own victim in time to help her niece Rose escape with young Willy Carson from a life like her own. Like life, the sea takes away but also gives, washes clean and renews.

And who knows? Perhaps the final image of Bond's *Lear* seemed more desperate to others than to him. Why should he not be an optimist? It was his two plays *Saved* and *Early Morning*, and the scandal aroused by the banning of such palpably serious, distinguished works of art, which finally brought down the great 200-year-old wall of fear the English had built between themselves and their own instincts, animality and artistic freedom. If Bond is the last of the illustrious company banned for extending the frontiers of art in the theatre, he is not the least. It is he who at last killed Goliath, freeing Britain from censorship. He is entitled to believe that, with courage, we may yet kill our other giants and demolish the remaining walls which divide us from ourselves.

DIGGING UP O'KEEFFE

Programme note for the Stratford Festival's
1981 production of *Wild Oats* by John O'Keeffe

I was browsing in the London Library one hot afternoon in the early '70s, at the end of a long day's play-hunting for the Royal Shakespeare Company, when I stumbled on John Bernard. It was somewhat like the meeting of Coleridge's Wedding Guest with the Ancient Mariner. I've never been able to resist actors' reminiscences, particularly those about touring in unlikely places. Bernard's *Retrospections of America* must be the most irresistible theatre gossip in that line ever put on paper. A comedian who forsook Drury Lane in the 1790s to try his fortunes in North America, Bernard travelled the infant United States for thirty years, playing barns, fit-ups and back-country courthouses from the Atlantic to the Ohio, and yarned about them as racily and irrepressibly as a nankeened David Niven. He was revealing about audiences in Charleston and Philadelphia (genteel and sophisticated), New York and Boston (rough but enthusiastic), and equally so about their taste in plays. Largely, they were conservative. Their favourites, he wrote, were the standard classic playwrights – "Shakespeare, Sheridan, Farquhar, Goldsmith and O'Keeffe."

The last name stopped me in my tracks, sniffing like a beagle. The others I knew, but O'Keeffe? I'd never heard of him. I crossed to the reference shelves to consult the *Oxford Companion to the Theatre*, and found a tantalizingly sparse eighteen-line entry. "Hazlitt called O'Keeffe 'the English Molière,'" it concluded skeptically, "but in view of the total disappearance of all his work from the stage, this comparison can hardly be justified." Hazlitt wrong and the *Oxford Companion* right? All experience cast doubt on the notion. I had to know more. That is how I took the trail which led to *Wild Oats*.

Hazlitt was wrong in one respect, it turned out. Like all the best writers of comedy in English from Congreve to Shaw, O'Keeffe was Irish. He was born in Dublin in 1747, son of a land-owning family which had mislaid its lands, and trained initially as an artist. (His brother became a fashionable painter of miniature portraits on ivory.) But at twenty-three his sight began to fail – he blamed an eye infection caught falling into the Liffey as a boy – and he turned his ambitions to the theatre. He apprenticed as an actor under Henry Mossop at the Smock Alley Theatre in Dublin, married the daughter of a Limerick actor-manager (to join the profession in those days, you really had to join a theatre family) and in 1777 sold a comedy filched from Goldsmith, *Tony Lumpkin in Town*, to George Colman, licensee of the Haymarket Theatre in London. Within ten years, he was the most popular playwright, after Sheridan, in the British Isles.

Why, then, did his work vanish from the stage while that of less popular contemporaries survived? Partly, this was the price he paid for his success. To protect his monopoly of his most profitable playwright, Colman bought O'Keeffe's copyrights outright and jealously refused his plays publication. After Colman's death, O'Keeffe published four volumes of them by subscription, but could afford to print only 500 copies, most of which disappeared into private hands. Three of his most popular pieces – *Wild Oats*, a horse-racing comedy called *Fountainebleau* and a romantic operetta, *The Castle in Andalusia* – were printed by Elizabeth Inchbald in the 1820s in her huge compendium of "standard" British plays, in whose twenty-second volume I found them buried. But most of the seventy-odd comedies, farces and operettas O'Keeffe turned out during his long career either were never published or slipped quickly from print. Although *Wild Oats*, *The Son-in-Law* and his short farce *The Poor Soldier* were among the most frequently-performed plays on British and American stages between 1780 and 1830, O'Keeffe died in comparative poverty in 1833.

For his last forty years, he was totally blind. He dictated his plays to amanuenses, among them his daughter Adelaide, and had to be escorted to their first nights by his son Tottenham. (His wife disappears from his memoirs, without explanation, during the

1780s.) According to Mrs Inchbald, "O'Keeffe, stone-blind, was led by his son down to the stage-door, to the lock of which he would anxiously place his ear to catch the quickest information how his work was received – and when, unhappily, hisses from the audience would sound louder than applause, in strong agitation he would press his hands to each side of his head, as if he had yet one sense too much. Thus he would remain, without sight or hearing, till some unexpected sally of humour in his drama would once more put the house in good temper, and they would begin to laugh and applaud; on which his son would pull him by the elbow and cry out, 'Now, father, listen again.'"

Young Tottenham seems to have been the light of his father's life in every sense. He dominates the two volumes of *Recollections* O'Keeffe published in 1826, and with his early death in 1806 the memoirs peter out pathetically. Only *Wild Oats* survived its author, until the end of the nineteenth century. As his friend and rival Sheridan said, O'Keeffe "turned the public taste from the dullness of sentiment into which it was rapidly falling, towards the sprightly channel of comic humour." During the Regency period, lively young imitators – Douglas Jerrold, Pierce Egan, Colman's son George Junior – mined his vein of debonair, rapid-fire nonsense with greater topicality and freedom from the conventional plot-situations O'Keeffe built on. But Rover, the strolling hero of *Wild Oats,* with his spangled torrent of jumbled quotation, held his own for decades among the scores of breezy, rattling scatterbrains he fathered – Dickens' Mr Jingle of *Pickwick Papers*, Dion Boucicault's feckless young dandies of *London Assurance*, the heroes of Maddison Morton's *Box and Cox*, and Gilbert's operettas. (A century later, his genes are still strong in the feather-headed, Shakespeare-flecked prattle of P.G. Wodehouse's Bertie Wooster.) Several leading Victorian comedians – Charles Matthews, Samuel Phelps and Charles Wyndham among them – played the role O'Keeffe created for his friend William "Gentleman" Lewis. The last was Edward Compton, father of the actress Fay Compton and the novelist Compton Mackenzie. When the Royal Shakespeare Company revived *Wild Oats* with great success in 1976, for the first time in ninety-three years, its Rover was Compton's great-grandson Alan Howard. O'Keeffe, author of the most affectionate comedy ever written about the theatre and its loyal Gypsy tribalism, would have liked that.

A DOUBLE BILL

Programme note for the Stratford Festival's
1985 production of *Oedipus Rex* and *The Critic*

History doesn't record who first thought of pairing Sophocles'
Oedipus Tyrannus in a double bill with Sheridan's *The Critic*, but it
makes clear that the idea was not Tyrone Guthrie's. In the last winter of World War II, when half London was queueing outside the
New Theatre to see the Old Vic productions of *Peer Gynt*, directed
by Guthrie, and *Richard III*, starring Laurence Olivier, Guthrie suggested to Olivier a way to top their current triumphs next season.
They should collaborate on a production of *Oedipus Rex*, Guthrie
directing, Olivier playing the doomed Theban king. Olivier seized
on the idea, and on the translation Guthrie urged on him: a prose
version by W.B. Yeats, spare and stony, which cut most of the choruses to emphasize the play's driving rhythm. Leaving Olivier to
work out details with his co-directors at the New, Ralph Richardson
and John Burrell, Guthrie travelled north to inspect the Vic's touring operation – since 1940, based in Lancashire, it had been playing
Shakespeare and other classics in blacked-out provincial cities –
and to direct *The Alchemist* for its company in Liverpool. He returned in April to a capital heady with the promise of victory, to
confer with the triumvirate at the New before Richardson and
Olivier led their company on a tour of liberated European cities.

Olivier met him with a new idea. Oppressed by the thought
of playing Oedipus' tragedy night after night without relief, he had
decided, with his colleagues, to follow it with Sheridan's riotous
farce. "Over my dead body!" Guthrie is said to have replied. And
that, metaphorically speaking, is where the double bill's first performance took place, on October 18, 1945. It was an historic occasion: the night which established Olivier as the English-speaking
theatre's greatest actor. But it was historic for other reasons. Be-

cause of it, many lives and public events turned out differently in the years that followed. It is a story of interest to Canadian audiences. But for *Oedipuff,* as the Old Vic company christened the double bill, there might never have been a Stratford Festival.

Guthrie planned his *Oedipus* as the master-stroke of a strategy he and the Old Vic governors had nursed since he inherited the theatre from Lilian Baylis in 1937. She boasted that she had made the Vic Britain's unofficial national theatre. Guthrie and his governors wished to make its status official. In 1944, that prospect suddenly seemed attainable. The war had provoked an amazing boom in the arts. Feeling their national identity imperilled, the British pulled their cultural treasures from the cupboard – Shakespeare, Trollope, Jane Austen, Elgar, Purcell – as if to remind themselves who they were and what they were fighting for. The surge in morale that went with this persuaded many people that the state should continue to foster the arts when peace came. There was talk of a national opera, national ballet and national theatre.

Lord Keynes, chairman of what was to become the Arts Council, championed the idea and was known to have commended it in high places – he was a friend of Churchill's – but he was believed to favour a system of subsidy to existing West End managements such as H.M. Tennent Ltd, which had staged a brilliant string of wartime revivals with John Gielgud: *Macbeth, The Importance of Being Earnest, Love for Love, The Duchess of Malfi.* He had been heard to refer to the Vic's touring productions as dowdy. This is why Guthrie and his governors, led by the theatre manager Bronson Albery, had raised the great company led by Olivier and Richardson, stars of the Vic's finest pre-war seasons, to show their flag in London – not at the bombed Old Vic, but at Albery's New Theatre, in the heart of the West End. Their superb 1944-45 season was a shot across Tennent's bow, and a reminder to Keynes and anyone else who needed reminding that there was another national theatre in the field.

After the historic success of *Peer Gynt* and *Richard III,* only one thing was left to prove. Olivier's Richard was recognized as one of the great performances in the history of the theatre, but primarily as a masterpiece of sardonic comedy. In tragedy Gielgud, the Hamlet of his generation, still held the crown. Guthrie, who had launched Olivier as a classical actor in Old Vic productions of *Hamlet*, *Henry V* and *Coriolanus* before the war, was determined to finish the job. He would show that a national theatre led by Olivier would surpass one led by Gielgud. *Oedipus* would reveal Olivier as a great tragedian, and display him as a hero-king sacrificing himself for his bleeding nation. As he had often said and written, Guthrie saw tragedy as the point at which the theatre merges with the sacred: a ritual in which the hopes, fears and collective anxieties of a people are gathered and purged. This was the relationship *Oedipus* was to establish between the Old Vic and British theatre-goers. Olivier's notion of adding a farcical afterpiece seemed to Guthrie blasphemy, and worse – strategically inept.

Was it? Looked at from another angle, Olivier may have known exactly what he was doing. Perhaps he wanted to provoke an explosion. Childless, Guthrie treated favourite young actors like adopted sons, and turned exigent and domineering if they failed to play the role in return. Olivier may have found his tutelary style oppressively close for comfort. There was a smell of jealousy in Guthrie's refusal ever to admit any talent in Olivier's wife, Vivien Leigh, or to have her in the wartime Old Vic. Olivier knew Guthrie's views on tragedy. He also knew that Guthrie's greatest enemy, the man he saw as his arch-rival in the theatre, was Michel Saint-Denis, the director to whom he turned immediately when Guthrie refused to touch the *Oedipus* double bill. What happened next may have been precisely what Olivier intended. Three weeks after VE Day, Guthrie resigned his position as administrator of the Old Vic. He and Olivier were never to work together again. There are many who believe that it was Olivier's cold-shouldering and manoeuvring which led Guthrie to throw in his hand, and his chance to become the first artistic director of a British national theatre.

If it was, Guthrie took his revenge. Three years later, the Old Vic governors suddenly and inexplicably fired Olivier, Richardson and Burrell. Their pretext was that Richardson and Olivier had taken long sabbaticals for filming, during which the Vic box office faltered. Clearly someone behind the scenes persuaded them that a national theatre could not run on glamour, under the leadership of film stars who needed several months a year away; and that actors who have once earned Hollywood incomes cannot be expected to renounce films for the stage. Guthrie admits in his autobiography that he said something of the sort to the governors. Burrell's widow to this day maintains that it was Guthrie who brought the triumvirate down.

Certainly it was to Guthrie that the governors turned, after a decent interval, to pick up the pieces scattered by their bombshell. But in ditching the triumvirate, he had ditched himself. When he came to assemble a new Vic company in 1951, the only Shakespearean star he could call on was Donald Wolfit, a rogue elephant who stamped his way out of his contract in a matter of weeks. Without the old allies who had let him down and whom he had betrayed in turn, Guthrie could not build the governors a national company. They did not renew his contract at the end of the 1951–52 season. It was at precisely this point, in May 1952, that Dora Mavor Moore cabled to ask whether he might advise the burghers of Stratford, Ontario, on the feasibility of getting up a Shakespeare festival.

Cheated of the national theatre which finally fell to Olivier in 1962, Guthrie tried to create one for Canada. But apart from the politics and personal emotions involved, had he a case against pairing *Oedipus* and *The Critic?* His chief objection was that for Olivier to play both the incestuous king and Sheridan's feather-brained playwright, Mr Puff, would turn the evening into an actor's conjuring trick, a feat, a gimmick. Some critics agreed. James Agate of the *Sunday Times* refused to discuss Olivier's Oedipus, claiming that *The Critic* wiped it from his mind. But on the whole, the bill was a huge success, and not just as a star turn. Audiences clearly came away exhilarated by exposure to the theatre's two polar extremes.

Critics have urged that tragedy and farce are simply two faces of one experience. In both, human beings are subjected violently to extremes of misfortune; but one genre makes us care, while the other makes us not care. "Nothing is so funny as unhappiness, I grant you," says Nell in Beckett's *Endgame*. It is all a question of how you look at it, who it's happening to.

Greek audiences felt involved with Oedipus because they knew his story was one episode in the history of a curse. Like all human beings, he was trapped in a web of fate woven before his birth, continuing past his death. His ancestor Cadmus, founder of Thebes, incurred the wrath of Ares, god of war, by killing the dragon he had set to guard Thebes' sacred spring. When Cadmus buried its teeth, twin armies sprang fighting from the furrows; that was to be Thebes' history, sons killing fathers, brothers killing brothers. For denying the godhead of Dionysus, Cadmus' grandson Pentheus was torn to pieces by his mother and her women in a Bacchic frenzy. Pentheus' nephew Laius was cursed by Pelops, founder of the house of Atreus, for abducting and seducing his youngest son. Oedipus, Greeks knew, was simply the instrument of the curse when he killed his father Laius, unwittingly married his mother and became accursed himself. In a society made up of clans, everyone could feel for the hapless inheritor of a family destiny.

The funniest part of *The Critic* is the performance of a tragedy. Sheridan points out to us delicately as he makes us laugh that he can do so because everything about Puff's chronicle of the Armada, and the tragic love of Tilburina for her Spanish grandee Whisk-erandos, belongs to a world opposite to that of human experience. It has no link to any life outside a theatre whose very existence is built on the lies Puff sells to morning papers. A kind of companion piece to *The School for Scandal*, the play satirizes people who live by inventing fictions not malicious but fatuously rosy, about a theatre which makes such fiction its staple diet. Because they choose a life wilfully unreal, it is impossible to care about them. If they were real we might weep.

What about the story of the double bill itself? Is it comic or tragic? Because Guthrie was cheated of his national theatre, we have Stratford. Olivier in the end got his, and left it feeling like King Lear, unthanked, outcast, misused. Meanwhile, the bill itself has become a tradition, inseparable as bacon and eggs. Olivier's feat, thought inimitable, has been imitated by a number of actors. The first was Derek Jacobi, at the Birmingham Playhouse in the 1970s. Olivier sent him an opening night telegram. It read "You cheeky bugger."

SWANKER

Review of *The Life of Kenneth Tynan* by Kathleen Tynan.
Originally published in the *London Review of Books*, December 1987

Kathleen Tynan says that she wavered for some time between writing a personal memoir of her sixteen years with her husband Kenneth and embarking on a full-dress biography, embracing the thirty-six before they met. As she foresaw, making the second choice has produced an odd, hybrid book, not quite one thing nor the other. At times deeply intimate, at others coolly dispassionate, her narrative becomes an antiphony of two voices in uneasy tension. Frequently, one feels that she might write more emotionally were it not for the biographer looking over her shoulder. Almost as often, one finds oneself reading passages of straight reporting as if they were playing the tricks of a novel, using flatness to imply feeling, disguising as unruffled objectivity the chilled revulsion of a wife.

For this is not, it must have leaked out by now, the traditional saint's life expected of literary widows. Mrs Tynan chose to write a biography, she says, because she felt the need to assert her husband's rightful place in twentieth-century English letters and theatre history, but she has not erected the conventional pious monument. It is hard to imagine Mary Shelley canvassing the opinions of former secretaries, asking how the Shelley ménage struck them at the time, or the second Mrs Hardy interviewing the novelist's former mistresses, discussing his sexual preferences. Mrs Tynan does all this and more, stopping short only (by whose decision she does not say) at comparing notes with her predecessor, the previous title-holder, Elaine Dundy. Before she dwindled into a wife, Kathleen Halton was an excellent journalist, from a family of some renown in the business, and she has done her leg-work conscientiously and well, excavating all the truth she could uncover about the erratic, divided egotist she married. But the objectivity with which she invaded the regions of his life not shared with her was, she recognizes, unnatural, and the strain she put on herself in doing so translates into an underlying strain running through her book like the San Andreas Fault.

Nonetheless, it's a compelling piece of writing, and her choice obviously was the right one. To tell only the story of her years with Tynan would have been to unfold a mystery with no key, the sort of cryptogram Tynan's favourite film, *Citizen Kane*, would have become had Orson Welles' studio bosses cut the childhood episodes which explain Kane's dying word, "Rosebud". The Tynan for whom she forsook her own first marriage in 1964 was a man glittering with success and his own pleasure in it: leading drama critic of the English-speaking world, newly-appointed dramaturg of Laurence Olivier's National Theatre, someone who could claim, like Oscar Wilde, a symbolic relation to his time. The husband whose agonizing death from emphysema she watched in California in 1980 (this is the book to give to a smoker you love for Christmas) was a lost, wasted man whose misery and sense of exile stare hauntingly out of the book's last photograph. The explanation for that change does not lie in the years during which it took place. To account for it, Mrs Tynan had to go back to the beginning: to the indulged Birmingham schoolboy who was always to maintain that he really was born on his first day at Oxford.

The time to which Ken Tynan bore a symbolic relation was the quarter-century following the Second World War, during which the generation of grammar-school children to whom the Education Act of 1944 opened Britain's older universities created a new society open to their talents. Tynan was the first, and flamboyantly the foremost, of their number. In fact, his father Sir Peter Peacock, chairman of the family chain of Midland drapery stores, could easily have sent him to a public school, and wished to. But his mother, Letitia Rose Tynan, feared that if he left home, he might discover his parents' guilty secret. She and Sir Peter were not married; the knight had an obdurate wife and four older children in Warrington, where he had served six terms as mayor. So Ken went to King

Edward's School, got a better education than he would have found at most boarding-schools, grew up heterosexual and entered Magdalen, Oxford, in 1945 on a demyship of £50 a year. His spending allowance, ten pounds a week, was larger than that of most undergraduates in those days and enabled him to become more conspicuous, famous for his technicolour suits (one green, one purple) and gold satin shirts. But essentially he was in the same situation as scores of clever provincial boys after the war, feeling their way into the new world which had given them equality with Etonians, Harrovians and Wykehamists, but left them to prove it.

Any age in which new classes thrust in among old ones is an age of dandyism. The vividest method of telling an old class you don't believe in their game, but can beat them at it anyway, is to out-swank them ironically. You can then move among them easily, using all the right noises and gestures, sharply caricatured to proclaim your difference. Tynan was, in effect, the earliest of the scholarship grubs who, with the help of new voices, fanciful wardrobes and an affectation of malicious exhibitionism, turned themselves into butterflies and swarmed through the old universities in the late '40s and '50s. The logic of their situation made them theatrical. Tynan happened already to be in love with films and theatre, and therefore became, so to speak, theatrical squared. Their situation also made them competitive. As Michael Young was to point out in *The Rise of the Meritocracy*, elites based on education lack the security of the old aristocracies of land and money. To live by one's wits is a nervous business: every younger brain, each new foot on the educational ladder, is a potential threat. Hence the competitive displays of educational firepower codified only half-jokingly in this period by Stephen Potter's *Lifemanship* books. Hence the cutthroat games of vocabulary-flashing and cultural reference pinned down by Harold Pinter and Joe Orton as Britain's post-war national sport. Tynan, a bookish, unathletic boy, made this kind of competition his own. A compulsive player of word games, he spattered his early writing with challenges to duels of literacy. A flip through his first collection of reviews turns up *cateran, cicisbeism, erethism, esurient, Galgenhumor* and *dompteuse*. (He over-reached with *erethism*, describing someone in a play as fathering a child in a moment of it. It would be difficult to do so in any other state.)

The most theatrical, the most competitive of his generation, he went further than almost all the rest. The penalty he paid was his inability to find his way back. His fellow meritocrats made the question of how to go home again, how to stay in touch with your roots, the great theme of British fiction and drama in the '50s and '60s. Tynan praised them but ignored it. Having turned his back on Birmingham, he never returned. His wife thinks he made the discovery of his illegitimacy, when he was twenty-one, the excuse for a course he probably would have followed anyway. Having invented a new self, made himself a changeling, he seized on the falsification attending his birth to slam the door of the past behind him forever. Some years earlier, he had discovered that his mother's first name was not Lilian, as she had pretended, but Letitia. Perhaps discovering that she shared the secret name of Wilde's Miss Prism helped too, making him feel entitled to the life of someone found in a handbag. His mother died in a home in Yorkshire in 1961, mentally deranged. Mrs Tynan quotes a passage of self-accusation, written years later, from his journals: "If she had come to London and lived with me in the Fifties, she could have been sustained by human contact . . . I could have postponed her death at the expense of my own absorption in self-advancement. I chose not to."

The point is not that he neglected his parents. We are all guilty there. It is that he hid from himself things from his Birmingham past which returned to haunt him. In making new selves for ourselves, we cannot avoid using old materials. Where, in those years of clothes rationing, did he find the stuffs for his purple suit and gold shirts but a draper's shelves? Elements of the life he chose to forget made their way, similarly metamorphosed, into the life he made for himself. In California, his wife says, he fell back when not dining out on the "brown foods" of his boyhood – sausages, kidneys, Worcester sauce, mulligatawny soup. Tastes and attitudes formed in his schooldays shaped what he became, assisting him in some ways, limiting him in others.

His wife's book is a moving personal story and a valuable strand of social history. But its chief use in the long run will be that it clarifies and explains the kind of critic Tynan was. He was imprinted for life by his first love, films. Like the rest of us who grew up on what we felt to be margins in the '30s, he made Hollywood, its gods and goddesses, its imaginary America of swing, white telephones and good-sport girls, his myth of the desirable centre. His first published writing, he admitted, was a letter sent to a film magazine when he was ten, asking the Warner Brothers for more of Humphrey Bogart, just seen in *The Petrified Forest*. His last, a *New Yorker* profile of Louise Brooks, reads like a farewell hymn to Aphrodite Cinematica, ageless epitome of all the girls loved over the years on thousands of silver screens. It seems to have been by way of film that he was drawn to his next love, old Broadway. As fans devour the implausible details of their idols' home life in Beverly Hills, he became fascinated by the earlier off-screen life of his favourite films, *The Philadelphia Story*, *The Women*, *The Man Who Came to Dinner*, in the New York theatre. The last, Kaufman and Hart's poisoned valentine to Alexander Woollcott, with its portrait of the critic as wit, tyrant and friend of the celebrated, clearly allured him. Echoes of its style appear frequently in his undergraduate writing, part of a generalized admiration for the world of the *New Yorker*, Cole Porter musicals and the Algonquin Round Table. I don't mock the progression. My own was identical.

Films implanted his obsession with stardom, the making and wearing of those golden masks with which his favourite performers – Dietrich, Garbo, Hepburn, Chaplin, Welles – vested themselves, like pharaohs, with power and timelessness. He became fascinated by the skills involved, the technique of imposing oneself on an audience, as hypnotists do, by a combination of bullying and seduction. Mildly sado-masochistic himself, he came to see this process as the exotic flower of which his condition was a bud, and to revere it with erotically-flavoured humility. Out of this came two of his central beliefs about acting: first, that all great actors have a strain of androgyny which enables them to seduce both sexes in an audience, as the boy playing Rosalind threatens to do in the epilogue to *As You Like It*; second, that all great acting is tinged with danger, with the possibility of cruelty or violence, or, as in the meeting of matador and bull in his favourite sport, a combination of both.

From his film-going too, I think, came one of his greatest virtues as a critic. He wrote about stage acting as if it were on the screen: that is to say, as if film's international language of movement were the essential, to which language itself was a late, added soundtrack. What he admired and described was actors' physical movement, often isolating it from language as if to discriminate the player's creation from the playwright's. This effect was heightened by his frequent use of animal similes. To emphasize the purity of the movement in itself, he would remove it from its human context and display it like the movement of an animal in a zoo. Anthony Quayle's Coriolanus reminded him of a young bull, Donald Wolfit's Iachimo of "a vast, gloating reptile," while to evoke Louise Brooks' Lulu in Pabst's silent film he summoned comparisons with a swan, a gazelle and a tropical fish. He could use animal imagery to be scathing, as well. Alan Badel's Romeo brought to his mind a restless marmoset, Dorothy Tutin's Ophelia "a mouse on the rack" and Claire Bloom's Jessica in an Old Vic *Merchant of Venice*, gazing adoringly but disconcertingly into Lorenzo's eyes, "a sea-lion awaiting a fish".

He almost resented actors such as Gielgud, whose movement had no animal quality for him to catch. Like film cameras, he preferred actors with thinking bodies to those whose heads control their performances. Implicitly, this committed him to preferring a cinematic realism on the stage – in the '50s he wrote of the need for "a theatre continuous with real life": but he also pictured the great, ultra-theatrical actors he admired as great beasts, holding your attention by sheer animal magnetism. The exercise of finding those animal parallels imposed a close, detailed attention to the stage which make his descriptions among the most vivid in theatrical criticism.

The king of his bestiary, of course, was Olivier. Of his *Titus Andronicus* in 1955, Tynan wrote: "All the grand, unplayable parts, after this, are open to him: Skelton's Magnificence, Ibsen's Brand, Goethe's Faust – anything, so long as we can see those lion eyes search for solace, that great jaw sag." Olivier was his star of stars, drawing from forgotten depths the pure fan-worship of the child who spent long Birmingham mornings in bed with *Film Pictorial*. Elaine Dundy has told of his excitement when he went to visit Olivier and Vivien Leigh at Notley Abbey in 1955 and heard for the first time of the possibility that Olivier might head a national theatre. When the time came in 1963, he offered himself as its dramaturg. "How shall we slaughter the little bastard?" snorted Olivier, handing his letter to Joan Plowright, whom he had married in the interim. Tynan had contributed, Olivier believed, to Vivien Leigh's mental breakdown by his derisive reviews. More recently, he had attacked the Chichester Festival, under cover of which Olivier was assembling his National company. Miss Plowright persuaded him to swallow his rage and accept the offer, and so the famous partnership began.

Kathleen Tynan says, with justice, that the full, balanced history of the partnership, and of Olivier's National Theatre, has yet to be written. The short chapter she devotes to Tynan's years with Olivier makes clear that the relationship misfired, but does not make clear how. Tynan alternated between humbling himself to Olivier and trying to bulldoze him with intellectual superiority in a way, she admits, that made it hard for Olivier to trust him. They never found a common language. The Oliviers would entertain the Tynans to family lunches on Sunday in Brighton, Olivier carving the roast in shirt-sleeves and braces, and Tynan would use the occasion to try and goad his employer into new displays of political or artistic adventurousness. "We were never Mick and Mack," says Olivier in retrospect. He refused Tynan permission in the '70s to write his biography or even a *New Yorker* profile of him, believing that he had betrayed confidences to a New York newspaper and perhaps aware of some of the disparaging things Tynan used to say behind his back to Fleet Street colleagues about the management of the National. But he points out what Tynan never knew: that when the National board were baying for Tynan's dismissal, after the *Soldiers* affair and *Oh Calcutta*, Olivier saved his skin by threatening his own resignation if Tynan went.

If your childhood dream is of snaring gods and goddesses, what do you do when you find one in your net? Whatever else may be possible, an equal relationship is not. The adorer wants to adore from below, and if denied this grows scornfully familiar. Like most players of Stephen Potter's games, Tynan had difficulty finding friends to whom he felt equal. Either he felt cleverer than other people, he confessed to his journal, and despised them, or he felt that other people were cleverer than him, and feared them. Olivier, it seems clear, offered Tynan friendship, but Tynan could not decide whether he adored his genius or despised his lack of education. The only relationship he could imagine was one in which, having hitched the star to his wagon, they soared together to ever more amazing heights of ambition and self-invention. Once or twice, when he prevailed on Olivier to play Othello and Edgar in Strindberg's *Dance of Death*, this happened. But for the most part Tynan's demands on Olivier to astonish him even further fell on the deaf ears of a man who, for the first time, was discovering the pleasures of ordinariness, domesticity and team play. Offered a place in this picture, Tynan backed off. He was not, as his wife says, a team player.

This would account for the uneasy, pantomime-horse nature of the National Theatre which Olivier and Tynan ran between them. It accomplished fine things, but the finest were seldom those to which Tynan's ambitions led it. What Olivier could have run best and most happily would have been a very British national theatre, exploring not too adventurously the byways of English and European drama. As it is, my brightest memories of the Olivier National, after his own star performances, are William Gaskill's superb revivals of *The Recruiting Officer* and *The Beaux' Stratagem*, John Dexter's *A Woman Killed with Kindness*, Coward's *Hay Fever*, Stoppard's *Jumpers*, Clifford Williams' all-male *As You Like It*, and Olivier's own productions of *Three Sisters* and *Juno and the Paycock*. All of those, I'm sure, were Tynan's choices, but one can imagine most of them happening with other dramaturgs. The National productions I can't imagine happening without Tynan and his ambitions for a theatre of European stature are those curiously ill-judged replicas of famous foreign productions – *Mother Courage, Hedda Gabler, A Flea in Her Ear*, the Brechtian *Coriolanus* (it was almost Brecht's *Coriolan*, but Olivier put his foot down) – and such items of imported avant-garderie as Arrabal's *The Architect and the Emperor of Assyria*. They are all plays well worth staging, even in borrowed mountings, but they belong to a Tynan, not an Olivier, National Theatre. It was the sense of such differences within the National's '60s seasons that made it seem less than whole-heartedly successful.

In the end, as we all know, Tynan tried to push Olivier too far, into staging Hochhuth's *Soldiers* with its accusation of Churchill's complicity in the death of General Sikorski, and Olivier was only able to protect him from his board by demoting him to "consultant". But, as *Oh Calcutta* went on to demonstrate, the difference between the two partners was not simply one of political judgment or artistic caution. One of Tynan's truly profound insights was that their belief in decency was what prevented Englishmen from making revolutions. Only by overthrowing the decencies could the country be changed. To someone of Olivier's generation, such a proposition smelled of treachery, as it had to – nothing new is brought about without betraying the old, some of it in oneself. It was at this point in Tynan's career that he began, his wife thinks, to be a man deeply divided against himself, forcing himself to outrage more and more deeply the decencies in himself that he felt he must outgrow. With half his mind, he planned a life of Wilhelm Reich, martyr of the orgasm; a pornographic film; an anthology of masturbation fantasies by various famous hands. With the other half, he blamed himself guiltily for the harm his insistence on sexual freedom was doing to his marriage, and wrote notes to the London producer of *Oh Calcutta* complaining of grossnesses, such as two actors miming buggery, which had crept into the performance.

The extent to which he had moved away from reality is revealed by the degree of shock he felt on discovering what his public image in England had become. This, as much as the onset of emphysema, says Mrs Tynan, was the motive for his self-exile to

California; he was particularly shocked by the attacks on him by John Osborne and William Gaskill in Logan Gourlay's collection of essays on Olivier. Mrs Tynan's last chapters make depressing reading. More and more, as his illness advanced, he took on the grotesque likeness of Kaufman and Hart's Sheridan Whiteside, the Man Who Came to Dinner: overbearing, querulous, tyrannical, the classic invalid determined to make everyone else suffer for his invalidism. "Beware, young man, of what you wish for in your youth," wrote Emerson in one of his essays, "for assuredly it will be given to you in your age."

That said, what is the place to be claimed for him in twentieth-century English letters and theatre history? The usual claim is that he was the finest theatre critic since Shaw. It's not a brilliant contest to win, against the blasé A.B. Walkley, the quasi-mystical Charles Morgan and the appalling James Agate, and personally I'd choose C.E. Montague of the *Guardian*; but let that go. He was certainly the most entertaining after Shaw, but there I'd say the comparison ends. He lacked the political centre from which Shaw's jokes sprang. All too often, his are simply Oxford revue skits and parodies, run up to make a clever column when a play stirs no special response. His politics were the result of his conquest by Brecht's aesthetic. Shaw's aesthetic was the result of his own politics.

The claims I'd make for him are different. His liveliness made the theatre he wrote about seem lively in a drab time, and therefore important. As a result, it began to behave as if it were important, and became so. One can't say he made the English theatre the best in the world in the post-war decades, but he made English audiences realize that it was and the quality of their relationship to their playwrights was for twenty years the envy of the world. And finally, he could draw in words. I think that's what the rest of us envied most. When he described Richardson's "cheese-face" or Gielgud's brusque, wrought-up manner of talking to other actors "as if he were going to tip them," he caught in a line of caricature what we had seen. That seems the important thing to tell posterity. The pictures he drew of Olivier, Gielgud, Richardson and Redgrave, of Edith Evans, Peggy Ashcroft, Sybil Thorndike and Maggie Smith, are true likenesses. We saw them too, and he can be believed.

OLIVIER REX

Review of *Olivier* by Anthony Holden. Originally published in the *London Review of Books*, September 1988

Anthony Holden's is the sixteenth book about Laurence Olivier, and his forward tells of two more biographers, John Cottrell and Garry O'Connor, too intent on their own deadlines to discuss their common quarry with him. All this activity may puzzle the lay person. Holden's final pages report Olivier alive, as well as can be expected at eighty-one, residing tranquilly in the Sussex countryside, still swimming occasional lengths of his pool in the altogether and attending the first nights of the three children who have followed Joan Plowright and himself into the theatre. Anyone likely to be interested in this book or its successors must remember that the actor published his own autobiography only six years ago, and a complementary professional memoir in 1986. In such situations, biographers usually hold their fire, waiting for time to unlock more secrets, death more tongues. Instead, Olivier's are behaving as if a landslide of new evidence, too hot to hold there, had fallen into their laps. What is going on?

The occasion of the scramble is indeed a windfall of new evidence, but Mr Holden is too courtly (his previous subjects include Prince Charles and the Queen Mum) to name it. He merely says demurely that he persuaded Olivier's friend, their shared publisher Lord Weidenfeld, that – how does he put it? – "between them [Olivier's] two books did not add up to a comprehensive, let alone objective, account of one of the most extraordinary lives, in any profession, of this century." Holden has a nice line in dry understatement, and knows this is the understatement of the decade. What he means is that he and his fellow-toilers in the biographical olive grove have been racing to make sense of the great heap of myth, obfuscation, blarney and coded revelation dumped on them in Olivier's *Confessions of an Actor*. Far from settling questions about himself, it raised them like flies. Perhaps it meant to. Had Olivier wished biographers to mushroom at his feet he could not have followed more closely the rules of mushroom cultivation: keep them in the dark and shovel manure on them.

The first question it raised was, "what sort of man would write a book like that?" The answer is: an actor. Olivier's *Confessions* are neither confession nor chronicle, but a performance, designed to amuse, impress, shock, wring and harrow. Reality figures in it, but only as actors evoke reality: by selection and amplification, blowing up details which in life would be too tiny for significance until the surface of everyday behaviour seems swollen with meaning. It is a technique which enabled Olivier, as so often on the stage, to hide in the spotlight. Promising a self-portrait, he painted across his own features a Kathakali mask of violent emotions, the grinning red, black and silver face of a tormented demon. This, his text declared with great cries of guilt, was the real Olivier: but what readers took in primarily was the enormous theatrical energy and gusto of the breast-beating. It was as if A.A. Milne's Tigger, for some fancy-dress occasion, had tried to pass himself off as the doleful, droop-eared Eeyore, but been betrayed by his invincible bounciness. According to Holden, Olivier's son Tarquin told friends privately when the book appeared that "it says absolutely nothing and gives everything away."

This is the reason for the rush to print of Holden and his rivals. The race is to deconstruct and translate Olivier's gestic text into terms accessible to those who deal in history, not drama – to reconcile it as far as possible with fact. Here Holden comes well-equipped. He has assembled all the facts available from previous biographies, as well as scores of entertaining new ones from his own researches and interviews with Olivier's friends and co-workers. It is the largest compilation between covers of what is known about the actor, and that is its value, a real one. As a reconciliation with reality of Olivier's mythic dance of himself, it is less successful. Holden never really gives the impression of seeing a subject's view of himself as one of the facts a biographer must deal with. Rather, he treats it as something the biographer must get out of his way. It is as if Herbert Spencer or John Stuart Mill, not Mrs Gaskell, herself a novelist, had descended on Haworth parsonage to decipher the lives of the makers of Gondal.

Holden is too new to the world of theatre talk to have got all his details right, let alone arrange them into the figure in Olivier's carpet. At the first dress rehearsal of *The Merchant of Venice* in 1970, he says, Olivier turned up with a hook nose and goatee modelled on George Arliss's Disraeli and had to be persuaded by his director, Jonathan Miller, to evolve in the succeeding weeks a characterization based on his own face. No one seems to have told Holden that dress rehearsals normally complete, not commence, the rehearsal process. He will surprise many who worked with Tyrone Guthrie by describing him as a "highly cerebral" director, and amuse showbiz New York mightily with the statement that, after their star-crossed *Romeo and Juliet* on Broadway in 1940, Olivier and Vivien Leigh went to lick their wounds for a month in Vermont with "the Alexander Woollcotts". The English period equivalent would be a month in the country with the Beverley Nicholses.

Holden is sometimes forgetful, evacuating the wartime Old Vic in one chapter to Burnley, in the next to Barnsley, and poor at sums. He gives the age of Olivier, born in 1907, as 39 when he achieved his triumph as Richard III in 1944. Tarquin Olivier, born in 1936, is credited with a visit at the age of seven to Notley Abbey, bought by his father in 1945. Nor has Holden checked all the stories he takes over from previous biographers. Like most of them, he tells how Olivier telephoned Ralph Richardson in the United States in August 1936 to ask if he should accept Guthrie's offer of a *Hamlet* at the Vic. The transatlantic operator must have had difficulty connecting them: on 6 August, Richardson began a year's run at the Haymarket in a thriller called *The Amazing Dr Clitterhouse*. Still, for such a bale of facts the level of error is not disgraceful. The most damaging result of Holden's unfamiliarity with the territory he has strayed into is his acceptance of one of the theatre's hoariest clichés: that the actor with a thousand faces has no personality of his own.

All actors suffer from our conviction that, having seen them on stage, we know them personally. I was once party to a discussion of the actor who provided the voice of Hal, the treacherous computer in Stanley Kubrick's film *2001*. "One can tell he has an enormous brain," one discutant said thoughtfully, "but do you feel he's completely reliable?" Similarly, Olivier has been plagued for forty years by half-memories of the first performance of his greatness: his Button Moulder in Guthrie's production of *Peer Gynt*, which opened the historic Old Vic season of 1944-45. It is the Button Moulder who tells Peer to peel an onion if he would see the soul at its centre, and laughs when Peer discovers that onions have no centre. Ever since 1944, people have written that Olivier is a theatrical chameleon, taking on the colours of his roles, invisible offstage for lack of an identity of his own. Olivier has said it himself sometimes; it must save time in interviews. By definition, all actors are less vivid, less certain, offstage than on. Vividness and decision are what they rehearse all those weeks to achieve. But Olivier didn't strike me as colourless the couple of times I met him off-duty. A boxer doesn't have to hit people for you to know he packs a wallop. Being close to Olivier felt like being close to a champion boxer – acting had developed his chest and shoulders out of proportion to the rest of his body – and as unsafe.

"Laurence Olivier is less gifted than Marlon Brando," wrote William Redfield in *Letters from an Actor*. "He is even less gifted than Richard Burton, Paul Scofield, Ralph Richardson and John Gielgud. But he is still the definitive actor of the twentieth century. Why? Because he wanted to be." Holden's book never reconciles his notion of Olivier the actor-as-onion with its pages of evidence that the force that through a hundred greenrooms drove his career was a huge, hungry, often ruthless will to succeed. Perhaps Holden has in mind E.M. Forster's conceit in *Howards End* that the Napoleons of the world have will without personality: never say "I" but only, like monstrous babies, "Want this," "Want that." Paying attention to Olivier's myth of himself in his *Confessions* would have dealt with that assumption. Illogically, in allusions and images,

Olivier enacts the dance of an Ego struggling to rise above the overmastering hunger of its Id. If his performance in the book has a through-line, it is the battle of his "I" with his "want".

Father Geoffrey Heald, the priest who introduced Olivier to acting at the choir school of All Saints Margaret Street, and who played Petruchio to his thirteen-year-old Katherina in *The Shrew*, told him to read Dickens — as an actor, he would never want for characterizations. The early chapters of Olivier's *Confessions* are written in Dickensian pastiche, even borrowing David Copperfield's opening speculation whether he would turn out the hero of his own life story. The object of this is to characterize the young Olivier as a Dickens child, a version of David, and his father, the widowed Reverend Gerard, as his Mr Murdstone, the icy cheeseparer who darkens his world after his adored mother's death when he was twelve. You can smile at the cunning which colours his boyhood Dickensian, but photographs of Olivier in early roles at the Birmingham Rep bear his mythmaking out. The young face scowling from beneath beetling eyebrows and unwashed hair is clearly underfed, underpraised and underloved. No one has ever made much sense of the oracular morsel passed like a torch from Felix Barker, Olivier's first biographer, to his successors: the story of how Elsie Fogerty, awarding the boy a scholarship to the Central Schook, ran her little finger from his hairline to the bridge of his nose, saying: "You have a weakness, here." Olivier, taking her literally, spent a lifetime re-building his nose with putty. Others have offered other, unkinder translations. The early pictures suggest she was simply warning him that he had developed a facial flinch: a shy habit of lowering his thick brows to veil the expression of his eyes. (Sixty years later, he is still doing it in Holden's jacket photograph of his television Lear.) In most of them, you can make out the intensity he is trying to hide: an adolescent compound of suspicion, defiance, and seething resolve to show them all, be revenged, escape to some larger, splendid life where attention will have to be paid to him.

What image he had of that life is harder to read. Obviously the theatre was much of it. But none of his biographers looks closely enough at the role in his personal mythology of his Uncle Sydney,

the first Lord Olivier, his family's highest achievement until he over-
took it. In his memory, Sydney is juxtaposed significantly to his
father's parsimonies: the bathwater his sons had to share, his razor-
thin slices of chicken. When Sydney visited his younger brother's
rectory of Letchworth, Gerard "spent the few household pennies
on vintage port and good food. Uncle Sydney was to have the
best." Sydney Olivier was a founder, with Shaw and Sidney Webb,
of the Fabian Society, and author of its essay on the moral basis of
socialism. A star of the Colonial Office, he was twice governor of
Jamaica and Secretary of State for India in the first Labour Government. Shaw called him one of the most powerfully attractive men
he had known, "distinguished enough to be unclassable . . . handsome and strongly sexed," with the air, even in old clothes, of a
Spanish grandee. It must have taken commanding qualities to get
away with his career in the Colonial Service, one of open opposi-
tion to the enrichment of white colonists by an exploitation of
black subjects. Rumbled finally and called home, he retired to a
small, exquisite Elizabethan house in Oxfordshire to write a blazing exposé of the relations between white capital and black labour
in southern Africa. In the few months he served Ramsay Mac-
Donald at the India Office, he embarked on a plan for Indian inde-
pendence, but was thwarted by Moslem intractability and the
Government's early fall. Olivier doesn't make clear how much he
understands of his uncle's remarkable career as an antibody of
empire, but evidently he took hungry note of the dignities that fall
to those who have done the state some service, and of Sydney's
style. In *On Acting* he tells how he modelled partly on Sydney his
1970 Shylock, the one man of integrity in an oppressive Victorian
setting of greed, luxury and speculation.

Rather than his roles colouring his life, his hunger and its
objects coloured the roles in which, because they gave scope to
the intensities he knitted his brows to veil, he was most successful.
In *Wuthering Heights*, he gave his first satisfactory screen performance.
Evidently the image of Heathcliff, the despised and outcast stable-
boy who returns rich from America, connected with him as the
swashbucklers and dapper young professionals of his previous films

had not. In *Henry V,* first at the Vic, then on celluloid, he found an objective correlative for his yearning to serve England conspicuously and be conspicuously rewarded for it. But the role he seems to regard as mythically his own, the image of his life's deepest truth, is Oedipus. The Sophoclean burden of the *Confessions* is that, of all men alive, Olivier has been the luckiest and unluckiest, the one who fell from the highest fortune to lowest. In Oedipus he evidently found expression for his unstanchable sense that the sorrows of his life were punishments for a great guilt incurred ascending fortune's wheel.

What guilt? Of all the empurpled, over-dramatized elements in his memoirs, Olivier's harping on his sinful unworthiness reads most hammily. Yet he seems to have found the heart of his best performances – Richard III, Macbeth, Andronicus, Othello, Edgar in Strindberg's *Dance of Death* – by drawing on this unexplained conviction of his own damnation. Clearly he believes it – believes that he owes his success to some Faustian deal with the devil, a debt he had to pay in torment. What debt? What Faustian contract? As Redfield implies, more than most actors Olivier gained his success by working for it, lifting more weights, breaking more bones, doing more voice exercises. What load on his conscience leads him to see himself as the twentieth-century incarnation of Thebes's incestuous king?

No Olivier biographer, and certainly not Olivier himself, has ever mentioned in print the principal reason why books about this actor are written and sold in quantities that will never be rivalled by works on Gielgud, Richardson or Alec Guinness. The nearest Holden comes is to retail a story from Gawn Grainger, the actor who helped Olivier edit *On Acting* from taped recollections, of watching the old man strip for his daily nude swim. Grainger could not keep his eyes from the tangle of operation scar tissue crisscrossing the septuagenarian torso. "Ah, yes!" cried Olivier. "This is the body they used to worship. They all fell for me in my day." It seems necessary that somebody should say, for the benefit of the posterity which will know only that he was a great actor, what enabled him to become one: that his films put him in the small company of those – Byron, Nijinsky, Valentino, the last Prince of Wales – with power over the sexual imagination of millions. Like an incubus, the Olivier of the '30s and '40s could enter the dreams of the young, the reveries of the less young, and bring them to orgasm. Had he lived three centuries earlier, he might have risked being burned.

Exactly when he realized that he had this power, and what he thought of it, is hard to make out. In his memoirs he goes to some lengths to convey that, when confronted with the two great Hollywood sex goddesses of his lifetime, Garbo and Monroe, they walked all over him. His first encounters with New York fans after *Wuthering Heights* simply repelled and frightened him into refusing to sign autographs, as if they had invaded his privacy, not he theirs. His subsequent films, *Rebecca, Pride and Prejudice* and *Lady Hamilton*, show him muffling his sexuality in withdrawn diffidence, with that effect of coquetry which led some contemporaries to describe him as flirtatious. But knowledge of his power is clearly present in the scenes where he woos Katherine of France in *Henry V* and Lady Anne in the film of *Richard III*. (It may even be there in his night scenes with his army before Agincourt.) The strongest, because most casual, evidence I saw him give of knowing it was in *The Master Builder* at the National Theatre in 1964. As Joan Plowright's Hilda told how Solness had possessed her dreams, seduced her in imagination, he nodded intently as he listened. She was telling him nothing new, merely confirming something he knew he was capable of. None of his contemporaries could have played that reaction as he did, so matter-of-factly. But of course the same knowledge was there, only half-hidden by disgust, in his playing of Archie Rice in *The Entertainer*. You can't leave me behind here in this theatre, Archie's gap-toothed leer told us. I'll follow you home into your sleep, and you won't like what happens when I get there.

Obviously part of his nature – the rectory child who swung the censer at All Saints – felt his power as a sin and curse. A maturer part may have felt, with more real guilt, that it was a fraud and imposture. Denys Blakelock, one of his earliest friends in the profession, told in his memoirs how Olivier won his mother's heart by his evident unfitness for a stage career. "He's such an *ugly* boy," she said pityingly, and Blakelock could not deny it. The twenty-year-old Olivier's hairline was simianly low, his eyebrows tangled over his nose, his front teeth had a gap wide enough to stick a straw in, and his starved frame looked even bonier in suits handed down by his uncles. By the time he left the Birmingham Rep for London, he had transformed himself. Photographs of the early '30s show a glossy young matinee idol with plucked eyebrows, romantic cheekbones, flawless smile and enough oil on his hair to service a Morris Minor. "Valentino taught me the importance of narcissism," he told Ken Tynan in a BBC interview in 1967. (He evidently studied film actors: his trick of rolling dead eyes upward till the whites showed came from Fritz Kortner.) He worked hard on himself, and the work paid off in matinee-idol parts: Beau Geste, Bothwell in a thing about Mary Stuart, and the John Barrymore caricature in Edna Ferber's and George Kaufman's *The Royal Family*. It was in the last that he was first seen, and marked down for her own, by Vivien Leigh.

There, it seems, lies the root of his guilt, the buried crime he thinks he spent his life expiating. By imposture, turning an unlovable self into a brilliantined dish for Hollywood's sex scouts, he attracted the love of the world's most beautiful woman and the wrath of the gods. Their life together, in his myth, is his punishment, their marriage the infernal machine, as Cocteau put it in his version of the Oedipus story, designed by fate to destroy a man. A stagey notion? The stage is his language, and what he is saying rings true enough. As he told the world in painful detail in the *Confessions*, he could not convince offstage in the role of a great lover. He must have felt seen through in other ways. Vivien Leigh had more schooling than he, and more to show for it: wit, taste, social grace, quickness with languages. She read books. He seldom mentions reading anything but plays and newspapers. The one thing he had of his own which she could not match was his talent. To undo his fraud and become a real hero for her, he made himself a great actor.

That was what drove them apart. On the most basic level, he tells in his memoirs, acting as he acted drained his sexual energies. Acting as she acted did not deplete hers. She read his belief that she could not love him unless he surpassed Kean and Irving as a message that he could not love her unless she excelled Rachel and Duse. Her knowledge that she could not – that she would never equal him professionally – fuelled the manic depression which, from 1945 on, led her downward into schizophrenia. (That was the year he played Oedipus.) The forms her madness increasingly took were raging abuse of him and compulsive infidelity with younger men picked up after the theatre – the role that became her personal myth was Blanche Dubois in *A Streetcar Named Desire*. Holden points out, with some justice, that in fact it was she who was destroyed, while Olivier survives. He takes this as testimony that her love was the greater; that his egotism armoured him against the slings and arrows of the life of emotions. I find that glib. What destroyed her was her disease. It is impertinent of anyone who has not done so to judge the actions of someone compelled to live intimately with a manic depressive. This is where more time needs to pass, more evidence become available. Vivien Leigh's friends are free to tell her story. Olivier's have had to leave his to him.

What Vivien Leigh destroyed in Olivier was his belief in himself as hero of the British Empire. From 1945 onward, the two of them were part of the national life as no actors had ever been before: received by royalty, friends of Churchill, treated in public almost as if royal themselves. It seemed natural that Olivier should speak the commentary for the film of the Queen's coronation in 1953. He had become an element of what Bagehot called the ceremonial aspect of the British constitution: the Performer Royal, slightly junior to the Poet Laureate, but of more use on state occasions than the Astronomer Royal, who can't even cast horoscopes. When he and Vivien Leigh led an Old Vic tour to Australia in 1948, their progress was vice-regal: banquets from premiers, speeches of greeting from the British nation to the Australian people, everything but launching ships. Touring of this kind had been invented by Henry Irving and his advance men, but never brought to such stateliness. Olivier started a diary which reflects the glory he took in it all. He had outstripped not only his predecessor as head of the profession, but also his Uncle Sydney. In Melbourne the diary breaks off. The reason Olivier gave was strain, a usefully ambiguous word. It covered both real exhaustion and the state of his marriage. It was in Australia, he maintained afterwards, that he lost his wife's love. She had taken to flirting publicly with young actors in the company. In private, they quarrelled emptily. Their next stop was Sydney, where Vivien Leigh would meet the man who demolished what remained of the great love, Peter Finch, and Olivier received the notorious letter from the chairman of the Vic's board of governors informing him that his services, and Ralph Richardson's, would not be required next season. The life of the Performer Royal had become a performance. It was after this that Olivier began agreeing with the interviewers that, yes, an actor is a hollow man, with no life to speak of offstage.

It was early in the '50s, too, that people started to tell stories about not recognizing him in street clothes. He let the matinee-idol beauty fade as swiftly as he had created it. It's interesting to study his make-up for his later roles. For heroes – Hamlet, Henry V, Coriolanus, Oedipus, Antony – he had always painted a fuller, more sensual upper lip over the thin one he inherited from his father. Part of a hero's being, he evidently felt, was physical seductiveness, sexual power. His 1955 Macbeth was the last role for which he did this, if you exclude his African Othello. From 1950 on, he specialized in playing heroes as character roles, to observe rather than fall in love with: heroes with something wrong with them, flaws, secret vices or burned-out cores. His guide to Shakespeare, characteristically, had always been A.C. Bradley's Edwardian analysis of the divided moral natures which destroy Hamlet, Macbeth, Antony and Lear. His forte as an actor became the illustration of such destruction: heroic magnificence driven and eaten from within.

It's hard to resist the conclusion that the unique national eminence he reached in the last third of his career resulted from the resonance between his great performances as flawed, dishonoured proconsuls and the British public's mixed feelings about the end of empire. During the war, as Nelson and Henry V, he had established a special relationship with his public by offering simple icons of British courage and decency winning the day. Now, as the Empire had to be let go, he provided images of the necessity for its surrender: instances of imperial virtue corrupted by passion or power – Antony, Macbeth, Coriolanus again, Othello and, perhaps most memorable of all, Titus Andronicus, the old hero who, meeting the onset of barbarism with cruelty to match its own, hastens the twilight of his civilization. Rich and complex, his performances gave British audiences the wide palette of emotions they needed to deal with the change to their world: shame and splendour, nobility and waste, loss and deliverance. His creations were of the scale the fall of empire demanded; better than Ian Smith or Enoch Powell. But among them also belongs his Archie Rice in *The Entertainer*, imperialist turned malcontent, lamenting the Empire's passing while railing at the dishonour it descended to at Suez. When he said, "don't clap too hard, ladies and gentlemen, it's a very old building," our scalps went cold. The intensity of his vision of a rotting kingdom pierced through the theatre walls out into the darkness of imperial London, eating the faces of statues and the façades of Whitehall, until we looked in imagination over the moonscape of the city after the raids.

It couldn't have worked had anyone at the time been very clear about what exactly his performances were doing for his audiences. Kenneth Tynan proved that when, in an excess of lucidity, he enmeshed Olivier in his efforts to acquire for the National Theatre Hochhuth's play *Soldiers*, with its portrait of Churchill as hero, machiavel and murderer. In spite of its ludicrous length and prosy naivety, the play tugged at the same roots, with some of the same power, as *Andronicus* and *The Entertainer*. The hope was that Richard Burton, the actor most like Olivier's heir, might play the Churchill role, and Tynan obviously expected Olivier to direct. It was a lunatic notion. Tynan must have known perfectly well that Lord Chandos, chairman of the National's board, had been Churchill's colleague in the war cabinet and so, if Hochhuth were dealing at all in fact, an accomplice in the crimes imputed to his chief. The interesting thing is the way Olivier floundered, confused, in the midst of the imbroglio. Clearly the play struck certain chords in him. Clearly he saw the reddened face of Chandos shouting at him that Tynan must go as the unacceptable face of the old empire's power. What he could not tell was whether the play itself was bad or good, or what he should do in the circumstances. He paltered, and in the end damaged his standing with the board irretrievably. His prestige in the country at large made him impossible to fire, but after the *Soldiers* affair a faction on the National's board obviously counted the days until he could be retired gracefully.

Did he himself recognize clearly his role as an imperial antibody, after the fashion of his Uncle Sydney? I doubt it. At some lesser crisis in the National's fortunes, his press officer asked if I would mind lunching with "Sir" so that he could let Fleet Street know how sharper than a serpent's tooth it is to have a thankless press. (And indeed, he played a pocket version of Lear in modern dress just for me; but that is another story.) One of the issues on his mind was whether his company was entitled to call itself the National Theatre of Great Britain. People had said it should bill itself abroad as the British National Theatre, the "Great" might cause offence. I started to make the harmless geographical distinction between Bretagne and Grand Bretagne, but he brushed it aside, too obsessed to listen. When he was at school, the map had been covered in pink, and Britain *was* great, dammit, and people were proud of it. He couldn't understand this new feeling in the country against greatness, could I explain it?

I didn't try, and hope no one else ever has. If anyone could have persuaded him that the word "great" has no objective meaning, but is simply a counter of patriarchal discourse designed to shore up the power of élites by "valorizing" their leaders and favoured aristocratic forms of art, he couldn't have been what he was. That is why it is important to listen to his myth of himself. He was a great actor because his acting was about greatness, both its dark and its golden faces. I wouldn't have forgone seeing it for the chance of a total reform of the Indo-European family of languages.

I hope the English will go on playing the role of Chorus his myth allots them. Evidently he took the trouble to find out what happens to Oedipus in the long run, in *Oedipus at Colonus*. By knowing greater suffering than any man alive, enacting it publicly for the purgation of his city, the outcast king finally achieves an unearthly peace, his sins forgiven his white hairs by the gods, in the company of his children. Indeed, the unique greatness of his ordeal invests him with mana, makes him a living treasure whose resting-place Thebes and Athens dispute, knowing that the land where his bones lie in honour will harbour a great fortune. Because he no longer had the force to convey its torments, it seemed to me, it was the old, redeemed Oedipus he chiefly played at the end of his television *Lear*. I hope his Chorus will know their lines when their cue comes.